INSTIGATIONS

INSTIGATIONS
OF
EZRA POUND

TOGETHER WITH

AN ESSAY
ON THE
CHINESE
WRITTEN
CHARACTER

BY

ERNEST FENOLLOSA

Essay Index Reprint Series

BOOKS FOR LIBRARIES PRESS
FREEPORT, NEW YORK

HOUSTON PUBLIC LIBRARY

First Published 1920
First Reprinting in this Series 1967
Second Reprinting 1969

STANDARD BOOK NUMBER:

8369-0795-7

LIBRARY OF CONGRESS CATALOG CARD NUMBER:

67-23261

PRINTED IN THE UNITED STATES OF AMERICA

TO
MY FATHER
HOMER L. POUND

TABLE OF CONTENTS

vii

A STUDY IN FRENCH POETS

INSTIGATIONS

I

A STUDY IN FRENCH POETS

THE time when the intellectual affairs of America could be conducted on a monolingual basis is over. It has been irksome for long. The intellectual life of London is dependent on people who understand the French language about as well as their own. America's part in contemporary culture is based chiefly upon two men familiar with Paris: Whistler and Henry James. It is something in the nature of a national disgrace that a New Zealand paper, "The Triad," should be more alert to, and have better regular criticism of, contemporary French publications than any American periodical has yet had.

I had wished to give but a brief anthology * of French poems, interposing no comment of my own between author and reader; confining my criticism to selection. But that plan was not feasible. I was indebted to MM. Davray and Valette for cordial semi-permissions to quote the "Mercure" publications.

Certain delicate wines will not travel; they are not always the best wines. Foreign criticism may sometimes correct the criticism *du cru*. I cannot pretend to

* *The Little Review*, February, 1918.

give the reader a summary of contemporary French opinion, but certain French poets have qualities strong enough to be perceptible to me, that is, to at least one alien reader; certain things are translatable from one language to another, a tale or an image will "translate"; music will, practically, never translate; and if a work be taken abroad in the original tongue, certain properties seem to become less apparent, or less important. Fancy styles, questions of local "taste," lose importance. Even though I know the overwhelming importance of technique, technicalities in a foreign tongue cannot have for me the importance they have to a man writing in that tongue; almost the only technique perceptible to a foreigner is the presentation of content as free as possible from the clutteration of dead technicalities, fustian à la Louis XV; and from timidities of workmanship. This is perhaps the only technique that ever matters, the only *mæstria*.

Mediocre poetry is, I think, the same everywhere; there is not the slightest need to import it; we search foreign tongues for *mæstria* and for discoveries not yet revealed in the home product. The critic of a foreign literature must know a reasonable amount of the bad poetry of the nation he studies if he is to attain any sense of proportion.

He will never be as sensitive to fine shades of language as the native; he has, however, a chance of being less bound, less allied to some group of writers. It would be politic for me to praise as many living Frenchmen as possible, and thereby to increase the number of my chances for congenial acquaintance on my next trip to Paris, and to have a large number of current French books sent to me to review.

But these rather broad and general temptations can

scarcely lead me to praise one man instead of another. If I have thrown over current French opinion, I must urge that foreign opinion has at times been a corrective. England has never accepted the continental opinion of Byron; the right estimate lies perhaps between the two. Heine is, I have heard, better read outside Germany than within. The continent has never accepted the idiotic British adulation of Milton; on the other hand, the idiotic neglect of Landor has never been rectified by the continent.

Foreign criticism, if honest, can never be quite the same as home criticism: it may be better or worse; it may have a value similar to that of a different decade or century and has at least some chance of escaping whims and stampedes of opinion.

I do not "aim at completeness." I believe that the American-English reader has heard in a general way of Baudelaire and Verlaine and Mallarmé; that Mallarmé, perhaps unread, is apt to be slightly overestimated; that Gautier's reputation, despite its greatness, is not yet as great as it should be.

After a man has lived a reasonable time with the two volumes of Gautier's poetry, he might pleasantly venture upon the authors whom I indicate in this essay; and he might have, I think, a fair chance of seeing them in proper perspective. I omit certain nebulous writers because I think their work bad; I omit the Parnassiens, Samain and Heredia, firstly because their work seems to me to show little that was not already implicit in Gautier; secondly, because America has had enough Parnassienism—perhaps second rate, but still enough. (The verses of La Comtesse de Noailles in the "Revue des Deux Mondes," and those of John Vance Cheney in "The Atlantic" once gave me an almost identical pleasure.)

I do not mean that all the poems here to be quoted are better than Samain's "Mon âme est une infante . . ." or his "Cléopatre."

We may take it that Gautier achieved hardness in *Emaux et Camées;* his earlier work did in France very much what remained for the men of "the nineties" to accomplish in England. Gautier's work done in "the thirties" shows a similar beauty, a similar sort of technique. If the Parnassiens were following Gautier they fell short of his merit. Heredia was perhaps the best of them. He tried to make his individual statements more "poetic"; but his whole, for all this, becomes frigid.

Samain followed him and began to go "soft"; there is in him just a suggestion of muzziness. Heredia is "hard," but there or thereabouts he ends. Gautier is intent on being "hard"; is intent on conveying a certain verity of feeling, and he ends by being truly poetic. Heredia wants to be poetic *and* hard; the hardness appears to him as a virtue in the poetic. And one tends to conclude, from this, that all attempts to be poetic in some manner or other, defeat their own end; whereas an intentness on the quality of the emotion to be conveyed makes for poetry.

I intend here a qualitative analysis. The work of Gautier, Baudelaire, Verlaine, Mallarmé, Samain, Heredia, and of the authors I quote here should give an idea of the sort of poetry that has been written in France during the last half century, or at least during the last forty years. If I am successful in my choice, I will indicate most of the best and even some of the half-good. Bever and Leautaud's anthology contains samples of some forty or fifty more poets.*

* A testimony to the effect of anthologies, and to the prestige of Van Bever and Leautaud in forming French taste, and at the

After Gautier, France produced, as nearly as I can understand, three chief and admirable poets: Tristan Corbière, perhaps the most poignant writer since Villon; Rimbaud, a vivid and indubitable genius; and Laforgue— a slighter, but in some ways a finer "artist" than either of the others. I do not mean that he "writes better" than Rimbaud; and Eliot has pointed out the wrongness of Symons's phrase, "Laforgue the eternal adult, Rimbaud the eternal child." Rimbaud's effects seem often to come as the beauty of certain silver crystals produced by chemical means. Laforgue always knows what he is at; Rimbaud, the "genius" in the narrowest and deepest sense of the term, the "most modern," seems, almost without knowing it, to hit on the various ways in which the best writers were to follow him, slowly. Laforgue is the "last word":—out of infinite knowledge of all the ways of saying a thing he finds the right way. Rimbaud, when right, is so because he cannot be bothered to exist in any other modality.

JULES LAFORGUE

(1860–'87)

LAFORGUE was the "end of a period"; that is to say, same time the most amazing response to my French number of the *Little Review,* was contained in a letter from one of the very poets I had chosen to praise:

"Je vous remercie de m'avoir révélé Laforgue que je connaissais seulement par les extraits publiés dans la première Anthologie en I volume par Van Bever et Leautaud."

This is also a reply to those who solemnly assured me that any foreigner attempting to criticize French poetry would meet nothing but ridicule from French authors.

I am free to say that Van B. and L.'s selections would have led me neither to Laforgue nor to Rimbaud. They were, however, my approach to many of the other poets, and their two volume anthology is invaluable.

he summed up and summarized and dismissed nineteenth-
century French literature, its foibles and fashions, as
Flaubert in "Bouvard and Pécuchet" summed up nine-
teenth-century general civilization. He satirized Flaubert's heavy "Salammbô" manner inimitably, and he manages to be more than a critic, for in process of this ironic
summary he conveys himself, *il raconte lui-même en
racontant son âge et ses moeurs,* he delivers the moods
and the passion of a rare and sophisticated personality:
"point ce 'gaillard-là' ni le Superbe . . . mais au fond
distinguée et franche comme une herbe"!

> Oh! laissez-moi seulement reprendre haleine,
> Et vous aurez un livre enfin de bonne foi.

> En attendant, ayez pitié de ma misère!
> Que je vous sois à tous un être bienvenu!
> Et que je sois absous pour mon âme sincère,
> Comme le fut Phryné pour son sincère nu.

He is one of the poets whom it is practically impossible
to "select." Almost any other six poems would be quite
as "representative" as the six I am quoting.

PIERROTS

(*On a des principes*)

ELLE disait, de son air vain fondamental:
"Je t'aime pour toi seul!"—Oh! là, là, grêle histoire;
Oui, comme l'art! Du calme, ô salaire illusoire
     Du capitaliste Idéal!

Elle faisait: "J'attends, me voici, je sais pas" . . .
Le regard pris de ces larges candeurs des lunes;

—Oh! là, là, ce n'est pas peut-être pour des prunes,
    Qu'on a fait ses classes ici-bas?
Mais voici qu'un beau soir, infortunée à point,
Elle meurt!—Oh! là, là; bon, changement de thème!
On sait que tu dois ressusciter le troisième
    Jour, sinon en personne, du moins
Dans l'odeur, les verdures, les eaux des beaux mois!
Et tu iras, levant encore bien plus de dupes
Vers le Zaïmph de la Joconde, vers la Jupe!
    Il se pourra même que j'en sois.

PIERROTS

III

COMME ils vont molester, la nuit,
Au profond des parcs, les statues,
Mais n'offrant qu'au moins dévêtues
Leur bras et tout ce qui s'ensuit,

En tête-à-tête avec la femme
Ils ont toujours l'air d'être un tiers,
Confondent demain avec hier,
Et demandent *Rien* avec âme!

Jurent "je t'aime" l'air là-bas,
D'une voix sans timbre, en extase,
Et concluent aux plus folles phrases
Par des: "Mon Dieu, n'insistons pas?"

Jusqu'à ce qu'ivre, Elle s'oublie,
Prise d'on ne sait quel besoin
De lune? dans leurs bras, fort loin
Des convenances établies.

COMPLAINTE DES CONSOLATIONS

Quia voluit consolari

Ses yeux ne me voient pas, son corps serait jaloux ;
Elle m'a dit : "monsieur . . ." en m'enterrant d'un
    geste ;
Elle est Tout, l'univers moderne et le céleste.
Soit, draguons donc Paris, et ravitaillons-nous,
    Tant bien que mal, du reste.

Les Landes sans espoir de ses regards brûlés,
Semblaient parfois des paons prêts à mettre à la voile . . .
Sans chercher à me consoler vers les étoiles,
Ah ! Je trouverai bien deux yeux aussi sans clés,
    Au Louvre, en quelque toile !

Oh ! qu'incultes, ses airs, rêvant dans la prison
D'un *cant* sur le qui-vive au travers de nos hontes !
Mais, en m'appliquant bien, moi dont la foi démonte
Les jours, les ciels, les nuits, dans les quatre saisons
    Je trouverai mon compte.

Sa bouche ! à moi, ce pli pudiquement martyr
Où s'aigrissent des nostalgies de nostalgies !
Eh bien, j'irai parfois, très sincère vigie,
Du haut de Notre-Dame aider l'aube, au sortir,
    De passables orgies.

Mais, Tout va la reprendre !—Alors Tout m'en absout.
Mais, Elle est ton bonheur !—Non ! je suis trop immense,
Trop chose.   Comment donc ! mais ma seule présence
Ici-bas, vraie à s'y mirer, est l'air de Tout :
    De la Femme au Silence.

LOCUTIONS DES PIERROTS

VI

Je te vas dire: moi, quand j'aime,
C'est d'un coeur, au fond sans apprêts,
Mais dignement élaboré
Dans nos plus singuliers problèmes.

Ainsi, pour mes moeurs et mon art,
C'est la période védique
Qui seule a bon droit revendique
Ce que j'en "attelle à ton char."

Comme c'est notre Bible hindoue
Qui, tiens, m'amène à caresser,
Avec ces yeux de cétacé,
Ainsi, bien sans but, ta joue.

This sort of thing will drive many bull-moose readers
to the perilous borders of apoplexy, but it may give
pleasure to those who believe that man is incomplete
without a certain amount of mentality. Laforgue is an
angel with whom our modern poetic Jacob must struggle.

COMPLAINTE DES PRINTEMPS

Permettez, ô sirène,
Voici que votre haleine
Embaume la verveine;
C'est l'printemps qui s'amène!

—Ce système, en effet, ramène le printemps,
Avec son impudent cortège d'excitants.

Otez donc ces mitaines ;
Et n'ayez, inhumaine,
Que mes soupirs pour traîne :
Ous'qu'il y a de la gêne . . .

—Ah ! yeux bleus méditant sur l'ennui de leur art !
Et vous, jeunes divins, aux soirs cruŝ de hasard !

Du géant à la naine,
Vois, tout bon sire entraine
Quelque contemporaine,
Prendre l'air, par hygiène . . .

—Mais vous saignez ainsi pour l'amour de l'exil !
Pour l'amour de l'Amour ! D'ailleurs, ainsi soit-il . . .

T'ai-je fait de la peine ?
Oh ! viens vers les fontaines
Où tournent les phalènes
Des Nuits Elyséennes !

—Pimbèche aux yeux vaincus, bellâtre aux beaux jarrets.
Donnez votre fumier à la fleur du Regret.

Voilà que son haleine
N'embaum' plus la verveine !
Drôle de phénomène . . .
Hein, à l'année prochaine ?

—Vierges d'hier, ce soir traineuses de foetus,
A genoux ! voici l'heure où se plaint l'Angelus.

Nous n'irons plus au bois,
Les pins sont éternels,
Les cors ont des appels! . . .
Neiges des pâles mois,
Vous serez mon missel!
—Jusqu'au jour de dégel.

COMPLAINTE DES PIANOS

Qu'on entend dans les Quartiers Aisés

Menez l'âme que les Lettres ont bien nourrie,
Les pianos, les pianos, dans les quartiers aisés!
Premiers soirs, sans pardessus, chaste flânerie,
Aux complaintes des nerfs incompris ou brisés.

Ces enfants, à quoi rêvent-elles,
Dans les ennuis des ritournelles?

— "Préaux des soirs,
Christs des dortoirs!

"Tu t'en vas et tu nous laisses,
Tu nous laiss's et tu t'en vas,
Défaire et refaire ses tresses,
Broder d'éternels canevas."

Jolie ou vague? triste ou sage? encore pure?
O jours, tout m'est égal? ou, monde, moi je veux?
Et si vierge, du moins, de la bonne blessure,
Sachant quels gras couchants ont les plus blancs aveux?

Mon Dieu, à quoi donc rêvent-elles?
A des Roland, à des dentelles?

— "Coeurs en prison,
Lentes saisons!

"Tu t'en vas et tu nous quittes,
Tu nous quitt's et tu t'en vas!
Couvents gris, choeurs de Sulamites,
Sur nos seins nuls croisons **nos bras**."

Fatales clés de l'être un beau jour apparues;
Psitt! aux hérédités en ponctuels ferments,
Dans le bal incessant de nos étranges rues;
Ah! pensionnats, théâtres, journaux, romans!

Allez, stériles ritournelles,
La vie est vraie et criminelle.

— "Rideaux tirés,
Peut-on entrer?

"Tu t'en vas et tu nous laisses,
Tu nous laiss's et tu t'en vas,
La source des frais rosiers baisse,
Vraiment! Et lui qui ne vient pas . . ."

Il viendra! Vous serez les pauvres coeurs en faute,
Fiancés au remords comme aux essais sans fond,
Et les suffisants coeurs cossus, n'ayant d'autre hôte
Qu'un train-train pavoisé d'estime et de chiffons

Mourir? peut-être brodent-elles,
Pour un oncle à dot, des bretelles?

— "Jamais! Jamais!
Si tu savais!

Tu t'en vas et tu nous quittes,
Tu nous quitt's et tu t'en vas,
Mais tu nous reviendras bien vite
Guérir mon beau mal, n'est-ce pas?"

Et c'est vrai! l'Idéal les fait divaguer toutes;
Vigne bohême, même en ces quartiers aisés.
La vie est là; le pur flacon des vives gouttes
Sera, *comme il convient,* d'eau propre baptisé.

Aussi, bientôt, se joueront-elles
De plus exactes ritournelles.

"— Seul oreiller!
Mur familier!

"Tu t'en vas et tu nous laisses,
Tu nous laiss's et tu t'en vas,
Que ne suis-je morte à la messe!
O mois, ô linges, ô repas!"

The journalist and his papers exist by reason of their "protective coloring." They must think as their readers think at a given moment.

It is impossible that Jules Laforgue should have written his poems in America in "the eighties." He was born in 1860, died in 1887 of *la misère,* of consumption and abject poverty in Paris. The vaunted sensitiveness of French perception, and the fact that he knew a reasonable number of wealthy and influential people, did nothing to prevent this. He had published two small volumes, one edition of each. The seventh edition of his collected poems is dated 1913, and doubtless they have been reprinted since then with increasing celerity.

Un couchant des Cosmogonies!
Ah! que la Vie est quotidienne . . .

Et, du plus vrai qu'on se souvienne,
Comme on fut piètre et sans génie. . . .

What is the man in the street to make of this, or of the
Complainte des Bons Ménages!

L'Art sans poitrine m'a trop longtemps bercé dupe.
Si ses labours sont fiers, que ses blés décevants!
Tiens, laisse-moi bêler tout aux plis de ta jupe
    Qui fleure le couvent.

Delicate irony, the citadel of the intelligent, has a curious effect on these people. They wish always to be exhorted, at all times no matter how incongruous and unsuitable, to do those things which almost any one will and does do whenever suitable opportunity is presented. As Henry James has said, "It was a period when writers besought the deep blue sea 'to roll.' "

The ironist is one who suggests that the reader should think, and this process being unnatural to the majority of mankind, the way of the ironical is beset with snares and with furze-bushes.

Laforgue was a purge and a critic. He laughed out the errors of Flaubert, i.e., the clogging and cumbrous historical detail. He left *Coeur Simple, L'Education, Madame Bovary, Bouvard.* His *Salome* makes game of the rest. The short story has become vapid because sixty thousand story writers have all set themselves to imitating De Maupassant, perhaps a thousand from the original.

Laforgue implies definitely that certain things in prose were at an end, and I think he marks the next phase after Gautier in French poetry. It seems to me that without a familiarity with Laforgue one can not appreciate—i. e., determine the value of—certain positives and certain negatives in French poetry since 1890.

He deals for the most part with literary poses and *clichés*, yet he makes them a vehicle for the expression of his own very personal emotions, of his own unperturbed sincerity.

Je ne suis pas "ce gaillard-là!" ni Le Superbe!
Mais mon âme, qu'un cri un peu cru exacerbe,
Est au fond distinguée et franche comme une herbe.

This is not the strident and satiric voice of Corbière, calling Hugo *"Garde National épique,"* and Lamartine *"Lacrymatoire d'abonnés."* It is not Tailhade drawing with rough strokes the people he sees daily in Paris, and bursting with guffaws over the Japanese in their mackintoshes, the West Indian mulatto behind the bar in the Quartier. It is not Georges Fourest burlesquing in a café; Fourest's guffaw is magnificent, he is hardly satirical. Tailhade draws from life and indulges in occasional squabbles.

Laforgue was a better artist than any of these men save Corbière. He was not in the least of their sort.

Beardsley's "Under the Hill" was until recently the only successful attempt to produce "anything like Laforgue" in our tongue. "Under the Hill" was issued in a limited edition. Laforgue's *Moralités Légendaires* was issued in England by the Ricketts and Hacon press in a limited edition, and there the thing has remained. Laforgue can never become a popular cult because tyros can not imitate him.

One may discriminate between Laforgue's tone and that of his contemporary French satirists. He is the

finest wrought; he is most "verbalist." Bad verbalism is
rhetoric, or the use of *cliché* unconsciously, or a mere
playing with phrases. But there is good verbalism, distinct from lyricism or imagism, and in this Laforgue is
a master. He writes not the popular language of any
country, but an international tongue common to the excessively cultivated, and to those more or less familiar
with French literature of the first three-fourths of the
nineteenth century.

He has done, sketchily and brilliantly, for French literature a work not incomparable to what Flaubert was
doing for "France" in *Bouvard and Pécuchet*, if one
may compare the flight of the butterfly with the progress
of an ox, both proceeding toward the same point of the
compass. He has dipped his wings in the dye of scientific terminology. Pierrot *imberbe* has

Un air d'hydrocéphale asperge.

The tyro can not play about with such things. Verbalism demands a set form used with irreproachable skill.
Satire needs, usually, the form of cutting rhymes to drive
it home.

Chautauquas, Mrs. Eddy, Dr. Dowies, Comstocks, Societies for the Prevention of All Human Activities, are
impossible in the wake of Laforgue. And he is therefore an exquisite poet, a deliverer of the nations, a
Numa Pompilius, a father of light. And to many people
this mystery, the mystery why such force should reside
in so fragile a book, why such power should coincide
with so great a nonchalance of manner, will remain forever a mystery.

> Que loin l'âme type
> Qui m'a dit adieu
> Parce que mes yeux
> Manquaient de principes!
>
> Elle, en ce moment.
> Elle, si pain tendre,
> Oh! peut-être engendre
> Quelque garnement.
>
> Car on l'a unie
> Avec un monsieur,
> Ce qu'il y a de mieux,
> Mais pauvre en génie.

Laforgue is incontrovertible. The "strong silent man" of the kinema has not monopolized all the certitudes.

TRISTAN CORBIERE

(1841–1875)

Corbière seems to me the greatest poet of the period. "La Rapsode Foraine et le Pardon de Sainte-Anne" is, to my mind, beyond all comment. He first published in '73, remained practically unknown until Verlaine's essay in '84, and was hardly known to "the public" until the Messein edition of his work in '91.

LA RAPSODE FORAINE ET LE PARDON DE SAINTE-ANNE

La Palud, 27 août, jour du Pardon.

> Bénite est l'infertile plage
> Où, comme la mer, tout est nud.

Sainte est la chapelle sauvage
De Sainte-Anne-de-la-Palud . . .

De la Bonne Femme Sainte Anne,
Grand'tante du petit Jésus,
En bois pourri dans sa soutane
Riche . . . plus riche que Crésus!

Contre elle la petite Vierge,
Fuseau frêle, attend l'*Angelus;*
Au coin, Joseph, tenant son cierge,
Niche, en saint qu'on ne fête plus . . .

C'est le Pardon.—Liesse et mystères—
Déjà l'herbe rase a des poux . . .
Sainte Anne, Onguent des belles-mères!
Consolation des époux! . . .

Des paroisses environnantes:
De Plougastel et Loc-Tudy,
Ils viennent tous planter leurs tentes,
Trois nuits, trois jours,—jusqu'au lundi.

Trois jours, trois nuits, la palud grogne,
Selon l'antique rituel,
—Choeur séraphique et chant d'ivrogne—
LE CANTIQUE SPIRITUEL.

Mère taillée à coups de hache,
Tout coeur de chêne dur et bon;
Sous l'or de ta robe se cache
L'âme en pièce d'un franc Breton!

—Vieille verte à la face usée
Comme la pierre du torrent,

Par des larmes d'amour creusée,
Séchée avec des pleurs de sang . . .

—Toi, dont la mamelle tarie
S'est refait, pour avoir porté
La Virginité de Marie,
Une mâle virginité!

—Servante-maîtresse altière,
Très haute devant le Très-Haut;
Au pauvre monde, pas fière,
Dame pleine de comme-il-faut!

—Bâton des aveugles! Béquille
Des vieilles! Bras des nouveau-nés!
Mère de madame ta fille!
Parente des abandonnés!

—O Fleur de la pucelle neuve!
Fruit de l'épouse au sein grossi!
Reposoir de la femme veuve . . .
Et du veuf Dame-de-merci!

—Arche de Joachim! Aïeule!
Médaille de cuivre effacé!
Gui sacré! Trèfle quatre-feuille!
Mont d'Horeb! Souche de Jessé!

—O toi qui recouvrais la cendre,
Qui filais comme on fait chez nous,
Quand le soir venait à descendre,
Tenant l'ENFANT sur tes genoux;

Toi qui fus là, seule, pour faire
Son maillot à Bethléem,
Et là, pour coudre son suaire
Douloureux, à Jérusalem! . . .

Des croix profondes sont tes rides,
Tes cheveux sont blancs comme fils . . .
—Préserve des regards arides
Le berceau de nos petits-fils . . .

Fais venir et conserve en joie
Ceux à naître et ceux qui sont nés,
Et verse, sans que Dieu te voie,
L'eau de tes yeux sur les damnés!

Reprends dans leur chemise blanche
Les petits qui sont en langueur . . .
Rappelle à l'éternel Dimanche
Les vieux qui traînent en longueur.

—Dragon-gardien de la Vierge,
Garde la crèche sous ton oeil.
Que, près de toi, Joseph-concierge
Garde la propreté du seuil!

Prends pitié de la fille-mère,
Du petit au bord du chemin . . .
Si quelqu'un leur jette la pierre,
Que la pierre se change en pain!

—Dame bonne en mer et sur terre,
Montre-nous le ciel et le port,
Dans la tempête ou dans la guerre . . .
O Fanal de la bonne mort!

Humble: à tes pieds n'as point d'étoile,
Humble . . . et brave pour protéger!
Dans la nue apparaît ton voile,
Pâle auréole du danger.

—Aux perdus dont la vie est grise,
(—Sauf respect—perdus de boisson)
Montre le clocher de l'église
Et le chemin de la maison.

Prête ta douce et chaste flamme
Aux chrétiens qui sont ici . . .
Ton remède de bonne femme
Pour tes bêtes-à-corne aussi!

Montre à nos femmes et servantes
L'ouvrage et la fécondité . . .
—Le bonjour aux âmes parentes
Qui sont bien dans l'éternité!

—Nous mettrons un cordon de cire,
De cire-vierge jaune autour
De ta chapelle et ferons dire
Ta messe basse au point du jour.

Préserve notre cheminée
Des sorts et du monde malin . . .
A Pâques te sera donnée
Une quenouille avec du lin.

Si nos corps sont puants sur terre,
Ta grâce est un bain de santé;
Répands sur nous, au cimetière,
Ta bonne odeur de sainteté.

—A l'an prochain!—Voici ton cierge:
(C'est deux livres qu'il a coûté)
. . . Respects à Madame la Vierge,
Sans oublier la Trinité.

. . . Et les fidèles, en chemise,
Sainte Anne, ayez pitié de nous!
Font trois fois le tour de l'église
En se traînant sur leurs genoux,

Et boivent l'eau miraculeuse
Où les Job teigneux ont lavé
Leur nudité contagieuse . . .
Allez: la Foi vous a sauvé!

C'est là que tiennent leurs cénacles
Les pauvres, frères de Jésus.
—Ce n'est pas la cour des miracles,
Les trous sont vrais: *Vide latus!*

Sont-ils pas divins sur leurs claies
Qu'auréole un nimbe vermeil
Ces propriétaires de plaies,
Rubis vivants sous le soleil! . . .

En aboyant, un rachitique
Secoue un moignon désossé,
Coudoyant un épileptique
Qui travaille dans un fossé.

Là, ce tronc d'homme où croît l'ulcère,
Contre un tronc d'arbre où croît le gui,
Ici, c'est la fille et la mère
Dansant la danse de Saint-Guy.

Cet autre pare le cautère
De son petit enfant malsain:
—L'enfant se doit à son vieux père . . .
—Et le chancre est un gagne-pain!

Là, c'est l'idiot de naissance,
Un *visité par Gabriel*,
Dans l'extase de l'innocence . . .
—L'innocent est (tout) près du ciel!—

—Tiens, passant, regarde: tout passe.
L'oeil de l'idiot est resté.
Car il est en état de grâce . . .
—Et la Grâce est l'Eternité!—

Parmi les autres, après vêpre,
Qui sont d'eau bénite arrosés,
Un cadavre, vivant de lèpre,
Fleurit, souvenir des croisés . . .

Puis tous ceux que les Rois de France
Guérissaient d'un toucher de doigts . . .
—Mais la France n'a plus de Rois,
Et leur dieu suspend sa clémence.
.   .   .   .   .   .
Une forme humaine qui beugle
Contre le *calvaire* se tient;
C'est comme une moitié d'aveugle:
Elle est borgne et n'a pas de chien . . .

C'est une rapsode foraine
Qui donne aux gens pour un liard
L' *Istoyre de la Magdalayne*,
Du *Juif Errant* ou d'*Abaylar*.

Elle hâle comme une plainte,
Comme une plainte de la faim,
Et, longue comme un jour sans pain,
Lamentablement, sa complainte . . .

—Ça chante comme ça respire,
Triste oiseau sans plume et sans nid
Vaguant où son instinct l'attire :
Autour des Bon-Dieu de granit . . .

Ça peut parler aussi, sans doute,
Ça peut penser comme ça voit :
Toujours devant soi la grand'route . . .
—Et, quand ç'a deux sous, ça les boit.

—Femme : on dirait, hélas !—sa nippe
Lui pend, ficelée en jupon ;
Sa dent noire serre une pipe
Eteinte . . . Oh, la vie a du bon !—

Son nom . . . ça se nomme Misère.
Ça s'est trouvé né par hasard.
Ça sera trouvé mort par terre . . .
La même chose—quelque part.

Si tu la rencontres, Poète,
Avec son vieux sac de soldat :
C'est notre soeur . . . donne—c'est fête—
Pour sa pipe, un peu de tabac ! . . .

Tu verras dans sa face creuse
Se creuser, comme dans du bois,
Un sourire ; et sa main galeuse
Te faire un vrai signe de croix.

                              (*Les Amours Jaunes.*)

It is not long since a "strong, silent" American, who had been spending a year or so in Paris, complained to me that "all French poetry smelt of talcum powder." He did not specifically mention Corbière, who, with perhaps a few dozen other French poets, may have been outside the scope of his research. Corbière came also to "Paris."

I

Bâtard de Créole et Breton,
Il vint aussi là—fourmilière,
Bazar où rien n'est en pierre,
Où le soleil manque de ton.

—Courage! On fait queue . . . Un planton
Vous pousse à la chaîne—derrière!—
—Incendie éteint, sans lumière;
Des seaux passent, vides ou non.—

Là, sa pauvre Muse pucelle
Fit le trottoir en *demoiselle.*
Ils disaient: Qu'est-ce qu'elle vend?

—Rien.—Elle restait là, stupide,
N'entendant pas sonner le vide
Et regardant passer le vent . . .

II

Là: vivre à coups de fouet!—passer
En fiacre, en correctionnelle;
Repasser à la ritournelle,
Se dépasser, et trépasser!—

—Non, petit, il faut commencer
Par être grand—simple ficelle—

Pauvre: remuer l'or à la pelle;
Obscur: un nom à tout casser! . . .

Le coller chez les mastroquets,
Et l'apprendre à des perroquets
Qui le chantent ou qui le sifflent—

—Musique!—C'est le paradis
Des mahomets ou des houris,
Des dieux souteneurs qui se giflent!

People, at least some of them, think more highly of his
Breton subjects than of the Parisian, but I can not see
that he loses force on leaving the sea-board; for example,
his "Frère et Soeur Jumeaux" seems to me "by the same
hand" and rather better than his "Roscoff." His language does not need any particular subject matter, or
prefer one to another. "Mannequin idéal, tête-de-turc
du leurre," "Fille de marbre, en rut!", "Je voudrais être
chien à une fille publique" are all, with a constant emis-
sion of equally vigorous phrases, to be found in the city
poems.   At his weakest he is touched with the style of
his time, i. e., he falls into a phrase à la Hugo,—but seldom.   And he is conscious of the will to break from
this manner, and is the first, I think, to satirize it, or at
least the first to hurl anything as apt and violent as
"garde nationale épique" or "inventeur de la larme
écrite" at the Romantico-rhetorico and the sentimento-
romantico of Hugo and Lamartine.   His nearest kinships
in our period are to Gautier and Laforgue, though it is
Villon whom most by life and temperament he must be
said to resemble.

Laforgue was, for four or five years, "reader" to the

ex-Kaiser's mama; he escaped and died of *la misère*.
Corbière had, I believe, but one level of poverty:

> Un beau jour—quel métier!—je faisais, comme ça
> Ma croisière.—Métier! . . . —Enfin. Elle passa.
> —Elle qui,—La Passante! Elle, avec son ombrelle!
> Vrai valet de bourreau, je la frôlai . . . —mais Elle
> Me regarda tout bas, souriant en dessous,
> Et—me tendit sa main, et . . . . .
> > m'a donné deux sous.

ARTHUR RIMBAUD

(1854–1891)

RIMBAUD's first book appeared in '73. His complete
poems with a preface by Verlaine in '95. Laforgue conveys his content by comment, Corbière by ejaculation, as
if the words were wrenched and knocked out of him by
fatality; by the violence of his feeling, Rimbaud presents
a thick suave color, firm, even.

Cinq heures du soir

AU CABARET VERT

> Depuis huit jours, j'avais déchiré mes bottines
> Aux cailloux aes chemins.   J'entrais à Charleroi,
> —*Au Cabaret Vert:* je demandai des tartines
> De beurre et du jambon qui fût à moitié froid.
>
> Bienheureux, j'allongeai les jambes sous la table
> Verte: je contemplai les sujets très naïfs
> De la tapisserie.—Et ce fut adorable,
> Quand la fille aux tétons énormes, aux yeux vifs,

—Celle-là, ce n'est pas un baiser qui l'épeure!—
Rieuse, m'apporta des tartines de beurre,
Du jambon tiède, dans un plat colorié,

Du jambon rose et blanc parfumé d'une gousse
D'ail,—et m'emplit la chope immense, avec sa mousse
Que dorait un rayon de soleil arriéré.

The actual writing of poetry has advanced little or not
at all since Rimbaud. Cézanne was the first to paint, as
Rimbaud had written,—in, for example, "Les Assis":

Ils ont greffé dans des amours epileptiques
Leur fantasque ossature aux grands squelettes noirs
De leurs chaises; leurs pieds aux barreaux rachitiques
S'entrelacent pour les matins et pour les soirs

Ces vieillards ont toujours fait tresse avec leurs sièges.

or in the octave of

VENUS ANADYOMENE

Comme d'un cercueil vert en fer-blanc, une tête
De femme à cheveux bruns fortement pommadés
D'une vieille baignoire émerge, lente et bête,
Montrant des déficits assez mal ravaudés;

Puis le col gras et gris, les larges omoplates
Qui saillent; le dos court qui rentre et qui ressort,
—La graisse sous la peau parait en feuilles plates
Et les rondeurs des reins semble prendre l'essor.

Tailhade has painted his "Vieilles Actrices" at greater

length, but smiling; Rimbaud does not endanger his intensity by a chuckle.   He is serious as Cézanne is serious.
Comparisons across an art are always vague and inexact, and there are no real parallels; still it is possible to think of Corbière a little as one thinks of Goya, without Goya's Spanish, with infinite differences, but with a macabre intensity, and a modernity that we have not yet surpassed. There are possible grounds for comparisons of like sort between Rimbaud and Cézanne.

Tailhade and Rimbaud were both born in '54; there is not a question of priority in date, I do not know who hit first on the form, but Rimbaud's "Chercheuses" is a very good example of a mould not unlike that into which Tailhade has cast his best poems.

LES CHERCHEUSES DE POUX

Quand le front de l'enfant plein de rouges tourmentes,
Implore l'essaim blanc des rêves indistincts,
Il vient près de son lit deux grandes soeurs charmantes
Avec de frêles doigts aux ongles argentins.

Elles asseoient l'enfant auprès d'une croisée
Grande ouverte où l'air bleu baigne un fouillis de fleurs,
Et, dans ses lourds cheveux où tombe la rosée,
Promènent leurs doigts fins, terribles et charmeurs.

Il écoute chanter leurs haleines craintives
Qui fleurent de longs miels végétaux et rosés
Et qu'interrompt parfois un sifflement, salives
Reprises sur la lèvre ou désirs de baisers.

Il entend leurs cils noirs battant sous les silences
Parfumés; et leurs doigts électriques et doux

Font crépiter, parmi ses grises indolences,
Sous leurs ongles royaux la mort des petits poux.

Voilà que monte en lui le vin de la Paresse,
Soupir d'harmonica qui pourrait délirer ;
L'enfant se sent, selon la lenteur des caresses,
Sourdre et mourir sans cesse un désir de pleurer.

The poem is "not really" like Tailhade's, but the comparison is worth while. Many readers will be unable to "see over" the subject matter and consider the virtues of the style, but we are, let us hope, serious people; besides, Rimbaud's mastery is not confined to "the unpleasant"; "Roman" begins:

I

On n'est pas sérieux, quand on a dix-sept ans.
—Un beau soir, foin des bocks et de la limonade,
Des cafés tapageurs aux lustres éclatants !
—On va sous les tilleuls verts de la promenade.

Les tilleuls sentent bon dans les bons soirs de juin !
L' air est parfois si doux, qu'on ferme la paupière ;
Le vent chargé de bruits,—la ville n'est pas loin—
A des parfums de vigne et des parfums de bière . . .

The sixth line is worthy ⌣ To-em-mei. But Rimbaud has not exhausted his idyllic moods or capacities in one poem. Witness:

COMEDIE EN TROIS BAISERS

Elle était fort déshabillée,
Et de grands arbres indiscrets
Aux vitres penchaient leur feuillée
Malinement, tout près, tout près.

Assise sur ma grande chaise,
Mi-nue elle joignait les mains.
Sur le plancher frissonnaient d'aise
Ses petits pieds si fins, si fins.

—Je regardai, couleur de cire
Un petit rayon buissonnier
Papillonner, comme un sourire
Sur son beau sein, mouche au rosier.

—Je baisai ses fines chevilles.
Elle eut un long rire très mal
Qui s'égrenait en claires trilles,
Une risure de cristal. . . .

Les petits pieds sous la chemise
Se sauvèrent: "Veux-tu finir!"
—La première audace permise,
Le rire feignait de punir!

—Pauvrets palpitant sous ma lèvre,
Je baisai doucement ses yeux:
—Elle jeta sa tête mièvre
En arrière: "Oh! c'est encor mieux! . . ."

"Monsieur, j'ai deux mots à te dire. . . ."
—Je lui jetai le reste au sein

Dans un baiser, qui la fit rire
D'un bon rire qui voulait bien . . .

—Elle était fort déshabillée
Et de grands arbres indiscrets,
Aux vitres penchaient leur feuillée
Malinement, tout près, tout près.

The subject matter is older than Ovid, and how many poems has it led to every silliness, every vulgarity! One has no instant of doubt here, nor, I think, in any line of any poem of Rimbaud's. How much I might have learned from the printed page that I have learned slowly from actualities. Or perhaps we never do learn from the page; but are only capable of recognizing the page after we have learned from actuality.

I do not know whether or no Rimbaud "started" the furniture poetry with "Le Buffet"; it probably comes, most of it, from the beginning of Gautier's "Albertus." I cannot see that the "Bateau Ivre" rises above the general level of his work, though many people seem to know of this poem (and of the sonnet on the vowels) who do not know the rest of his work. Both of these poems are in Van Bever and Léautaud. I wonder in what other poet will we find such firmness of coloring and such certitude.

TABLE

Laforgue 1860-1887; published 1885
Corbière 1840-1875; published 1873 and 1891
Rimbaud 1854-1891; published 1873
Remy de Gourmont 1858-1915
Merril 1868-1915

Tailhade 1854-1919
Verhaeren 1855-1916
Moréas 1856-1911
Living:
Vielé-Griffin 1864
Jammes 1868
De Régnier 1864
Spire 1868
Younger Men:
Klingsor, Romains, Vildrac
Other Dates:
Verlaine 1844-1896
Mallarmé 1842-1898
Samain 1858-1900
Elskamp, born 1862

REMY DE GOURMONT

(1858-1915)

As in prose, Remy de Gourmont found his own form, so also in poetry, influenced presumably by the medieval sequaires and particularly by Goddeschalk's quoted in his (De Gourmont's) work c.i "Le Latin Mystique," he recreated the "litanies." It was one of the great gifts of "symbolisme," of the doctrine that one should "suggest" not "present"; it is, in his hand, an effective indirectness. The procession of all beautiful women moves before one in the "Litanies de la Rose"; and the rhythm is incomparable. It is not a poem to lie on the page, it must come to life in audition, or in the finer audition which one may have in imagining sound. One must "hear" it, in one way or another, and out of that

intoxication comes beauty. One does no injustice to
De Gourmont by giving this poem alone. The "Litany
of the Trees" is of equal or almost equal beauty. The
Sonnets in prose are different; they rise out of natural
speech, out of conversation. Paul Fort perhaps began
or rebegan the use of conversational speech in rhyming
prose paragraphs, at times charmingly.

LITANIES DE LA ROSE

A Henry de Groux.

Fleur hypocrite,
Fleur du silence.
Rose couleur de cuivre, plus frauduleuse que nos joies,
rose couleur de cuivre, embaume-nous dans tes men-
songes, fleur hypocrite, fleur du silence.
Rose au visage peint comme une fille d'amour, rose au
cœur prostitué, rose au visage peint, fais semblant d'être
pitoyable, fleur hypocrite, fleur du silence.
Rose à la joue puérile, ô vierges des futures trahisons,
rose à la joue puérile, innocente et rouge, ouvre les rets
de tes yeux clairs, fleur hypocrite, fleur du silence.
Rose aux yeux noirs, miroir de ton néant, rose aux
yeux noirs, fais-nous croire au mystère, fleur hypocrite,
fleur du silence.
Rose couleur d'or pur, ô coffre-fort de l'idéal, rose
couleur d'or pur, donne-nous la clef de ton ventre, fleur
hypocrite, fleur du silence.
Rose couleur d'argent, encensoir de nos rêves, rose
couleur d'argent prends notre cœur et fais-en de la
fumée, fleur hypocrite, fleur du silence.
Rose au regard saphique, plus pâle que les lys, rose au
regard saphique, offre-nous le parfum de ton illusoire
virginité, fleur hypocrite, fleur du silence.

Rose au front pourpre, colère des femmes dédaignées, rose au front pourpre dis-nous le secret de ton orgueil, fleur hypocrite, fleur du silence.

Rose au front d'ivoire jaune, amante de toi-même, rose au front d'ivoire jaune, dis-nous le secret de tes nuits virginales, fleur hypocrite, fleur du silence.

Rose aux lèvres de sang, ô mangeuse de chair, rose aux lèvres de sang, si tu veux notre sang, qu'en ferions-nous? bois-le, fleur hypocrite, fleur du silence.

Rose couleur de soufre, enfer des désirs vains, rose couleur de soufre, allume le bûcher où tu planes, âme et flamme, fleur hypocrite, fleur du silence.

Rose couleur de pêche, fruit velouté de fard, rose sournoise, rose couleur de pêche, empoisonne nos dents, fleur hypocrite, fleur du silence.

Rose couleur de chair, déesse de la bonne volonté, rose couleur de chair, fais-nous baiser la tristesse de ta peau fraîche et fade, fleur hypocrite, fleur du silence.

Rose vineuse, fleur des tonnelles et des caves, rose vineuse, les alcools fous gambadent dans ton haleine: souffle-nous l'horreur de l'amour, fleur hypocrite, fleur du silence.

Rose violette, ô modestie des fillettes perverses, rose violette, tes yeux sont plus grands que le reste, fleur hypocrite, fleur du silence.

Rose rose, pucelle au cœur désordonné, rose rose, robe de mousseline, entr'ouvre tes ailes fausses, ange, fleur hypocrite, fleur du silence.

Rose en papier de soie, simulacre adorable des grâces incréées, rose en papier de soie, n'es-tu pas la vraie rose, fleur du silence.

Rose couleur d'aurore, couleur du temps, couleur de rien, ô sourire du Sphinx, rose couleur d'aurore, sourire

ouvert sur le néant, nous t'aimerons, car tu mens, fleur
hypocrite, fleur du silence.

Rose blonde, léger manteau de chrôme sur des épaules
frêles, ô rose blonde, femelle plus forte que les mâles,
fleur hypocrite, fleur du silence!

Rose en forme de coupe, vase rouge où mordent les
dents quand la bouche y vient boire, rose en forme de
coupe, nos morsures te font sourire et nos baisers te
font pleurer, fleur hypocrite, fleur du silence.

Rose toute blanche, innocente et couleur de lait, rose
toute blanche, tant de candeur nous épouvante, fleur
hypocrite, fleur du silence.

Rose couleur de bronze, pâte cuite au soleil, rose
couleur de bronze, les plus durs javelots s'émoussent sur
ta peau, fleur hypocrite fleur du silence.

Rose couleur de feu, creuset spécial pour les chairs
réfractaires, rose couleur de feu, ô providence des
ligueurs en enfance, fleur hypocrite, fleur du silence.

Rose incarnate, rose stupide et pleine de santé, rose
incarnate, tu nous abreuves et tu nous leurres d'un vin
très rouge et très bénin, fleur hypocrite, fleur du silence.

Rose en satin cerise, munificence exquise des lèvres
triomphales, rose en satin cerise, ta bouche enluminée a
posé sur nos chairs le sceau de pourpre de son mirage,
fleur hypocrite, fleur du silence.

Rose au cœur virginal, ô louche et rose adolescence qui
n'a pas encore parlé, rose au cœur virginal, tu n'as rien
à nous dire, fleur hypocrite, fleur du silence.

Rose groseille, honte et rougeur des péchés ridicules,
rose groseille, on a trop chiffonné ta robe, fleur hypocrite,
fleur du silence.

Rose couleur du soir, demi-morte d'ennui, fumée
crépusculaire, rose couleur du soir, tu meurs d'amour

en baisant tes mains lasses, fleur hypocrite, fleur du silence.

Rose bleue, rose iridine, monstre couleur des yeux de la Chimère, rose bleue, lève un peu tes paupières : as-tu peur qu-on te regarde, les yeux dans les yeux, Chimère, fleur hypocrite, fleur du silence!

Rose verte, rose couleur de mer, ô nombril des sirènes, rose verte, gemme ondoyante et fabuleuse, tu n'es plus que de l'eau dès qu'un doigt t'a touchée, fleur hypocrite, fleur du silence.

Rose escarboucle, rose fleurie au front noir du dragon, rose escarboucle, tu n'es plus qu'une boucle de ceinture, fleur hypocrite, fleur du silence.

Rose couleur de vermillon, bergère énamourée couchée dans les sillons, rose couleur de vermillon, le berger te respire et le bouc t'a broutée, fleur hypocrite, fleur du silence.

Rose des tombes, fraîcheur émanée des charognes, rose des tombes, toute mignonne et rose, adorable parfum des fines pourritures, tu fais semblant de vivre, fleur hypocrite, fleur du silence.

Rose brune, couleur des mornes acajous, rose brune, plaisirs permis, sagesse, prudence et prévoyance, tu nous regardes avec des yeux rogues, fleur hypocrite, fleur du silence.

Rose ponceau, ruban des fillettes modèles, rose ponceau, gloire des petites poupées, es-tu niaise ou sournoise, joujou des petits frères, fleur hypocrite, fleur du silence.

Rose rouge et noire, rose insolente et secrète, rose rouge et noire, ton insolence et ton rouge ont pâli parmi les compromis qu'invente la vertu, fleur hypocrite, fleur du silence.

Rose ardoise, grisaille des vertus vaporeuses, rose ardoise, tu grimpes et tu fleuris autour des vieux bancs solitaires, rose du soir, fleur hypocrite, fleur du silence.

Rose pivoine, modeste vanité des jardins plantureux, rose pivoine, le vent n'a retroussé tes feuilles que par hasard, et tu n'en fus pas mécontente, fleur hypocrite, fleur du silence.

Rose neigeuse, couleur de la neige et des plumes du cygne, rose neigeuse, tu sais que la neige est fragile et tu n'ouvres tes plumes de cygne qu'aux plus insignes, fleur hypocrite, fleur du silence.

Rose hyaline, couleur des sources claires jaillies d'entre les herbes, rose hyaline, Hylas est mort d'avoir aimé tes yeux, fleur hypocrite, fleur du silence.

Rose opale, ô sultane endormie dans l'odeur du harem, rose opale, langueur des constantes caresses, ton cœur connaît la paix profonde des vices satisfaits, fleur hypocrite, fleur du silence.

Rose améthyste, étoile matinale, tendresse épiscopale, rose améthyste, tu dors sur des poitrines dévotes et douillettes, gemme offerte à Marie, ô gemme sacristine, fleur hypocrite, fleur du silence.

Rose cardinale, rose couleur du sang de l'Eglise romaine, rose cardinale, tu fais rêver les grands yeux des mignons et plus d'un t'épingla au nœud de sa jarretière, fleur hypocrite, fleur du silence.

Rose papale, rose arrosée des mains qui bénissent le monde, rose papale, ton cœur d'or est en cuivre, et les larmes qui perlent sur ta vaine corolle, ce sont les pleurs du Christ, fleur hypocrite, fleur du silence.

Fleur hypocrite,
Fleur du silence.

DE REGNIER

(born 1864)

DE RÉGNIER is counted a successor to the Parnassiens,

and has indeed written much of gods and of marble fountains, as much perhaps of the marble decor, as have other contemporaries of late renaissance and of more modern house furniture. His "J'ai feint que les dieux m'aient parlé" opens charmingly. He has in the "Odelettes" made two darts into vers libre which are perhaps worth many more orderly pages, and show lyric sweetness.

ODELETTE

Si j'ai parlé
De mon amour, c'est à l'eau lente
Qui m'écoute quand je me penche
Sur elle; si j'ai parlé
De mon amour, c'est au vent
Qui rit et cuchote entre les branches;
Si j'ai parlé de mon amour, c'est à l'oiseau
Qui passe et chante
Avec le vent;
Si j'ai parlé
C'est à l'écho.

Si j'ai aimé de grand amour,
Triste ou joyeux,
Ce sont tes yeux;
Si j'ai aimé de grand amour,
Ce fut ta bouche grave et douce,
Ce fut ta bouche;
Si j'ai aimé de grand amour,
Ce furent ta chair tiède et tes mains fraîches,
Et c'est ton ombre que je cherche.

He has joined himself to the painters of contemporary things in:

L'ACCUEIL

Tous deux étaient beaux de corps et de visages,
L'air francs et sages
Avec un clair sourire dans les yeux,
Et, devant eux,
Debout **en leur** jeunesse svelte et prompte,
Je me **sentais** courbé et j'avais presque honte
D'être si vieux.

Les ans
Sont lourds aux épaules et pèsent
Aux plus fortes
De tout le poids des heures mortes,
Les ans
Sont durs, et brève
La vie et l'on a vite des cheveux blancs;
Et j'ai déjà vécu beaucoup de jours.
Les ans sont lourds. . . .

Et tous deux me regardaient, surpris de voir
Celui qu'ils croyaient autre en leur pensée
Se lever pour les recevoir
Vêtu de bure et le front nu
Et non pas, comme en leur pensée,
Drapé de pourpre et lauré d'or

Et je leur dis: "Soyez tous deux les bienvenus."
Ce fut alors
Que je leur dis:
"Mes fils, quoi, vous avez monté la côte
Sous ce soleil cuisant d'août
Jusqu'à ma maison haute,

O vous
Qu'attend là-bas peut-être, au terme du chemin
Le salut amoureux de quelque blanche main!
Si vous avez pour moi allongé votre route
Peut-être, au moins mes chants vous auront-ils aidés,
De leurs rythmes présents en vos mémoires,
A marcher d'un jeune pas scandé
Je n'ai jamais désiré d'autre gloire
Sinon que les vers du poète
Plussent à la voix qui les répète.
Si les miens vous ont plu: merci,
Car c'est pour cela que, chantant
Mon rêve, après l'avoir conçu en mon esprit,
Depuis vingt ans,
J'habite ici."

Et, d'un geste, je leur montrai la chambre vide
Avec son mur de pierre et sa lampe d'argile
Et le lit où je dors et le sol où, du pied,
Je frappe pour apprendre au vers estropié
A marcher droit, et le calame de roseau
Dont la pointe subtile aide à fixer le mot
Sur la tablette lisse et couverte de cire
Dont la divine odeur la retient et l'attire
Et le fait, dans la strophe en fleurs qu'il ensoleille,
Mystérieusement vibrer comme une abeille.

Et je repris:
"Mes fils,
Les ans
Sont lourds aux épaules et pèsent
Aux plus fortes
De tout le poids des heures mortes.
Les ans

Sont durs, la vie est brève
Et l'on a vite des cheveux blancs,
Si quelque jour,
En revenant d'où vous allez,
Vous rencontriez sur cette même route,
Entre les orges et les blés,
Des gens en troupe
Montant ici avec des palmes à la main,
Dites-vous bien
Que si vous les suiviez vous ne me verriez pas
Comme aujourd'hui debout en ma robe de laine
Qui se troue à l'épaule et se déchire au bras,
Mais drapé de pourpre hautaine
Peut-être—et mort
Et lauré d'or!"

Je leur ai dit cela, pour qu'ils le sachent,
Car ils sont beaux tous deux de corps et de visages,
L'air francs et sages
Avec un clair sourire aux yeux,
Parce qu'en eux
Peut-être vit quelque désir de gloire,
Je leur ai parlé ainsi pour qu'ils sachent
Ce qu'est la gloire,
Ce qu'elle donne,
Ce qu'il faut croire
De son vain jeu,
Et que son dur laurier ne pose sa couronne
Que sur le front inerte et qui n'est plus qu'un peu
Déjà d'argile humaine où vient de vivre un Dieu.

Here we have the modern tone in De Régnier. My
own feeling at the moment is that his hellenics, his verse
on classical and ancient subjects, is likely to be over-

shadowed by that of Samain and Heredia. I have
doubts whether his books will hold against the Cléopatra
sonnets, or if he has equaled, in this vein, the poem
beginning "Mon âme est une infante en robe de parade."
But in the lyric odelette, and in this last given poem
in particular, we find him leading perhaps onward toward
Vildrac, and toward a style which might be the basis for
a certain manner F. M. Hueffer has used in English vers
libre, rather than remembering the Parnassiens.

EMILE VERHAEREN

VERHAEREN has been so well introduced to America
by his obituary notices that I can scarcely hope to com-
pete with them in this limited space. One can hardly
represent him better than by the well known:

LES PAUVRES

Il est ainsi de pauvres cœurs
avec en eux, des lacs de pleurs,
qui sont pâles, comme les pierres
d'un cimetière.

Il est ainsi de pauvres dos
plus lourds de peine et de fardeaux
que les toits des cassines brunes,
parmi les dunes.

Il est ainsi de pauvres mains,
comme feuilles sur les chemins,
comme feuilles jaunes et mortes,
devant la porte.

Il est ainsi de pauvres yeux
humbles et bons et soucieux
et plus tristes que ceux des bêtes,
sous la tempête.

Il est ainsi de pauvres gens,
aux gestes las et indulgents
sur qui s'acharne la misère,
au long des plaines de la terre.

VIELE-GRIFFIN

Two men, half-Americans, Vielé-Griffin and Stuart Merril, won for themselves places among the recent French poets. Vielé-Griffin's poem for the death of Mallarmé is among his better known works:

IN MEMORIAM STEPHANE MALLARMÉ

Si l'on te disait: Maître!
Le jour se lève;
Voici une aube encore, la même, pâle;
Maître, j'ai ouvert la fenêtre,
L'aurore s'en vient encor du seuil oriental,
Un jour va naître!
—Je croirais t'entendre dire: Je rêve.

Si l'on te disait: Maître, nous sommes là,
Vivants et forts,
Comme ce soir d'hier, devant ta porte;
Nous sommes venus en riant, nous sommes là,
Guettant le sourire et l'étreinte forte,
—On nous répondrait: Le Maître est mort.

Des fleurs de ma terrasse,
Des fleurs comme au feuillet d'un livre,
Des fleurs, pourquoi?
Voici un peu de nous, la chanson basse
Qui tourne et tombe,
—Comme ces feuilles-ci tombent et tournoient—
Voici la honte et la colère de vivre
Et de parler des mots—contre ta tombe.

His curious and, perhaps not in the bad sense, old-fashioned melodic quality shows again in the poem beginning:

> Lâche comme le froid et la pluie,
> Brutal et sourd comme le vent,
> Louche et faux comme le ciel bas,
> L'Automne rôde par ici,
> Son bâton heurte aux contrevents;
> Ouvre la porte, car il est là.
> Ouvre la porte et fais-lui honte,
> Son manteau s'effiloche et traîne,
> Ses pieds sont alourdis de boue;
> Jette-lui des pierres, quoi qu'il te conte,
> Ne crains pas ses paroles de haine:
> C'est toujours un rôle qu'il joue.

. . . . . .

It is embroidery à la Charles D'Orléans; one must take it or leave it.

STUART MERRIL

I know that I have seen somewhere a beautiful and effective ballad of Merril's. His "Chambre D'Amour"

would be more interesting if Samain had not written
"L'Infante," but Merril's painting is perhaps interesting
as comparison. It begins:

> Dans la chambre qui fleure un peu la bergamote,
> Ce soir, lasse, la voix de l'ancien clavecin
> Chevrote des refrains enfantins de gavotte.

There is a great mass of this poetry full of highly
cultured house furnishing; I think Catulle Mendès also
wrote it. Merril's "Nocturne" illustrates a mode of
symbolistic writing which has been since played out and
parodied:

> La blême lune allume en la mare qui luit,
> Miroir des gloires d'or, un émoi d'incendie.
> Tout dort.   Seul, à mi-mort, un rossignol de nuit
> Module en mal d'amour sa molle mélodie.
> Plus ne vibrent les vents en le mystère vert
> Des ramures. La lune a tu leurs voix nocturnes :
> Mais à travers le deuil du feuillage entr'ouvert
> Pleuvent les bleus baisers des astres taciturnes.

.   .   .   .   .   .

There is no need to take this sort of tongue-twisting
too seriously, though it undoubtedly was so taken in
Paris during the late eighties and early nineties. He is
better illustrated in "La Wallonie," vide infra.

LAURENT TAILHADE

1854-1919

TAILHADE's satires seem rough if one come upon them
straight from reading Laforgue; and Laforgue will seem,
and is presumably, the greatly finer artist; but one

should not fail to note certain definite differences.
Laforgue is criticizing, and conveying a mood. He is
more or less literary, playing with words. Tailhade is
painting contemporary Paris, with verve. His eye is
on the thing itself. He has, au fond, not very much
in common with Laforgue. He was born six years before Laforgue and in the same year as Rimbaud. Their
temperaments are by no means identical. I do not
know whether Tailhade wrote "Hydrotherapie" before
Rimbaud had done "Les Chercheuses." Rimbaud in
that poem identifies himself more or less with the child
and its feeling. Tailhade is detached. I do not say
this as praise of either one or the other. I am only
trying to keep things distinct.

HYDROTHERAPIE

Le vieux monsieur, pour prendre une douche ascendante,
A couronné son chef d'un casque d'hidalgo
Qui, malgré sa bedaine ample et son lumbago,
Lui donne un certain air de famille avec Dante.

Ainsi ses membres gourds et sa vertebre à point
Traversent l'appareil des tuyaux et des lances,
Tandis que des masseurs, tout gonflés d'insolences,
Frottent au gant de crin son dos où l'acné point.

Oh! l'eau froide! la bonne et rare panacée
Qui, seule, raffermit la charpente lassée
Et le protoplasma des sénateurs pesants!

Voici que, dans la rue, au sortir de sa douche,
Le vieux monsieur qu'on sait un magistrat farouche
Tient des propos grivois aux filles de douze ans.

QUARTIER LATIN

Dans le bar où jamais le parfum des brévas
Ne dissipa l'odeur de vomi qui la navre
Triomphent les appas de la mère Cadavre
Dont le nom est fameux jusque chez les Howas.

Brune, elle fut jadis vantée entre les brunes,
Tant que son souvenir au Vaux-Hall est resté.
Et c'est toujours avec beaucoup de dignité
Qu'elle rince le zinc et détaille les prunes.

A ces causes, son cabaret s'emplit le soir,
De futurs avoués, trop heureux de surseoir
Quelque temps à l'étude inepte des *Digestes,*

Des Valaques, des riverains du fleuve Amoor
S'acoquinent avec des potards indigestes
Qui s'y viennent former aux choses de l'amour.

RUS

Ce qui fait que l'ancien bandagiste renie
Le comptoir dont le faste alléchait les passants,
C'est son jardin d'Auteuil où, veufs de tout encens,
Les zinnias ont l'air d'être en tôle vernie.

C'est là qu'il vient, le soir, goûter l'air aromal
Et, dans sa rocking-chair, en veston de flanelle,
Aspirer les senteurs qu'épanchent sur Grenelle
Les fabriques de suif et de noir animal.

Bien que libre-penseur et franc-maçon, il juge
Le dieu propice qui lui donna ce refuge
Où se meurt un cyprin emmy la pièce d'eau,
Où, dans la tour mauresque aux lanternes chinoises,
—Tout en lui préparant du sirop de framboises—
Sa "demoiselle" chante un couplet de Nadaud.

From this beneficent treatment of the amiable burgess;
from this perfectly poetic inclusion of modernity, this
unrhetorical inclusion of the factories in the vicinity of
Grenelle (inclusion quite different from the allegorical
presentation of workmen's trousers in sculpture, and the
grandiloquent theorizing about the socialistic up-lift or
down-pull of smoke and machinery), Tailhade can move
to personal satire, a personal satire impersonalized by
its glaze and its finish.

RONDEL

Dans les cafés d'adolescents
Moréas cause avec Frémine :
L'un, d'un parfait cuistre a la mine,
L'autre beugle des contre-sens.

Rien ne sort moins de chez Classens
Que le linge de ces bramines.
Dans les cafés d'adolescents,
Moréas cause avec Frémine.

Désagrégeant son albumine,
La Tailhède offre quelque encens :
Maurras leur invente Commine

Et ça fait roter les passants,
Dans les cafés d'adolescents.

But perhaps the most characteristic phase of Tailhade is in his pictures of the bourgeoisie. Here is one depicted with all Tailhadian serenity. Note also the opulence of his vocables.

DINER CHAMPETRE

Entre les siègès où des garçons volontaires
Entassent leurs chalants parmi les boulingrins,
La famille Feyssard, avec des airs sereins,
Discute longuement les tables solitaires.

La demoiselle a mis un chapeau rouge vif
Dont s'honore le bon faiseur de sa commune,
Et madame Feyssard, un peu hommasse et brune,
Porte une robe loutre avec des reflets d'if.

Enfin ils sont assis! Or le père commande
Des écrevisses, du potage au lait d'amande,
Toutes choses dont il rêvait depuis longtemps.

Et, dans le ciel couleur de turquoises fanées,
Il voit les songes bleus qu'en ses esprits flottant
A fait naître l'ampleur des truites saumonées.

All through this introduction I am giving the sort of French poem least likely to have been worn smooth for us; I mean the kind of poem least represented in English. Landor and Swinburne have, I think, forestalled Tailhade's hellenic poems in our affections. There are also his ballades to be considered.

A STUDY IN FRENCH POETS

FRANCIS JAMMES

(born 1868)

THE bulk of Jammes' unsparable poetry is perhaps larger than that of any man still living in France. The three first books of poems, and "Le Triomphe de la Vie" containing "Existences," the more than "Spoon River" of France, must contain about six hundred pages worth reading. "Existences" can not be rendered in snippets. It is not a series of poems, but the canvass of a whole small town or half city, unique, inimitable and "to the life," full of verve. Only those who have read it and "L'Angelus de l'Aube," can appreciate the full tragedy of Jammes' débâcle. Paul Fort had what his friends boasted as "tone," and he has diluted himself with topicalities; in Jammes' case it is more charitable to suppose some organic malady, some definite softening of the brain, for he seems perfectly simple and naïve in his débâcle. It may be, in both cases, that the organisms have broken beneath the strain of modern existence. But the artist has no business to break.

Let us begin with Jammes' earlier work:

> J'aime l'âne si doux
> marchant le long des houx.
> Il prend garde aux abeilles
> et bouge ses oreilles;
> et il porte les pauvres
> et des sacs remplis d'orge
> Il va, près des fossés
> d'un petit pas cassé.
> Mon amie le croit bête

parce qu'il est poëte.
Il réflechit toujours,
Ses yeux sont en velours.
Jeune fille au doux cœur
tu n'as pas sa douceur.

.   .   .   .

The fault is the fault, or danger, which Dante has
labeled "muliebria"; of its excess Jammes has since
perished. But the poem to the donkey can, in certain
moods, please one. In other moods the playful simplicity, at least in excess, is almost infuriating. He runs
so close to sentimentalizing—when he does not fall into
that puddle—that there are numerous excuses for those
who refuse him altogether. "J'allai à Lourdes" has
pathos. Compare it with Corbière's "St. Anne" and the
decadence is apparent; it is indeed a sort of half-way
house between the barbaric Breton religion and the ultimate deliquescence of French Catholicism in Claudel,
who (as I think it is James Stephens has said) "is
merely lying on his back kicking his heels in it."

J' ALLAI A LOURDES

J'allai à Lourdes par le chemin de fer,
le long du gave qui est bleu comme l'air.

Au soleil les montagnes semblaient d'étain.
Et l'on chantait: sauvez! sauvez! dans le train,

Il y avait un monde fou, exalté,
plein de poussière et du soleil d'été.

Des malheureux avec le ventre en avant
étendaient leurs bras, priaient en les tordant.

Et dans une chaire où était du drap bleu,
un prêtre disait: "un chapelet à Dieu!"

Et un groupe de femmes, parfois, passait,
qui chantait: sauvez! sauvez! sauvez! sauvez!

Et la procession chantait. Les drapeaux
se penchaient avec leurs devises en or.

Le soleil était blanc sur les escaliers
dans l'air bleu, sur les cloches déchiquetées.

Mais sur un brancard, portée par ses parents,
son pauvre père tête nue et priant,

et ses frères qui disaient: "ainsi soit-il,"
une jeune fille sur le point de mourir.

Oh! qu'elle était belle! elle avait dix-huit ans,
et elle souriait; elle était en blanc.

Et la procession chantait. Des drapeaux
se penchaient avec leurs devises en or.

Moi je serrais les dents pour ne pas pleurer,
et cette fille, je me sentais l'aimer.

Oh! elle m'a regardé un grand moment,
une rose blanche en main, souriant.

Mais maintenant où es-tu? dis, où es-tu,
Es-tu morte? je t'aime, toi qui m'as vu.

Si tu existes, Dieu, ne la tue pas.
elle avait des mains blanches, de minces bras.

Dieu ne la tue pas!—et ne serait-ce que
pour son père nu-tête qui priait Dieu.

Jammes goes to pieces on such adjectives as "pauvre"
and "petite," just as DeRégnier slips on "cher," "aimée"
and "tiède"; and in their train flock the herd whose adjectival centre appears to waver from "nue" to "frémis-
sante." And there is, in many French poets, a fatal
proclivity to fuss just a little too much over their subjects. Jammes has also the furniture tendency, and to
it we owe several of his quite charming poems. However the strongest impression I get to-day, reading his
work in inverse order (i. e. "Jean de Noarrieu" before
these earlier poems), is of the very great stylistic advance made in that poem over his earlier work.

But he is very successful in saying all there was to be
said in:—

LA JEUNE FILLE

La jeune fille est blanche,
elle a des veines vertes
au poignets, dans ses manches
    ouvertes.
On ne sait pas pourquoi
elle rit. Par moments
elle crie et cela
    est perçant.
Est-ce qu'elle se doute
qu'elle vous prend le cœur
en cueillant sur la route
    des fleurs.

On dirait quelquefois
qu'elle comprend des choses.
Pas toujours.   Elle cause
        tout bas
"Oh! ma chère! oh! là, là . . .
 . . . Figure-toi . . . mardi
je l'ai vu . . . j'ai ri"—Elle dit
        comme ça.
Quand un jeune homme souffre,
d'abord elle se tait:
elle ne rit plus, tout
        etonnée.
Dans les petits chemins
elle remplit ses mains
de piquants de bruyères
        de fougères.
Elle est grande, elle est blanche,
elle a des bras très doux,
Elle est très droite et penche
        le cou.

The poem beginning:

Tu seras nue dans le salon aux vieilles choses,
fine comme un fuseau de roseau de lumière
et, les jambes croisées, auprès du feu rose
        tu écouteras l'hiver

loses, perhaps, or gains little by comparison with that of
Heinrich von Morungen, beginning:

Oh weh, soll mir nun nimmermehr
hell leuchten durch die Nacht
noch weisser denn ein Schnee

ihr Leib so wohl gemacht?
Der trog die Augen mein,
ich wähnt, es sollte sein
des lichten Monden Schein,
da tagte es.

Morungen had had no occasion to say "Je pense à
Jean-Jacques," and it is foolish to expect exactly the
same charm of a twentieth-century poet that we find in
a thirteenth-century poet. Still it is not necessary to be
Jammes-crazy to feel

IL VA NEIGER . . .

Il va neiger dans quelques jours.   Je me souviens
de l'an dernier.   Je me souviens de mes tristesses
au coin du feu.   Si l'on m'avait demandé: qu'est-ce?
j'aurais dit: laissez-moi tranquille.   Ce n'est rien.
J'ai bien réfléchi, l'année avant, dans ma chambre,
pendant que la neige lourde tombait dehors.
J'ai réfléchi pour rien.   A présent comme alors
je fume une pipe en bois avec un bout d'ambre.

Ma vieille commode en chêne sent toujours bon.
Mais moi j'étais bête parce que ces choses
ne pouvaient pas changer et que c'est une pose
de vouloir chasser les choses que nous savons.

Pourquoi donc pensons-nous et parlons-nous?   C'est
    drôle;
nos larmes et nos baisers, eux, ne parlent pas,
et cependant nous les comprenons, et les pas
d'un ami sont plus doux que de douces paroles.

If I at all rightly understand the words "vouloir chasser les choses que nous savons" they are an excellent warning against the pose of simplicity over-done that has been the end of Maeterlinck, and of how many other poets whose poetic machinery consists in so great part of pretending to know less than they do.

Jammes' poems are well represented in Miss Lowell's dilutation on *Six French Poets,* especially by the well-known "Amsterdam" and "Madame de Warens," which are also in Van Bever and Léautaud. He reaches, as I have said, his greatest verve in "Existences" in the volume "Le Triomphe de la Vie."

I do not wish to speak in superlatives, but "Existences," if not Jammes' best work, and if not the most important single volume by any living French poet, either of which it well may be, is at any rate indispensable. It is one of the first half dozen books that a man wanting to know contemporary French work must indulge in. One can *not* represent it in snippets. Still I quote "Le Poète" (his remarks at a provincial soirée):

Cest drôle . . . Cette petite sera bête
comme ces gens-là, comme son père et sa mére.
Et cependant elle a une grâce infinie.
Il y a en elle l'intelligence de la beauté.
C'est délicieux, son corsage qui n'existe pas,
son derrière et ses pieds. Mais elle sera bête
comme une oie dans deux ans d'ici. Elle va jouer.

(*Benette joue la valse des elfes*)

In an earlier scene we have a good example of his rapidity in narrative.

La Servante
Il y a quelqu'un qui veut parler à monsieur.

Le Poète
Qui est-ce?

La Servante
Je ne sais pas.

Le Poète
Un homme ou une femme?

La Servante
Un homme.

Poète
Un commis-voyageur, Vous me le foutez belle!

La Servante
Je ne sais pas, monsieur.

Poète
Faites entrer au salon.
Laissez-moi achever d'achever ces cerises.

(Next Scene)

Le Poète (dans son salon)
A qui ai-je l'honneur de parler, monsieur?

Le Monsieur
Monsieur, je suis le cousin de votre ancienne
maitresse.

Le Poète
De quelle maîtresse? Je ne vous connais pas.
Et puis qu'est-ce que vous voulez?

Le Monsieur
Monsieur, écoutez-moi.
On m'a dit que vous êtes bon.

Poète
Ce n'est pas vrai.

La Pipe du Poète
Il me bourre avec une telle agitation
que je ne vais jamais pourvoir tirer de l'air.

Poète
D'abord, de quelle maitresse me parlez-vous?
De qui, prétendez-vous?   Non.   Vous prétendez de
qui j'ai été l'amant?

Le Monsieur
De Néomie.

Poète

De Néomie,

Le Monsieur
Oui, monsieur.

Poète
Où habitez-vous?
Le Monsieur
J'habite les environs de Mont-de-Marsan.

Poète
Enfin que voulez-vous?
Le Monsieur
Savoir si monsieur serait
assez complaisant pour me donner quelque chose.

Poète
Et si je ne vous donne le pas, qu'est-ce que vous
ferez?

Le Monsieur
Oh! Rien monsieur. Je ne vous ferai rien. Non . . .

Le Poète
Tenez, voilà dix francs, et foutez-moi la paix.
(*Le monsieur s'en va, puis le poète sort.*)

The troubles of the Larribeau family, Larribeau and
the *bonne*, the visit of the "Comtese de Pentacosa," who
is also staved off with ten francs, are all worth quoting.

The whole small town is "Spoon-Rivered" with equal
verve. "Existences" was written in 1900.

MOREAS

It must not be thought that these very "modern" poets
owe their modernity merely to some magic chemical
present in the Parisian milieu. Moréas was born in
1856, the year after Verhaeren, but his Madeline-aux-
serpents might be William Morris on Rapunzel:

> Et votre chevelure comme des grappes d'ombres,
> Et ses bandelettes à vos tempes,
> Et la kabbale de vos yeux latents,—
> Madeline-aux-serpents, Madeline.
> Madeline, Madeline,
> Pourquoi vos lèvres à mon cou, ah, pourquoi
> Vos lèvres entre les coups du hache du roi!
> Madeline, et les cordaces et les flûtes,
> Les flûtes, les pas d'amour, les flûtes, vous les
> voulûtes,
> Hélas! Madeline, la fête, Madeline,
> Ne berce plus les flots au bord de l'Ile,
> Et mes bouffons ne crèvent plus des cerceaux
> Au bord de l'Ile, pauvres bouffons.
> Pauvres bouffons que couronne la sauge!
> Et mes litières s'effeuillent aux ornières, toutes mes
> litières a grand pans
> De nonchaloir, Madeline-aux-serpents . . .

A difference with Morris might have arisen, of course,
over the now long-discussed question of vers libre, but
who are we to dig up that Babylon? The school-boys'
papers of Toulouse had learnt all about it before the old

gentlemen of *The Century* and *Harper's* had discovered
that such things exist.

One will not have understood the French poetry of
the last half-century unless one makes allowance for
what they call the Gothic as well as the Roman or classic
influence. We should probably call it (their "Gothic")
"medievalism," its tone is that of their XIII century
poets, Crestien de Troies, Marie de France, or perhaps
even D'Orléans (as we noticed in the quotation from
Vielé-Griffin). Tailhade in his "Hymne Antique" displays what we would call Swinburnism (Greekish).
Tristan Klingsor (a nom de plume showing definite ten-
dencies) exhibits these things a generation nearer to us:

> Dans son rêve le vieux Prince de Touraine
> voit passer en robe verte à longue traine
> Yeldis aux yeux charmeurs de douce reine.

> . . . . . .

> or
> Au verger où sifflent les sylphes d'automne
> mignonne Isabelle est venue de Venise
> et veut cueillir des cerises et des pommes.

> . . . . . .

He was writing rhymed vers libre in 1903, possibly
stimulated by translations in a volume called "Poésie
Arabe." This book has an extremely interesting preface.
I have forgotten the name of the translator, but in ex-
cusing the simplicity of Arab songs he says: "The young
girl in Germany educated in philosophy in Kant and
Hegel, when love comes to her, at once exclaims 'Infinite!', and allies her vocabulary with the transcendental.

The little girl in the tents 'ne savait comparer fors que sa gourmandise.' " In Klingsor for 1903, I find:

> Croise tes jambes fines et nues
> Dans ton lit,
> Frotte de tes mignonnes mains menues
> Le bout de ton nez;
> Frotte de tes doigts potelés et jolis,
> Les deux violettes de tes yeux cernés,
> Et rêve.
> Du haut du minaret arabe s'échappe
> La mélopée triste et brève
> De l'indiscret muezzin
> Qui nasillonne et qui éternue,
> Et toi tu bâilles comme une petite chatte,
> Tu bâilles d'amour brisée,
> Et tu songes au passant d'Ormuz ou d'Endor
> Qui t'a quittée ce matin
> En te laissant sa légère bourse d'or
> Et les marques bleues de ses baisers.

Later he turns to Max Elkskamp, addressing him as if he, Klingsor, at last had "found Jesus":

> Je viens vers vous, mon cher Elkskamp
> Comme un pauvre varlet de cœur et de joie
> Vient vers le beau seigneur qui campe
> Sous sa tente d'azur et de soie.

. . . . . .

However I believe Moréas was a real poet, and, being stubborn, I have still an idea which got imbedded in my head some years ago: I mean that Klingsor is a poet.

As for the Elkskamp phase and cult, I do not make much
of it. Jean de Bosschère has written a book upon
Elkskamp, and he assures me that Elkskamp is a great
and important poet, and some day, perhaps, I may understand it. De Bosschère seems to me to see or to feel
perhaps more keenly than any one else certain phases
of modern mechanical civilization: the ant-like madness
of men bailing out little boats they never will sail in,
shoeing horses they never will ride, making chairs they
never will sit on, and all with a frenzied intentness. I
may get my conviction as much from his drawings as
from his poems. I am not yet clear in my mind about
it. His opinion of Max Elkskamp can not be too lightly
passed over. Vide infra "De Bosschère on Elkskamp."

OF OUR DECADE

Early in 1912 *L'Effort,* since called *L'Effort Libre,*
published an excellent selection of poems mostly by men
born since 1880: Arcos, Chennevière, Duhamel, Spire,
Vildrac, and Jules Romains, with some of Léon Bazal-
gette's translations from Whitman.

SPIRE

(born 1868)

André Spire, writing in the style of the generation
which has succeeded him, is well represented in this collection by his "Dames Anciennes." The contents of his
volumes are of very uneven value: Zionist propaganda,
addresses, and a certain number of well-written poems.

INSTIGATIONS

DAMES ANCIENNES

En hiver, dans la chambre claire,
Tout en haut de la maison,
Le poêle de faïence blanche,
Cerclé de cuivre, provincial, doux,
Chauffait mes doigts et mes livres.
Et le peuplier mandarine,
Dans le soir d'argent dédoré,
Dressait, en silence, ses branches,
Devant ma fenêtre close.

—Mère, le printemps aux doigts tièdes
A soulevé l'espagnolette
De mes fenêtres sans rideaux.
Faites taire toutes ces voix qui montent
Jusqu'à ma table de travail.

—Ce sont les amies de ma mère
Et de la mère de ton père,
Qui causent de leurs maris morts,
Et de leurs fils partis.

—Avec, au coin de leurs lévres,
Ces moustaches de café au lait?
Et dans leurs mains ces tartines?
Dans leurs bouches ces Kouguelofs?

—Ce sont des cavales anciennes
Qui mâchonnent le peu d'herbe douce
Que Dieu veut bien leur laisser.

—Mère, les maîtres sensibles
Lâchent les juments inutiles

Dans les prés, non dans mon jardin!

—Sois tranquille, mon fils, sois tranquille,
Elles ne brouteront pas tes fleurs.

—Mère, que n'y occupent-elles leurs lèvres,
Et leurs trop courtes dents trop blanches
De porcelaine trop fragile!

—Mon fils, fermez votre fenêtre.
Mon fils, vous n'êtes pas chrétien!

VILDRAC

VILDRAC'S "Gloire" is in a way commentary on
Romains' Ode to the Crowd; a critique of part, at least,
of unanimism.

Il avait su gagner à lui
Beaucoup d'hommes ensemble,

.   .   .   .   .   .

Et son bonheur était de croire,
Quand il avait quitté la foule,
Que chacun des hommes l'aimait
Et que sa présence durait
Innombrable et puissante en eux,

.   .   .   .   .   .

Or un jour il en suivit un
Qui retournait chez soi, tout seul,
Et il vit son regard s'éteindre
Dès qu'il fut un peu loin des autres.

.   .   .   .   .   .

(The full text of this appeared in *Poetry* Aug., 1913.)
Vildrac's two best-known poems are "Une Auberge"
and "Visite"; the first a forlorn scene, not too unlike a
Van Gogh, though not done with Van Gogh's vigor.

C'est seulement parce qu'on a soif qu'on entre y boire;
C'est parce qu'on se sent tomber qu'on va s'y asseoir.
On n'y est jamais à la fois qu'un ou deux
Et l'on n'est pas forcé d'y raconter son histoire.

.   .   .   .   .   .

Celui qui entre . . .

.   .   .   .   .   .

mange lentement son pain
Parce que ses dents sont usées;
Et il boit avec beaucoup de mal
Parce qu'il a de peine plein sa gorge.

Quand il a fini,
Il hésite, puis timide
Va s'asseoir un peu
A côté du feu.

Ses mains crevassées épousent
Les bosselures dures de ses genoux.

Then of the other man in the story:

"qui n'était pas des nôtres. . . .
"Mais comme il avait l'air cependant d'être des nôtres!"

The story or incident in "Visite" is that of a man stir-

ring himself out of his evening comfort to visit some
pathetic dull friends.

.   .   .   .   .   .

Ces gens hélas, ne croyaient pas
Qu'il fût venu à l'improviste
Si tard, de si loin, par la neige . . .
Et ils attendaient l'un et l'autre
Que brusquement et d'un haleine il exposât
La grave raison de sa venue.

Only when he gets up to go, "ils osèrent comprendre"

.   .   .   .   .   .

Il leur promit de revenir.

.   .   .   .   .   .

Mais avant de gagner la porte
Il fixa bien dans sa mémoire
Le lieu où s'abritait leur vie.
Il regarda bien chaque objet
Et puis aussi l'homme et la femme,
Tant il craignait au fond de lui
De ne plus jamais revenir.

The relation of Vildrac's verse narratives to the short
story form is most interesting.

JULES ROMAINS

The reader who has gone through Spire, Romains, and
Vildrac, will have a fair idea of the poetry written by
this group of men. Romains has always seemed to me,
and is, I think, generally recognized as, the nerve-centre,
the dynamic centre of the group.

Les marchands sont assis aux portes des boutiques;
Ils regardent.   Les toits joignent la rue au ciel
Et les pavés semblent féconds sous le soleil
                        Comme un champ de maïs.
Les marchands ont laissé dormir près du comptoir
Le désir de gagner qui travaille dès l'aube.
On dirait que, malgré leur âme habituelle,
Une autre âme s'avance et vient au seuil d'eux-mêmes
Comme ils viennent au seuil de leurs boutiques noires.

We are regaining for cities a little of what savage
man has for the forest. We live by instinct; receive
news by instinct; have conquered machinery as primitive man conquered the jungle. Romains feels this,
though his phrases may not be ours. Wyndham Lewis
on giants is nearer Romains than anything else in English, but vorticism is, in the realm of biology, the hypothesis of the dominant cell. Lewis on giants comes
perhaps nearer Romains than did the original talks about
the Vortex. There is in inferior minds a passion for
unity, that is, for a confusion and melting together of
things which a good mind will want kept distinct. Un-
informed English criticism has treated Unanimism as if
it were a vague general propaganda, and this criticism
has cited some of our worst and stupidest versifiers as
a corresponding manifestation in England. One can
only account for such error by the very plausible hypothesis that the erring critics have not read "Puissances
de Paris."

Romains is not to be understood by extracts and fragments. He has felt this general replunge of mind into
instinct, or this development of instinct to cope with a
metropolis, and with metropolitan conditions; in so far

as he has expressed the emotions of this consciousness he is poet; he has, aside from that, tried to formulate this new consciousness, and in so far as such formulation is dogmatic, debatable, intellectual, hypothetical, he is open to argument and dispute; that is to say he is philosopher, and his philosophy is definite and defined. Vildrac's statement "Il a changé la pathétique" is perfectly true. Many people will prefer the traditional and familiar and recognizable poetry of writers like Klingsor. I am not dictating people's likes and dislikes. Romains has made a new kind of poetry. Since the scrapping of the Aquinian, Dantescan system, he is perhaps the first person who had dared put up so definite a philosophical frame-work for his emotions.

I do not mean, by this, that I agree with Jules Romains; I am prepared to go no further than my opening sentence of this section, concerning our growing, or returning, or perhaps only newly-noticed, sensitization to crowd feeling; to the metropolis and its peculiar sensations. Turn to Romains:

Je croyais les murs de ma chambre imperméables.
Or ils laissent passer une tiède bruine
Qui s'épaissit et qui m'empêche de me voir,
Le papier à fleurs bleues lui cède. Il fait le bruit
Du sable et du cresson qu'une source traverse.
L'air qui touche mes nerfs est extrêmement lourd.
Ce n'est pas comme avant le pur milieu de vie
Ou montait de la solitude sublimée.

Voila que par osmose
Toute l'immensité d'alentour le sature.

.   .   .   .

Il charge mes poumons, il empoisse les choses,
Il sépare mon corps des meubles familiers,

. . . . . .

Les forces du dehors s'enroulent à mes mains.

In "Puissances de Paris" he states that there are
beings more "real than the individual." Here, I can but
touch upon salients.

Rien ne cesse d'être intérieur.
La rue est plus intime à cause de la brume.

Lines like Romains', so well packed with thought, so
careful that you will get the idea, can not be poured out
by the bushel like those of contemporary rhetoricians,
like those of Claudel and Fort. The best poetry has
always a content, it may not be an intellectual content;
in Romains the intellectual statement is necessary to keep
the new emotional content coherent.

The opposite of Lewis's giant appears in:

Je suis l'esclave heureux des hommes dont l'haleine
Flotte ici. Leur vouloirs s'écoule dans mes nerfs;
Ce qui est moi commence à fondre.

This statement has the perfectly simple order of
words. It is the simple statement of a man saying things
for the first time, whose chief concern is that he shall
speak clearly. His work is perhaps the fullest statement
of the poetic consciousness of our time, or the scope of
that consciousness. I am not saying he is the most
poignant poet; simply that in him we have the fullest
poetic exposition.

You can get the feel of Laforgue or even of Corbière

from a few poems; Romains is a subject for study. I
do not say this as praise, I am simply trying to define
him. His "Un Etre en Marche" is the narrative of a
girls' school, of the "crocodile" or procession going out
for its orderly walk, its collective sensations and adventures.
Troupes and herds appear in his earlier work:

> Le troupeau marche, avec ses chiens et son berger,
> Il a peur. Çà et là des réverbères brûlent,
> Il tremble d'être poursuivi par les étoiles.

> . . . . . .

> La foule traine une écume d'ombrelles blanches

> . . . . . .

> La grande ville s'évapore,
> Et pleut à verse sur la plaine
>   Qu'elle sature.

His style is not a "model," it has the freshness of
grass, not of new furniture polish. In his work many
nouns meet their verbs for the first time, as, perhaps, in
the last lines above quoted. He needs, as a rule, about
a hundred pages to turn round in. One can not give
these poems in quotation; one wants about five volumes
of Romains. In so far as I am writing "criticism," I
must say that his prose is just as interesting as his verse.
But then his verse is just as interesting as his prose.
Part of his method is to show his subject in a series of
successive phases, thus in L'Individu:

V

> Je suis un habitant de ma ville, un de ceux
> Qui s'assoient au théâtre et qui vont par les rues

> . . . . . .

VI

Je cesse lentement d'être moi. Ma personne
Semble s'anéantir chaque jour un peu plus
C'est à peine si je le sens et m'en étonne.

His poetry is not of single and startling emotions,
but—for better or worse—of progressive states of consciousness. It is as useless for the disciple to try and
imitate Romains, without having as much thought of his
own, as it is for the tyro in words to try imitations of
Jules Laforgue. The limitation of Romains' work, as
of a deal of Browning's, is that, having once understood
it, one may not need or care to re-read it. This restric-
tion applies also in a wholly different way to "Endymion"; having once filled the mind with Keats' color,
or the beauty of things described, one gets no new thrill
from the re-reading of them in not very well-written
verse. This limitation applies to all poetry that is not
implicit in its own medium, that is, which is not indis-
solubly bound in with the actual words, word music, the
fineness and firmness of the actual writing, as in Villon,
or in "Collis O Heliconii."

But one can not leave Romains unread. His interest
is more than a prose interest, he has verse technique,
rhyme, terminal syzygy, but that is not what I mean.
He is poetry in:

On ne m'a pas donné de lettres, ces jours-ci;
Personne n'a songé, dans la ville, à m'écrire,
Oh! je n'espérais rien; je sais vivre et penser
Tout seul, et mon esprit, pour faire une flambée,
N'attend pas qu'on lui jette une feuille noircie.

Mais je sens qu'il me manque un plaisir familier,
J'ai du bonheur aux mains quand j'ouvre une enveloppe ;

.   .   .   .   .   .

But such statements as :

TENTATION

Je me plais beaucoup trop à rester dans les gares ;
Accoudé sur le bois anguleux des barrières,
Je regarde les trains s'emplir de voyageurs.

.   .   .   .   .   .

and :

Mon esprit solitaire est une goutte d'huile
Sur la pensée et sur le songe de la ville
Qui me laissent flotter et ne m'absorbent pas.

.   .   .   .   .   .

would not be important unless they were followed by
exposition.   The point is that they are followed by exposition, to which they form a necessary introduction,
defining Romains' angle of attack ; and as a result the
force of Romains is cumulative.   His early books gather
meaning as one reads through the later ones.

And I think if one opens him almost anywhere one
can discern the authentic accent of a man saying something, not the desultory impagination of rehash.

Charles Vildrac is an interesting companion figure to
his brilliant friend Romains.   He conserves himself, he
is never carried away by Romains' theories.   He ad-
mires, differs, and occasionally formulates a corrective
or corollary as in "Gloire."

Compare this poem with Romains' "Ode to the Crowd
Here Present" and you get the two angles of vision.
Henry Spiess, a Genevan lawyer, has written an interesting series of sketches of the court-room. He is a
more or less isolated figure. I have seen amusing and
indecorous poems by George Fourest, but it is quite
probable that they amuse because one is unfamiliar with
their genre; still "La Blonde Négresse" (the heroine of
his title), his satire of the symbolo-rhapsodicoes in the
series of poems about her: "La négresse blonde, la
blonde négresse," gathering into its sound all the swish
and woggle of the sound-over-sensists: the poem on
the beautiful blue-behinded baboon; that on the gentleman "qui ne craignait ni la vérole ni dieu"; "Les pianos
du Casino au bord de la mer" (Laforgue plus the four-
hour touch), are an egregious and diverting guffaw.
(I do not think the book is available to the public. J. G.
Fletcher once lent me a copy, but the edition was limited
and the work seems rather unknown.)

Romains is my chief concern. I can not give a full
exposition of Unanimism on a page or two. Among all
the younger writers and groups in Paris, the group cen-
tering in Romains is the only one which seems to me
to have an energy comparable to that of the *Blast* group
in London,* the only group in which the writers for *Blast*
can be expected to take very much interest.

Romains in the flesh does not seem so energetic as
Lewis in the flesh, but then I have seen Romains only
once and I am well acquainted with Lewis. Romains is,
in his writing, more placid. the thought seems more
passive, less impetuous. As for those who will not
have Lewis "at any price," there remains to them no
other course than the acceptance of Romains, for these

* Statement dated Feb., 1918.

two men hold the two tenable positions: the Mountain and the Multitude.

It might be fairer to Romains to say simply he has chosen, or specialized in, the collected multitude as a subject matter, and that he is quite well on a mountain of his own.

My general conclusions, redoing and reviewing this period of French poetry, are (after my paw-over of some sixty new volumes as mentioned, and after re-reading most of what I had read before):

1. As stated in my opening, that mediocre poetry is about the same in all countries; that France has as much drivel, gas, mush, etc., poured into verse, as has any other nation.

2. That it is impossible "to make a silk purse out of a sow's ear," or poetry out of nothing; that all attempts to "expand" a subject into poetry are futile, fundamentally; that the subject matter must be coterminous with the expression. Tasso, Spenser, Ariosto, prose poems, diffuse forms of all sorts are all a preciosity, a parlor-game, and dilutations go to the scrap heap.

3. That Corbière, Rimbaud, Laforgue are permanent; that probably some of De Gourmont's and Tailhade's poems are permanent, or at least reasonably durable; that Romains is indispensable, for the present at any rate; that people who say they "don't like French poetry" are possibly matoids, and certainly ignorant of the scope and variety of French work. In the same way people are ignorant of the qualities of French people; ignorant that if they do not feel at home in Amiens (as I do not), there are other places in France; in the Charente if you walk across country you meet people exactly like the nicest people you can meet in the American country and *they are not "foreign."*

All France is not to be found in Paris. The adjective "French" is current in America with a dozen erroneous or stupid connotations. If it means, as it did in the mouth of my contemporary, "talcum powder" and surface neatness, the selection of poems I have given here would almost show the need of, or at least a reason for, French Parnassienism; for it shows the French poets violent, whether with the violent words of Corbière, or the quiet violence of the irony of Laforgue, the sudden annihilations of his "turn-back" on the subject. People forget that the incision of Voltaire is no more all of French Literature than is the *robustezza* of Brantôme. (Burton of the "Anatomy" is our only writer who can match him.) They forget the two distinct finenesses of the Latin French and of the French "Gothic," that is of the eighteenth century, of Bernard (if one take a writer of no great importance to illustrate a definite quality), or of D'Orleans and of Froissart in verse. From this delicacy, if they can not be doing with it, they may turn easily to Villon or Basselin. Only a general distaste for literature can be operative against all of these writers.

UNANIMISME

The English translation of Romains' "Mort de Quelqu'un" has provoked various English and American essays and reviews. His published works are "L'Ame des Hommes," 1904; "Le Bourg Régénéré," 1906; "La Vie Unanime," 1908; "Premier Livre de Prières," 1909; "La Foule qui est Ici," 1909; in 1910 and 1911 "Un Etre en Marche," "Deux Poèmes," "Manuel de Deification," "L'armée dans la Ville," "Puissances de Paris," and "Mort de Quelqu'un," employing the three excellent publishing houses of the *Mercure*, Figuiere and Sansot.

His "Reflexions" at the end of "Puissances de Paris" are so good a formulation of the Unanimiste Aesthetic, .or *"Pathetique,"* that quotation of them will do more to disabuse readers misled by stupid English criticism than would any amount of talk about Romains. I let him speak for himself:

REFLEXIONS

"Many people are now ready to recognize that there are in the world beings more real than man. We admit the life of entities greater than our own bodies. Society is not merely an arithmetical total, or a collective designation. We even credit the existence of groups intermediate between the individual and the state. But these opinions are put forth by abstract deduction or by experimentation of reason.

"People employ them to complete a system of things and with the complacencies of analogy. If they do not follow a serious study of social data, they are at least the most meritorious results of observations; they justify the method, and uphold the laws of a science which struggles manfully to be scientific.

"These fashions of knowing would seem both costly and tenuous. Man did not wait for physiology to give him a notion of his body, in which lack of patience he was intelligent, for physiology has given him but analytic and exterior information concerning things he had long known from within. He had been conscious of his organs long before he had specified their modes of activity. As spirals of smoke from village chimneys, the profound senses of each organ had mounted toward him; joy, sorrow, all the emotions are deeds more fully of consciousness than are the thoughts of man's reason.

Reason makes a concept of man, but the heart perceives the flesh of his body.

"In like manner we must know the groups that englobe us, not by observation from without, but by an organic consciousness. And it is by no means sure that the rhythms will make their nodes in us, if we be not the centres of groups. We have but to become such. Dig deep enough in our being, emptying it of individual reveries, dig enough little canals so that the souls of the groups will flow of necessity into us.

"I have attempted nothing else in this book. Various groups have come here into consciousness. They are still rudimentary, and their spirit is but a perfume in the air. Beings with as little consistence as la Rue du Havre, and la Place de la Bastile, ephemeral as the company of people in an omnibus, or the audience at L'Opéra Comique, can not have complex organism or thoughts greatly elaborate. People will think it superfluous that I should unravel such shreds in place of re-carding once more the enormous heap of the individual soul.

"Yet I think the groups are in the most agitated stage of their evolution. Future groups will perhaps deserve less affection, and we shall conceal the basis of things more effectively. Now the incomplete and unstable contours have not yet learned to stifle any tendency (any inclination). Every impact sets them floating. They do not coat the infantile matter with a hard or impacting envelope. A superior plant has realized but few of the possibilities swarming in fructificatory mould. A mushroom leads one more directly to the essential life quality than do the complexities of the oak tree.

"Thus the groups prepare more future than is strictly required. Thus we have the considerable happiness of watching the commencement of reign, the beginning of

an organic series which will last as did others, for a
thousand ages, before the cooling of the earth. This
is not a progression, it is a creation, the first leap-out of
a different series. Groups will not continue the activities of animals, nor of men; they will start things afresh
according to their own need, and as the consciousness
of their substance increases they will refashion the
image of the world.

"The men who henceforth can draw the souls of groups
to converge within themselves, will give forth the coming dream, and will gather, to boot, certain intuitions of
human habit. Our ideas of the being will undergo a
correction; will hesitate rather more in finding a distinction between the existent and non-existent. In passing successively from the Place de l'Europe to the Place
des Vosges, and then to a gang of navvies, one perceives
that there are numerous shades of difference between
nothing and something. Before resorting to groups one
is sure of discerning a being of a simple idea. One
knows that a dog exists, that he has an interior and
independent unity; one knows that a table or a mountain
does not exist; nothing but our manner of speech cuts
it off from the universal non-existing. But streets demand all shades of verbal expression (from the non-
existing up to the autonomous creature).

"One ceases to believe that a definite limit is the indispensable means of existence. Where does la Place de
la Trinité begin? The streets mingle their bodies. The
squares isolate themselves with great difficulty. The
crowd at the theatre takes on no contour until it has
lived for some time, and with vigor. A being (être)
has a centre, or centres in harmony, but a being is not
compelled to have limits. He exists a great deal in one
place, rather less in others, and, further on, a second

being commences before the first has left off. Every
being has, somewhere in space, its maximum. Only
ancestored individuals possess affirmative contours, a
skin which cuts them off from the infinite.

"Space is no one's possession. No being has succeeded
in appropriating one scrap of space and saturating it
with his own unique existence. Everything over-crosses,
coincides, and cohabits. Every point is a perch for a
thousand birds. Paris, the rue Montmartre, a crowd, a
man, a protoplasm are on the same spot of pavement.
A thousand existences are concentric. We see a little
of some of them.

"How can we go on thinking that an individual is a
solitary thing which is born, grows, reproduces itself
and dies? This is a superior and inveterate manner of
being an individual. But groups are not truly born.
Their life makes and unmakes itself like an unstable
state of matter, a condensation which does not endure.
They show us that life, at its origin, is a provisory attitude, a moment of exception, an intensity between two
relaxations, not continuity, nothing decisive. The first
entireties take life by a sort of slow success, and extin-
guish themselves without catastrophe, the single elements
do not perish because the whole is disrupted.

"The crowd before the Baraque Foraine starts to live
little by little, as water in a kettle begins to sing and
evaporate. The passages of the Odeon do not live by
night, each day they are real, a few hours. At the start
life seems the affair of a moment, then it becomes inter-
mittent. To be durable; to become a development and
a destiny; to be defined and finished off at each end
by birth and death, it needs a deal of accustomedness.

"The primitive forms are not coequal. There is a
natural hierarchy among groups. Streets have no set

middle, no veritable limitations; they hold a long vacillating sort of life which night flattens out almost to nothingness. Cross-roads and squares take on contour, and gather up the nodes of their rhythms. Other groups have a fashioned body, they endure but a little space, but they have learned, almost, to die; they even resurrect themselves as by a jerk or dry spasm, they begin the habit of being, they strive toward it, and this puts them out of breath.

"I have not yet met a group fully divine. None has had a real consciousness, none has addressed me, saying: I exist. The day when the first group shall take its soul in its hands, as one lifts up a child in order to look in its face, that day there will be a new god upon earth. This is the god I await, with my labor of annunciation."

This excerpt from Romains gives the tone of his thought. In so far as he writes in the present tense he carries conviction. He broaches truly a "new," or at least contemporary *"pathétique."* He utters, in original vein, phases of consciousness whereinto we are more or less drifting, in measure of our proper sensibility.

I retain, however, my full suspicion of agglomerates.

DE BOSSCHERE'S STUDY OF ELSKAMP *

I confessed in my February essay my inability to make anything of Max Elskamp's poetry, and I have tacitly confessed my inability to find any formula for hawking De Bosschère's own verse to any public of my acquaintance; De Bosschère's study of Elskamp, however, requires no advocacy; I do not think it even re-

* *"Max Elskamp"; essai par Jean De Bosschère. Bibliothèque de l'Occident, 17 rue Eblé, Paris. fr. 3.50.*

quires to be a study of Max Elskamp; it drifts as quiet
canal water; the protagonist may or not be a real man.

"Ici, la solitude est plus accentuée: souvent, pendant
de longues minutes, les rues sont désertes. . . . Les
portes ne semblent pas, ainsi que dans les grandes villes,
s'ouvrir sur un poumon de vie, et être une cellule vivante
de la rue. Au contraire, toutes sont fermées. Aussi
bien, les façades de ce quartier sont pareilles aux murs
borgnes. Un mince ruban de ciel roux et gris, à peine
bleu au printemps, découpe les pignons, se tend sur le
marché désert et sur le puits profond des cours."

From this Antwerp, De Bosschère derives his subject,
as Gautier his "Albertus" from

Un vieux bourg flamand tel que peint Tèniers;
trees bathing in water.

"Son univers était limité par: 'le grand peuplier'; une
statue de Pomone, 'le grand rocher,' et 'la grand
grenouille'; ceci était un coin touffu où il y avait de l'eau
et où il ne vit jamais qu'une seule grenouille, qu'il croyait
immortelle." De Bosschère's next vision of Elskamp is
when his subject is pointed out as "le poète décadent,"
for no apparent reason save that he read Mallarmé at a
time when Antwerp did not. The study breaks into a
cheerful grin when Elskamp tells of Mallarmé's one
appearance in the sea-port:

"Le bruit et les cris qui furent poussés pendant la
conférence de Mallarmé, l'arrêtèrent plusieurs fois.
L'opinion du public sur sa causerie est contenue en ces
quelques mots, dits par un général retraité, grand joueur
de billard, et qui du reste ne fit qu'une courte absence
de la salle de jeu, pour écouter quelques phrases du
poète. 'Cet homme est ivre ou fou,' dit il fort haut,
en quittant la salle, où son jugement fit loi. Anvers,
malgré un léger masque de snobisme, qui pourrait

tromper, n'a pas changé depuis. Mallarmé, même pour les *avertis*, est toujours l'homme ivre ou fou."

The billiard player is the one modern touch in the book; for the rest Elskamp sails with sea-captains, apparently in sailing ships to Constantinople, or perhaps one should call it Byzantium. He reads Juan de la Cruz and Young's Night Thoughts, and volumes of demonology, in the properly dim library of his maternal grandfather, "Sa passion en rhétorique fut pour Longfellow, il traduisait 'Song of (sic) Hiawatots.' "

The further one penetrates into De Bosschère's delightful narrative the less real is the hero; the less he needs to be real. A phantom has been called out of De Foe's period, delightful phantom, taking on the reality of the fictitious; in the end the author has created a charming figure, but I am as far as ever from making head or tail of the verses attributed to this creation. I have had a few hours' delightful reading, I have loitered along slow canals, behind a small window sits Elskamp doing something I do not in the least understand.

II

So was I at the end of the first division "Sur la Vie" de Max Elskamp. The second division, concerned with "Oeuvre et Vie," but raised again the questions that had faced me in reading Elskamp's printed work. He has an undercurrent, an element everywhere present, differentiating his poems from other men's poems. De Bosschère scarcely helps me to name it. The third division of the book, at first reading, nearly quenched the curiosity and the interest aroused by the first two-thirds. On second reading I thought better of it. Elskamp, plunged in the middle ages, in what seems almost an atrophy, as much as an atavism, becomes a little more plausible. (For what. it is worth, I read the chapter upon a day of almost complete exhaustion.)

"Or, quand la vision lâche comme une proie vidée le saint, il demeure avec les hommes."

"Entre le voyant et ceux qui le sanctifient il y a un précipice insondable. Seul l'individu est béatifié par sa croyance; mais il ne peut *l'utiliser* au temporel ni la partager avec les hommes, et c'est peut-être la forme unique de la justice sur terre."

The two sentences give us perhaps the tone of De Bosschère's critique "Sur le Mysticisme" of Elskamp.

It is, however, not in De Bosschère, but in *La Wallonie* that I found the clue to this author:

CONSOLATRICE DES AFFLIGÉS

Et l'hiver m'a donné la main,
J'ai la main d'Hiver dans les mains,

et dans ma tête, au loin, il brûle
les vieux étés de canicule;

et dans mes yeux, en candeurs lentes,
très blanchement il fait des tentes,

dans mes yeux il fait des Sicile,
puis des îles, encore des îles.

Et c'est tout un voyage en rond
trop vite pour la guérison

à tous les pays où l'on meurt
au long cours des mers et des heures;

et c'est tout un voyage au vent
sur les vaisseaux de mes lits blancs

qui houlent avec des étoiles
à l'entour de toutes les voiles.

or j'ai le goût de mer aux lèvres
comme une rancœur de genièvre

bu pour la très mauvaise orgie
des départs dans les tabagies;

puis ce pays encore me vient:
un pays de neiges sans fin. . . .

Marie des bonnes couvertures,
faites-y la neige moins dure

et courir moins comme des lières
mes mains sur mes draps blancs de fièvre.
—*Max Elskamp in "La Wallonie,"* 1892.

The poem appears in Van Bever and Léautaud's anthology and there may be no reason for my not having thence received it; but there is, for all that, a certain value in finding a man among his native surroundings, and in finding Elskamp at home, among his contemporaries, I gained first the advantage of comprehension.

ALBERT MOCKEL AND "LA WALLONIE" *

I recently received a letter from Albert Mockel, written with a graciousness not often employed by English and American writers in communication to their

* *Little Review,* Oct., 1918.

juniors. Indeed, the present elder generation of American "respectable" authors having all their lives approached so nearly to death, have always been rather annoyed that American letters did not die utterly in *their* personal desiccations. Signs of vitality; signs of interest in, or cognizance of other sections of this troubled planet have been steadily and papier-mâchéedly deprecated. The rubbish bins of *Harper's* and the *Century* have opened their lids not to new movements but only to the diluted imitations of new movers, etc.

La Wallonie, beginning as *L'Elan Littéraire* in 1885, endured seven years. It announced for a full year on its covers that its seventh year was its last. Albert Mockel has been gracious enough to call it "Notre *Little Review* à nous," and to commend the motto on our cover, in the letter here following:

109, *Avenue de Paris*   *8 mai,* 1918
La Malmaison Rueil
Monsieur et cher confrère,
   Merci de votre amiable envoi. La *Little Review* m'est sympathique à l'extrème. En la feuilletant j'ai cru voir renaître ce temps doré de ferveur et de belle confiance où, adolescent encore, et tâtonnant un peu dans les neuves régions de l'Art, je fondai à Liége notre *Little Review* à nous, *La Wallonie.* Je retrouve justement quelques livraisons de cette revue et je vous les envoie; elles ont tout au moins le mérite de la rareté.
   Vous mon cher confrère, déjà ne marchez plus à tâtons mais je vous soupçonne de n'être pas aussi terriblement, aussi criminellement jeune que je l'étais à cette époque-là. Et puis trente ans ont passé sur la littérature, et c'est de la folie d'hier qu'est faite la sagesse d'aujourd'hui. Alors le Symbolisme naissait; grace à la collabora-

tion de mes amis, grace à Henri de Régnier et Pierre M. Olin qui dirigèrent la revue avec moi, *La Wallonie* en fut l'un des premiers foyers. Tout était remis en question. On aspirait à plus de liberté à une forme plus intense et plus complete plus musicale et plus souple, à une expression nouvelle de l'éternelle beauté. On s'ingeniait on cherchait . . . Tâtonnementse? Certes et ils étaient inévitables. Mais vif et ardent effort, désintéressement absolu, foi juvénile et surtout "No compromise with the public taste" . . . N'y a-t-il point là quelques traits de ressemblance avec l'œuvre que vous tentez aujourd'hui en Amérique, et, à trente années d'intervale, une sorte de cousinage? C'est pourquoi mon cher confrère, j'ai lu avec tant de plaisir la *Little Review* dont vous avec eu la gentillesse de m'adresser la collection.

Croyez-moi sympathiquement vôtre,

ALBERT MOCKEL.

With a native mistrust of *la belle phrase;* of *"temps doré," "ferveur," "belle confiance,"* etc., and with an equally native superiority to any publication not printed LARGE, I opened *La Wallonie.* The gropings, "tatonnements," to which M. Mockel so modestly refers, appear to have included some of the best work of Mallarmé, of Stuart Merrill, of Max Elskamp and Emile Verhaeren. Verlaine contributed to *La Wallonie,* De Regnier was one of its editors . . . Men of since popular fame—Bourget, Pierre Louys, Maeterlinck—appeared with the rarer spirits.

If ever the "amateur magazine" in the sense of magazine by lovers of art and letters, for lovers of art and letters, in contempt of the commerce of letters, has vindicated itself, that vindication was *La Wallonie.* Verhaeren's "Les Pauvres" first appeared there as the second part of the series: "Chansons des Carrefours" (Jan., '92) . . . The Elskamp I have just quoted appeared there with other poems of Max Elskamp. Mallarmé is represented by the exquisite:

SONNET

Ses purs ongles très haut dédiant leur onyx,
L'Angoisse ce minuit, soutient, lampadophore,
Maint rêve vespéral brûle par le phénix
Que ne recueille pas de cinéraire amphore

Sur les crédences, au salon vide: nul ptyx,
Aboli bibelot d'inanité sonore,
(Car le maître est allé puiser des pleurs au Styx
Avec ce seul objet dont le Néant s'honore.)

Mais proche la croisée au nord vacante, un or
Agonise selon peut-être le décor
Des licornes ruant du feu contre une nixe,

Elle, défunte nue en le miroir encor
Que, dans l'oubli fermé par le cadre, se fixe
De scintillations sitôt le septuor.
    —*Mallarmé in "La Wallonie,"* Jan., 1889.

An era of Franco-Anglo-American intercourse is marked by his address to:

THE WHIRLWIND

Pas les rafales à propos
De rien comme occuper la rue

Sujette au noir vol des chapeaux ;
Mais une danseuse apparue

Tourbillon de mousseline ou
Fureur éparses en écumes
Que soulève par son genou
Celle même dont nous vécûmes

Pour tout, hormis lui, rebattu
Spirituelle, ivre, immobile
Foudroyer avec le tutu,
Sans se faire autrement de bile

Sinon rieur que puisse l'air
De sa jupe éventer Whistler.
          —*Mallarmé in "Wallonie," Nov., 1890.*

If I owe Albert Mockel a great debt in having illuminated my eye for Elskamp I owe him no less the pleasure
of one of Merrill's most delicate triumphs in the opening of

BALLET

Pour Gustave Moreau

En casque de cristal rose les baladines,
Dont les pas mesurés aux cordes des kinnors
Tintent sous les tissus de tulle roidis d'ors,
Exultent de leurs yeux pâles de xaladines.

Toisons fauves sur leurs lèvres incarnadines,
Bras lourds de bracelets barbares, en essors
Moelleux vers la lueur lunaire des décors,
Elles murmurent en malveillantes sourdines :

"Nous sommes, ô mortels, danseuses du Désir,
Salomés dont les corps tordus par le plaisir
Leurrent vos heurs d'amour vers nos pervers arcanes.

Prosternez-vous avec des hosannas, ces soirs!
Car, surgissant dans des aurores d'encensoirs,
Sur nos cymbales nous ferons tonner vos crânes."
—*Stuart Merrill in "La Wallonie," July, '98.*

The period was "glauque" and "nacre," it had its pet
and too-petted adjectives, the handles for parody; but
it had also a fine care for sound, for sound fine-wrought,
not mere swish and resonant rumble, not
"Dolores, O hobble and kobble Dolores.
O perfect obstruction on track."
The particular sort of fine workmanship shown in
this sonnet of Merrill's has of late been too much let
go by the board. One may do worse than compare it
with the Syrian syncopation of Διώνα and Ἄδων ιν in
Bion's Adonis.

Hanton is gently didactic:

LE BON GRAIN

"Déjà peinent maints moissonneurs dont
la mémoire est destinée à vivre."
—*Celestin Demblon.*

Amants des rythmes en des strophes cadencées,
Des rimes rares aux splendeurs évocatoires,
Laissant en eux comme un écho de leurs pensées,
Comme un parfum de leurs symboles en histoires:

Tels les poètes vont cherchant en vrais glaneurs
Les blonds épis qui formeront leur riche écrin.
Ils choisiront, comme feraient les bons vanneurs,
Parmi les blés passés au crible, le beau grain.

Et germera cette semence bien choisie,
Entre les roses et les lys, pour devenir
Riche moisson de la fertile fantaisie.

L'ardent soleil de Messidor fera jaunir
Les tiges souples d'une forte poésie
Qui dresseront leurs fiers épis vers l'avenir!
—*Edmond Hanton in "La Wallonie," July, '88.*

Delaroche is, at least in parts, utterly incomprehensible, but there is an interesting experiment in sound-sequence which begins:

SONNETS SYMPHONIQUES

En la langueur
accidentelle
de ta dentelle
où meurt mon coeur

Un profil pleure
et se voit tel
en le pastel
du divin leurre

Qu'or végétal
de lys s'enlise
au froid santal

Si n'agonise
occidental
qui s'adonise.
—*Achille Delaroche in "La Wallonie," Feb.,* '89.

I do not know that we will now be carried away by
Albert Saint-Paul's chinoiserie, or that she-devils are so
much in fashion as when Jules Bois expended, certainly,
some undeniable emotion in addressing them:

PETALES DE NACRE

En sa robe où s'immobilisent les oiseaux,
Une émerge des fleurs comme une fleur plus grande.
Comme une fleur penchée au sourire de l'eau,

Ses mains viennent tresser la traînante guirlande
Pour enchaîner le Dragon vert—et de légende!
Qui de ses griffes d'or déchire les roseaux,

Les faisceaux de roseaux: banderolles et lances.

Et quand le soir empourprera le fier silence
De la forêt enjôleuse de la Douleur,
Ses doigts, fuseaux filant au rouet des murmures
Les beaux anneaux fleuris liant les fleurs aux fleurs,

Ses doigts n'auront saigné qu'aux épines peu dures.
—*Albert Saint-Paul in "La Wallonie," Jan.,* '91.

POUR LA DEMONE

Un soir de joie, un soir d'ivresse, un soir de fête,
—Et quelle fête, et quelle ivresse, et quelle joie!—

Tu vins. L'impérial ennui sacrait ta tête;
Et tu marchais dans un bruit d'armure et de soie.

Tu dédaignas tous les bijoux et l'oripeau
De ruban, de dentelle et d'éphémère fleur. . . . .
Hermétique,* ta robe emprisonnait ta peau.
Oui, la fourrure seule autour de ta pâleur.

Tu parus. Sous tes yeux que le kh'ol abomine,
Le bal fut la lugubre et dérisoire histoire.
Les hommes des pantins qu'un vice mène et mine.
Les femmes, coeurs et corps fanés, — — et quel déboire!

POUR LA DEMONE

v.

Elle est folle, c'est sûr, elle est folle la chère;
Elle m'aime à n'en pas douter, mais elle est folle,
Elle m'aime et. compatissez à ma misère,
Avec tous, avec toutes, elle batifole.

Un passe. . . . Elle s'élance à lui, coeur présumé. . . .
Elle s'offre et le provoque, puis elle fuit
Vers ailleurs . . . si fidèle encore au seul-aimé,
Mais elle est folle et je m'éplore dans la nuit.

Pour quelque amie aux délicatesses félines,
Elle glisse vers les caresses trop profondes.
. . . "Tu vas, folle, oublier mes rancoeurs orphelines."
Mais sa lèvre pensive hésite aux toisons blondes.

> —*Jules Bois in "La Wallonie," Sept.,* '90.

* *Laforgue?*

In part we must take our reading of *La Wallonie* as a study of the state of symbolism from 1885 to '92.

Rodenbach displays the other leaf of the diptych: the genre, the homely Wallon landscape, more familiar to the outer world in Verhaeren, but not, I think, better painted.

PAYSAGES SOUFFRANTS

II.

A Emilie Verhaeren.

Là-bas, tant de petits hameaux sous l'avalanche
De la neige qui tombe adoucissante et blanche,
Tant de villages, tant de chaumines qui sont
Pour le reste d'un soir doucement assoupies,
Car le neige s'étend en de molles charpies
Sur les blessures des vieilles briques qui n'ont
Rien senti d'une Soeur sur leur rougeur qui saigne!
Mais, ô neige, c'est toi la Soeur au halo blanc
Qui consoles les murs malades qu'on dédaigne
Et mets un peu d'ouate aux pierres s'éraflant.

Las! rien ne guérira les chaumines—aieules
Qui meurent de l'hiver et meurent d'être seules. . . .
Et leurs âmes bientôt, au gré des vents du nord.
Dans la fumée aux lents départs, seront parties
Cependant que la neige, à l'heure de leur mort,
Leur apporte ses refraîchissantes hosties!

—*Georges Rodenbach in "La Wallonie," Jan., '88.*

Rodenbach is authentic.
Vielé-Griffin, who, as Stuart Merrill, has always been

known in France as "an American," contributed largely
to *La Wallonie.* His "Au Tombeau d'Hélène" ends:

HELENE

Me voici:
J'étais là dès hier, et dès sa veille,
Ailleurs, ici;
Toute chair, a paré, un soir, mon âme vieille
Comme l'éternité du désir que tu vêts.
La nuit est claire au firmament . . .
Regarde avec tes yeux levés:
Voici—comme un tissu de pâle feu fatal
Qui fait épanouir la fleur pour la flétrir—
Mon voile où transparaît tout assouvissement
Qui t'appelle à la vie et qui t'en fait mourir.
La nuit est claire au firmament vital . . .

Mes mythes, tu les sais:
Je suis fille du Cygne,
Je suis la lune dont s'exubèrent les mers
Qui montent, tombent, se soulèvent;
Et c'est le flot de vie exultante et prostrée,
le flot des rêves,
le flot des chairs,
le flux et le reflux de la vaste marée.

Mon doute—on dit l'Espoir—fait l'action insigne:
Je suis reine de Sparte et celle-là de Troie,
Par moi, la douloureuse existence guerroie
Je meus toute inertie aux leurres de ma joie,
Hélène, Séléné, flottant de phase en phase,
Je suis l'Inaccédée et la tierce Hypostase
Et si je rejetais, désir qui m'y convies,

Mon voile qui promet et refuse l'extase,
Ma nudité de feu résorberait les Vies. . . .
—*Viele-Griffin in "La Wallonie," Dec., '91.*
(Complete number devoted to his poems.)

Mockel is represented by several poems rather too long
to quote,—"Chantefable un peu naive," "L'Antithèse."
suggestive of the Gourmont litany; by prose comment,
by work over various pseudonyms. "A Clair Matin" is
a suitable length to quote, and it is better perhaps to
represent him here by it than by fragments which I had
first intended to cut from his longer poems.

A CLAIR MATIN

La nuit au loin s'est effacée
comme les lignes tremblantes d'un rêve;
la nuit s'est fondue au courant du Passé
et le jour attendu se lève.

Regardez! en les courbes molles des rideaux
une heure attendue se révèle
et ma fenêtre enfin s'éclaire,
cristalline du gîvre où se rit la lumière.

Une parure enfantine de neiges
habille là-bas d'immobiles eaux
et c'est les cortèges des fées nouvelles
à tire d'ailes, à tire d'ailes
du grand lointain qui toutes reviennent
aux flocons de ce jour en neiges qui s'épèle.

Des courbes de mes rideaux clairs
—voici! c'est un parfum de ciel!—

blanc des guirlandes de l'hiver
le jeune matin m'est apparu
avec un visage de fiancée.

Des fées
(ah je ne sais quelles mortelles fées)
jadis elles vinrent toucher la paupière
d'un être enfantin qui mourut.
Son âme, où se jouait en songes la lumière,
diaphane corolle épanouie au jour
son âme était vive de toute lumière!
Lui, comme un frère il suivait ma course
et nous allions en confiants de la montagne à la vallée
par les forêts des chênes, des hêtres
—car eux, les ancêtres, ils ont le front grave
ils virent maints rêves des autres âges
et nous parlent, très doucement, comme nos Pères.

Mais voyez! à mes rideaux pâles
le matin glisse des sourires;
car la Fiancée est venue
car la Fiancée est venue
avec un simple et très doux visage,
avec des mots qu'on n'entend pas,
en silence la Fiancée est apparue
comme une grande soeur de l'enfant qui mourut;
et les hêtres, les chênes royaux des forêts
par douce vocalise égrenant leur parure,
les voix ressuscitées en la plaine sonore
et toute la forêt d'aurore
quand elle secoue du crépuscule sa chevelure.
tout chante, bruit, pétille et rayonne
car la céleste Joie que la clarté délivre
d'un hymne répercute aux miroirs du futur

le front pàle où scintille en étoiles le givre.
—*Albert Mockel in "La Wallonie," Dernier fascicule,*
    '92.

I have left Gide and Van Lerberghe unquoted, un-
mentioned, but I have, I dare say, given poems enough
to indicate the quality and the scope of the poetry in
La Wallonie.

In prose their cousinage is perhaps more quickly apparent. Almost the first sentence I come upon (I suspect it is Mockel's) runs as follows:

"*La Revue des deux Mondes* publie un roman de Georges
Ohnet ce qui ne surprendra personne."

This is the proper tone to use when dealing with elderly
muttonheads; with the *Harpers* of yester year. *La Wallonie* found it out in the eighties. The symboliste movement flourished on it. American letters did not flour-
ish, partly perhaps for the lack of it, and for the lack
of unbridled uncompromising magazines run by young
men who did not care for *réputations surfaites,* for
elderly stodge and stupidity.

If we turn to Mockel's death notice for Jules Laforgue
we will find *La Wallonie* in '87 awake to the value of
contemporary achievement:

JULES LAFORGUE

Nous apprenons avec une vive tristesse, la mort de
Jules Laforgue, l'un des plus curieux poètes de la littérature aux visées nouvelles. Nous l'avons désigné,
jà deux mois: un Tristan Corbière plus argentin, moins
âpre . . . Et telle est bien sa caractéristique. Sans le

moindre soupçon d'imitation ou de réminiscences, Jules Laforgue a sauvegardé une originalité vivace. Seulement, cette originalité, par bien des saillies, touche à celle de Tristan Corbière. C'est une même raillerie de la Vie et du Monde; mais plus de sombre et virile amertume émouvait en l'auteur des Amours Jaunes, dont cette pièce donnera quelque idée:

LE CRAPAUD

Un chant dans une nuit sans air . . .
—La lune plaque en métal clair
Les découpures du vert sombre.
. . . Un chant; comme un écho, tout vif
Enterré, là, sous le massif . . .
—Ca se tait; viens, c'est là, dans l'ombre . . .
Un crapaud!
       —Pourquoi cette peur,
Près de moi, ton soldat fidèle!
Vois-le, poète tondu, sans aile,
Rossignol de la boue . . .
       —Horreur!—
. . . Il chante.—Horreur!!—Horreur pourquoi?
Vois-tu pas son oeil de lumière . . .
Non, il s'en va, froid, sous sa pierre.

.   .   .   .   .

Bonsoir—ce crapaud-là c'est moi.

Chez Laforgue, il y a plus de gai sans-souci, de coups de batte de pierrot donnés à toutes choses, plus de "vaille-que-vaille la vie," dit d'un air de moqueuse résignation. Sa rancoeur n'est pas qui encombrante. Il était un peu l'enfant indiscipliné que rit à travers les gronderies, et fait la moue à sa fantaisie; mais son haussement d'épaules

gamin, et ses "Après tout?" qu'il jette comme une
chiquenaude au visage du Temps, cachent toujours au
fond de son coeur un lac mélancolique, un lac de tristesse
et d'amours flétris, où vient se refléter sa claire imagination. Témoins ces fragments pris aux *Complaintes* :
Mon coeur est une urne où j'ai mis certains défunts,
Oh! chut, refrains de leurs berceaux! et vous, parfums.

.   .   .   .   .

Mon coeur est un Néron, enfant gâté d'Asie,
Qui d'empires de rêve en vain se rassasie.
Mon coeur est un noyé vidé d'âme et d'essors,
Qu'étreint la pieuvre Spleen en ses ventouses d'or.
C'est un feu d'artifice, hélas! qu'avant la fête,
A noyé sans retour l'averse qui s'embête.
Mon coeur est le terrestre Histoire-Corbillard
Que traînent au néant l'instinct et le hazard
Mon coeur est une horloge oubliée à demeure
Qui, me sachant défunt, s'obstine à marquer l'heure.

.   .   .   .   .

Et toujours mon coeur ayant ainsi déclamé,
En revient à sa complainte : Aimer, être aimé!

Et cette pièce, d'une ironie concentrée :

COMPLAINTE DES BONS MENAGES

L'Art sans poitrine m'a trop longtemps bercé dupe.
Si ses labours sont fiers, que ses blés décevants!
Tiens, laisse-moi bêler tout aux plis de ta jupe
            Qui fleure le couvent.
La Génie avec moi, serf, a fait des manières;
Toi, jupe, fais frou-frou, sans t'inquièter pourquoi . . .

.   .   .   .   .

Mais l'Art, c'est l'Inconnu! qu'on y dorme et s'y vautre,
On ne peut pas l'avoir constamment sur les bras!

Et bien, ménage au vent! Soyons Lui, Elle et l'Autre.
Et puis n'insistons pas.
Et puis? et puis encore un pied de nez melancolique
à la destinée:
Qui m'aima jamais? Je m'entête
Sur ce refrain bien impuissant
Sans songer que je suis bien bête
De me faire du mauvais sang:

Jules Laforgue a publié outre les *Complaintes,* un
livret de vers dégingandés, d'une raillerie splénétique, à
froid, comme celle qui sied aux hommes du Nord. Mais
il a su y ajouter ce sans-façon de choses dites à l'aven-
ture, et tout un parfum de lumière argentine, comme
les rayons de *Notre-Dame la Lune* qu'il célèbre. Le
manque de place nous prive d'en citer quelques pages.
Nous avons lu aussi cette étrange Nuit d'Etoiles: le *Conseil Féerique,* un assez court poême édité par la "Vogue";
divers articles de revue, entre lesquels cette page en-
soleillée, parue dans la Revue Indépendante: *Pan et la
Syrinx.* Enfin un nouveau livre était annoncé: *de la
Pitié, de la Pitié!,* déjà préparé par l'une des Invoca-
tions du volume précédent, et dont nous croyons voir
l'idée en ces vers des *Complaintes:*

Vendange chez les Arts enfantins; sois en fête
D'une fugue, d'un mot, d'un ton, d'un air de tête.
.   .   .   .   .   .
Vivre et peser selon le Beau, le Bien, le Vrai?
O parfums, ô regards, ô fois! soit, j'essaierai.
.   .   .   .   .   .
. . . Va, que ta seule étude
Soit de vivre sans but, fou de mansuétude—
—*Albert Mockel in "La Wallonie,"* 1887.

I have quoted but sparingly, and I have thought quotation better than comment, but despite the double meagreness I think I have given evidence that *La Wallonie* was worth editing.

It began as *L'Elan Littéraire* with 16 pages, and an edition of 200 copies; it should convince any but the most stupid that size is not the criterion of permanent value, and that a small magazine may outlast much bulkier printings.

After turning the pages of *La Wallonie*, perhaps after reading even this so brief excerpt, one is ready to see some sense in even so lyric a phrase as "temps doré, de ferveur et de belle confiance."

In their seven years' run these editors, one at least beginning in his "teens," had published a good deal of the best of Verhaeren, had published work by Elskamp, Merrill, Griffin, Louys, Maeterlinck, Verlaine Van Lerberghe, Gustave Kahn, Moréas, Quillard, André Gide; had been joined in their editing board by De Régnier (remember that they edited in Liège, not in Paris; they were not at the hub of the universe, but in the heart of French Belgium); they had not made any compromise. Permanent literature, and the seeds of permanent literature, had gone through proof-sheets in their office.

There is perhaps no greater pleasure in life, and there certainly can have been no greater enthusiasm than to have been young and to have been part of such a group of writers working in fellowship at the beginning of such a course, of such a series of courses as were implicated in *La Wallonie*.

If the date is insufficiently indicated by Mallarmé's allusion to Whistler, we may turn to the art notes:

"eaux-fortes de Mlle Mary Cassatt . . . Lucien Pis-

saro, Sisley . . . lithographies de Fantin-Latour . . .
Odillon Redon."

"J'ai été un peu à Paris, voir Burne Jones, Moreau,
Delacroix . . . la danse du ventre, et les adorables Java-
naises. C'est mon meilleur souvenir, ces filles 'très
parées' dans l'étrange demi-jour de leur case et qui tournent lentement dans la stridente musique avec de si énig-
matique inflexions de mains et de si souriantes pour-
suites les yeux dans les yeux."

Prose poetry, that doubtful connection, appears at
times even to advantage:

"Séléné, toi l'essence et le regard des infinis, ton mal
nous serait la félicité suprême. O viens à nous, Tanit,
Vierge Tanit, fleur métallique épanouie aux plaines
célestes!"—*Mockel*.

II

HENRY JAMES

This essay on James is a dull grind of an affair, a Baedecker to a continent.

I set out to explain, not why Henry James is less read than formerly—I do not know that he is. I tried to set down a few reasons why he ought to be, or at least might be, more read.

Some may say that his work was over, well over, finely completed; there is mass of that work, heavy for one man's shoulders to have borne up, labor enough for two life-times; still we would have had a few more years of his writing. Perhaps the grasp was relaxing, perhaps we should have had no strongly-planned book; but we should have had paragraphs here and there, and we should have had, at least, conversation, wonderful conversation; even if we did not hear it ourselves, we should have known that it was going on somewhere. The massive head, the slow uplift of the hand, *gli occhi onesti e tardi,* the long sentences piling themselves up in elaborate phrase after phrase, the lightning incision, the pauses, the slightly shaking admonitory gesture with its "wu-a-wait a little, wait a little, something will come;" blague and benignity and the weight of so many years' careful, incessant labor of minute observation always there to enrich the talk. I had heard it but seldom, yet it was all unforgettable.

The man had this curious power of founding affection in those who had scarcely seen him and even in many who had not, who but knew him at second hand.

No man who has not lived on both sides of the Atlantic can well appraise Henry James; his death marks the end of a period. The *Times* says: "The Americans will understand his changing his nationality," or something of that sort. The "Americans" will understand nothing whatsoever about it. They have understood nothing about it. They do not even know what they lost. They have not stopped for eight minutes to consider the meaning of his last public act. After a year of ceaseless labor, of letter writing. of argument, of striving in every way to bring in America on the side of civilization, he died of apoplexy. On the side of civilization—civilization against barbarism, civilization, not Utopia, not a country or countries where the right always prevails in six weeks! After a life-time spent in trying to make two continents understand each other, in trying, and only his thoughtful readers can have any conception of how he had tried, to make three nations intelligible one to another. I am tired of hearing pettiness talked about Henry James's style. The subject has been discussed enough in all conscience, along with the minor James. Yet I have heard no word of the major James, of the hater of tyranny; book after early book against oppression, against all the sordid petty personal crushing oppression, the domination of modern life; not worked out in the diagrams of Greek tragedy, not labeled "epos" or "Aeschylus." The outbursts in *The Tragic Muse*, the whole of *The Turn of the Screw*, human liberty, personal liberty, the rights of the individual against all sorts of intangible bondage!* The passion of it, the continual passion of it in this man who, fools said, didn't "feel." I have never yet found a man of emotion against whom idiots didn't raise this cry.

And the great labor, this labor of translation, of making America intelligible, of making it possible for individuals to meet across national borders. I think half the American idiom is recorded in Henry James's writing, and whole decades of American life that otherwise would have been utterly lost, wasted, rotting in the unhermetic jars of bad writing, of inaccurate writing. No English reader will ever know how good are his New York and his New England; no one who does not see his grandmother's friends in the pages of the American books. The whole great assaying and weighing, the research for the significance of nationality, French, English, American.

"An extraordinary old woman, one of the few people who is really doing anything good." There were the cobwebs about connoisseurship, etc., but what do they matter? Some yokel writes in the village paper, as Henley had written before, "James's stuff was not worth doing." Henley has gone pretty completely. America has not yet realized that never in history had one of her

---

* This holds, despite anything that may be said of his fuss about social order, social tone. I naturally do not drag in political connotations, from which H. J. was, we believe, wholly exempt. What he fights is "influence", the impinging of family pressure, the impinging of one personality on another; all of them in highest degree damn'd, loathsome and detestable. Respect for the peripheries of the individual may be, however, a discovery of our generation; I doubt it, but it seems to have been at low ebb in some districts (not rural) for some time.

great men abandoned his citizenship out of shame. It
was the last act—the last thing left. He had worked all
his life for the nation and for a year he had labored
for the national honor. No other American was of sufficient importance for his change of allegiance to have
constituted an international act; no other American
would have been welcome in the same public manner.
America passes over these things, but the thoughtful
cannot pass over them.

Armageddon, the conflict? I turn to James's *A Bundle
of Letters;* a letter from "Dr. Rudolph Staub" in Paris,
ending:

"You will, I think, hold me warranted in believing
that between precipitate decay and internecine enmities,
the English-speaking family is destined to consume itself and that with its decline the prospect of general
pervasiveness to which I alluded above, will brighten
for the deep-lunged children of the fatherland!"

We have heard a great deal of this sort of thing
since; it sounds very natural. My edition of the volume
containing these letters was printed in '83, and the imaginary letters were written somewhat before that. I do
not know that this calls for comment. Henry James's
perception came thirty years before Armageddon. That
is all I wish to point out. Flaubert said of the War of
1870: "If they had read my *Education Sentimentale,*
this sort of thing wouldn't have happened." Artists are
the antennæ of the race, but the bullet-headed many will
never learn to trust their great artists. If it is the business of the artist to make humanity aware of itself;
here the thing was done, the pages of diagnosis. The
multitude of wearisome fools will not learn their right
hand from their left or seek out a meaning.

It is always easy for people to object to what they
have not tried to understand.

I am not here to write a full volume of detailed criticism, but two things I do claim which I have not seen in
reviewers' essays. First, that there was emotional greatness in Henry James's hatred of tyranny; secondly, that
there was titanic volume, weight, in the masses he sets
in opposition within his work. He uses forces no whit
less specifically powerful than the proverbial "doom of
the house,"—Destiny, *Deus ex machina,*—of great traditional art. His art was great art as opposed to over-
elaborate or over-refined art by virtue of the major
conflicts which he portrays. In his books he showed race
against race, immutable; the essential Americanness, or
Englishness or Frenchness—in *The American,* the difference between one nation and another; not flag-waving
and treaties, not the machinery of government, but
"why" there is always misunderstanding, why men of
different race are not the same.

We have ceased to believe that we conquer anything
by having Alexander the Great make a gigantic "joy-
ride" through India. We know that conquests are made
in the laboratory, that Curie with his minute fragments
of things seen clearly in test tubes in curious apparatus,
makes conquests. So, too, in these novels, the essential
qualities which make up the national qualities, are found
and set working, the fundamental oppositions made clear.
This is no contemptible labor. No other writer had so
essayed three great nations or even thought of attempting it.

Peace comes of communication. No man of our time
has so labored to create means of communication as did
the late Henry James. The whole of great art is a strug-

gle for communication. All things that oppose this are evil, whether they be silly scoffing or obstructive tariffs.

And this communication is not a leveling, it is not an elimination of differences. It is a recognition of differences, of the right of differences to exist, of interest in finding things different. Kultur is an abomination; philology is an abomination, all repressive uniforming education is an evil.

A SHAKE DOWN

I have forgotten the moment of lunar imbecility in which I conceived the idea of a "Henry James" number.* The pile of typescript on my floor can but annoyingly and too palpably testify that the madness has raged for some weeks.

Henry James was aware of the spherical form of the planet, and susceptible to a given situation, and to the tone and tonality of persons as perhaps no other author in all literature. The victim and the votary of the "scene," he had no very great narrative sense, or at the least, he attained the narrative faculty but *per aspera*, through very great striving.

It is impossible to speak accurately of "his style," for he passed through several styles which differ greatly one from another; but in his last, his most complicated and elaborate, he is capable of great concision; and if, in it, the single sentence is apt to turn and perform evolutions for almost pages at a time, he nevertheless manages to say on one page more than many a more "direct" author would convey only in the course of a chapter.

* *Little Review*, Aug., 1918.

His plots and incidents are often but adumbrations or symbols of the quality of his "people," illustrations invented, contrived, often factitiously and almost transparently, to show what acts, what situations, what contingencies would befit or display certain characters. We are hardly asked to accept them as happening.

He did not begin his career with any theory of art for art's sake, and a lack of this theory may have damaged his earlier work.

If we take "French Poets and Novelists" as indication of his then (1878) opinions, and novels of the nineties showing a later bias, we might contend that our subject began his career with a desire to square all things to the ethical standards of a Salem mid-week Unitarian prayer meeting, and that to almost the end of his course he greatly desired to fit the world into the social exigencies of Mrs. Humphry Ward's characters.

Out of the unfortunate cobwebs he emerged into his greatness, I think, by two causes: first by reason of his hatred of personal intimate tyrannies working at close range; and secondly, in later life, because the actual mechanism of his scriptorial processes became so bulky, became so huge a contrivance for record and depiction, that the old man simply couldn't remember or keep his mind on or animadvert on anything but the authenticity of his impression.

I take it as the supreme reward for an artist; the supreme return that his artistic conscience can make him after years spent in its service, that the momentum of his art, the sheer bulk of his processes, the (*si licet*) size of his fly-wheel, should heave him out of himself, out of his personal limitations, out of the tangles of heredity and of environment, out of the bias of early training, of early predilections, whether of Florence,

A. D. 1300, or of Back Bay of 1872, and leave him simply the great true recorder.

And this reward came to Henry James in the ripeness of his talents; even further perhaps it entered his life and his conversation. The stages of his emergence are marked quite clearly in his work. He displays himself in *French Poets and Novelists,* constantly balancing over the question of whether or no the characters presented in their works are, or are not, fit persons to be received in the James family back-parlor.

In *The Tragic Muse* he is still didactic quite openly. The things he believes still leap out nakedly among the people and things he is portraying; the parable is not yet wholly incarnate in the narrative.

To lay all his faults on the table, we may begin with his self-confessed limitation, that "he never went down town." He displayed in fact a passion for high life comparable only to that supposed to inhere in the readers of a magazine called *Forget-me-not.*

Hardy, with his eye on the Greek tragedians, has produced an epic tonality, and *The Mayor of Casterbridge* is perhaps more easily comparable to the Grettir Saga than to the novels of Mr. Hardy's contemporaries. Hardy is, on his other side, a contemporary of Sir Walter Scott.

Balzac gains what force his crude writing permits him by representing his people under the ἀνάγκη of modernity, cash necessity; James, by leaving cash necessity nearly always out of the story, sacrifices, or rather fails to attain, certain intensities.

He never manages the classic, I mean as Flaubert gives us in each main character: *Everyman.* One may conceivably be bored by certain pages in Flaubert, but one takes from him a solid and concrete memory, a property. Emma Bovary and Frederic and M. Arnoux are respectively every woman and every man of their period. Maupassant's *Bel Ami* is not. Neither are Henry James's people. They are always, or nearly always, the bibelots.

But he does, nevertheless, treat of major forces, even of epic forces, and in a way all his own. If Balzac tried to give a whole civilization, a whole humanity, James was not content with a rough sketch of one country.

As Armageddon has only too clearly shown, national qualities are the great gods of the present and Henry James spent himself from the beginning in an analysis of these potent chemicals; trying to determine from the given microscopic slide the nature of the Frenchness, Englishness, Germanness, Americanness, which chemicals too little regarded, have in our time exploded for want of watching. They are the permanent and fundamental hostilities and incompatibles. We may rest our claim for his greatness in the magnitude of his protagonists, in the magnitude of the forces he analyzed and portrayed. This is not the bare matter of a number of titled people, a few duchesses and a few butlers.

Whatever Flaubert may have said about his *Education Sentimentale* as a potential preventive of the débâcle of 1870, *if people had* read it, and whatever Gautier's friend may have said about *Emaux et Camées* as the last resistance to the Prussians, from Dr. Rudolph Staub's paragraph in *The Bundle of Letters* to the last and almost only public act of his life, James displayed a steady perception and a steady consideration of the qualities of different western races, whose consequences none of us can escape.

And these forces, in precisely that they are not political and executive and therefore transient, factitious,

but in precisely that they are the forces of race temperaments, are major forces and are indeed as great protagonists as any author could have chosen.   They are
firmer ground than Flaubert's when he chooses public
events as in the opening of the third part of *Education
Sentimentale*.

The portrayal of these forces, to seize a term from
philology, may be said to constitute "original research"
—to be Henry James's own addendum; not that this
greatly matters.   He saw, analyzed, and presented them.
He had most assuredly a greater awareness than was
granted to Balzac or to Mr. Charles Dickens or to M.
Victor Hugo who composed the *Légende des Siècles*.

His statement that he never went down town has been
urged greatly against him.   A butler is a servant, tem-
pered with upper-class contacts.   Mr. Newman, the
American, has emerged from the making of wash-tubs;
the family in *The Pupil* can scarcely be termed upper-
class, however, and the factor of money, Balzac's,
ἀνάγκη, scarcely enters his stories.

We may leave Hardy writing Sagas.   We may admit
that there is a greater *robustezza* in Balzac's messiness,
simply because he is perpetually concerned, inaccurately,
with the factor of money, of earning one's exiguous
living.

We may admit the shadowy nature of some of James's
writing, and agree whimsically with R. H. C. (in the
New Age) that James will be quite comfortable after
death, as he had been dealing with ghosts all his life.

James's third donation is perhaps a less sweeping
affair and of more concern to his compatriots than to
any one who might conceivably translate him into an
alien tongue, or even to those who publish his writings in
England.

He has written history of a personal sort, social history well documented and incomplete, and he has put America on the map both in memoir and fiction, giving to her a reality such as is attained only by scenes recorded in the arts and in the writing of masters. Mr. Eliot has written, and I daresay most other American admirers have written or will write, that, whatever any one else thinks of Henry James, no one but an American can ever know, really know, how good he is at the bottom, how good his "America" is.

No Englishman can, and in less degree can any continental, or in fact any one whose family was not living on, say, West 23rd Street in the old set-back, two-story-porched red brick vine-covered houses, etc., when Henry James was being a small boy on East 23rd Street; no one whose ancestors had not been presidents or professors or founders of Ha'avwd College or something of that sort, or had not heard of a time when people lived on 14th Street, or had known of some one living in Lexington or Newton "Old Place" or somewhere of that sort in New England, or had heard of the New York that produced "Fanny," New York the jocular and uncritical, or of people who danced with General Grant or something of that sort, would quite know *Washington Square* or *The Europeans* to be so autochthonous, so authentic to the conditions. They might believe the things to be "real," but they would not know how closely they corresponded to an external reality.

Perhaps only an exile from these things will get the range of the other half of James's presentations! Europe to the Transpontine, New York of brown stone that he detested, the old and the new New York in *Crapey Cornelia* and in *The American Scene*, which more than any other volumes give us our peculiar heri-

tage, an America with an interest, with a tone of time
not overstrained, not jejunely over-sentimentalized,
which is not a redoing of school histories or the laying
out of a fabulous period; and which is in relief, if you
like, from Dickens or from Mark Twain's *Mississippi*.
He was not without sympathy for his compatriots as
is amply attested by Mr. and Mrs. B. D. Hayes of New
York (vide *The Birthplace*) with whom he succeeds,
I think, rather better than with most of his princely con-
tinentals. They are, at any rate, his bow to the Happy
Genius of his country—as distinct from the gentleman
who displayed the "back of a banker and a patriot," or
the person whose aggregate features could be designated
only as a "mug."

In his presentation of America he is greatly attentive, and, save for the people in *Coeur Simple*, I doubt
if any writer has done more of "this sort of thing" for
his country, this portrayal of the typical thing in timbre
and quality—balanced, of course, by the array of spit-
toons in the Capitol ("The Point of View").

Still if one is seeking a Spiritual Fatherland, if one
feels the exposure of what he would not have scrupled
to call, two clauses later, such a wind-shield, "The
American Scene" greatly provides it. It has a mermaid
note, almost to outvie the warning, the sort of nickel-
plate warning which is hurled at one in the saloon of
any great transatlantic boat; the awfulness that engulfs
one when one comes, for the first time unexpectedly on
a pile of all the *Murkhn* Magazines laid, shingle-wise
on a brass-studded, screwed-into-place, baize-covered
steamer table. The first glitter of the national weapons
for driving off quiet and all closer signs of intelligence.*

* I differ, beyond that point, with our author. I enjoy ascent
as much as I loathe descent in an elevator. I do not mind the

Attempting to view the jungle of the work as a whole, one notes that, despite whatever cosmopolitan upbringing Henry James may have had, as witness "A Small Boy's Memoirs" and "Notes of Son and Brother," he nevertheless began in "French Poets and Novelists" with a provincial attitude that it took him a long time to work free of. Secondly we see various phases of the "style" of his presentation or circumambiance.

There is a small amount of prentice work. Let us say "Roderick Hudson," "Casamassima." There are lucky first steps in "The American" and "Europeans," a precocity of result, for certainly some of his early work is as permanent as some of the ripest, and more so than a deal of the intervening. We find (for in the case before us criticism must be in large part a weeding-out) that his first subject matter provides him with a number of good books and stories: "The American," "The Europeans," "Eugene Pickering," "Daisy Miller," "The Pupil," "Brooksmith," "A Bundle of Letters," "Washington Square," "The Portrait of a Lady," before 1880, and rather later, "Pandora," "The Four Meetings," perhaps "Louisa Pallant." He ran out of his first material.

We next note a contact with the "Yellow Book," a dip into "cleverness," into the epigrammatic genre, the bare epigrammatic style. It was no better than other writers, not so successful as Wilde. We observe him to be not so hard and fine a satirist as is George S. Street.

We come then to the period of allegories ("The Real Thing," "Dominick Ferrand," "The Liar"). There en-

click of brass doors. I had indeed for my earliest toy, if I was not brought up in it, the rather slow and well-behaved elevator in a quiet and quietly bright huge sanatorium. The height of high buildings, the chasms of New York are delectable; but this is beside the point; one is not asked to share the views and tastes of a writer.

sues a growing discontent with the short sentence, epigram, etc., in which he does not at this time attain distinction; the clarity is not satisfactory, was not satisfactory to the author, his *donné* being radically different from that of his contemporaries. The "story" not being really what he is after, he starts to build up his medium; a thickening, a chiaroscuro is needed, the long sentence; he wanders, seeks to add a needed opacity, he overdoes it, produces the cobwebby novel, emerges or justifies himself in "Maisie" and manages his long-sought form in "The Awkward Age." He comes out the triumphant stylist in the "American Scene" and in all the items of "The Finer Grain" collection and in the posthumous "Middle Years."

This is not to damn incontinent all that intervenes, but I think the chief question addressed to me by people of good-will who do not, but are yet ready and willing to, read James, is: Where the deuce shall I begin? One cannot take even the twenty-four volumes, more or less selected volumes of the Macmillan edition all at once, and it is, alas, but too easy to get so started and entoiled as never to finish this author or even come to the best of him.

The laziness of an uncritical period can be nowhere more blatant than in the inherited habit of talking about authors as a whole. It is perhaps the sediment from an age daft over great figures or a way of displaying social gush, the desire for a celebrity at all costs, rather than a care of letters.

To talk in any other way demands an acquaintance with the work of an author, a price few conversationalists care to pay, *ma che!* It is the man with inherited opinions who talks about "Shelley," making no distinction between the author of the Fifth Act of "The Cenci" and of the "Sensitive Plant." Not but what there may be a personal *virtu* in an author—appraised, however, from the best of his work when, that is, it is correctly appraised. People ask me what James to read. He is a very uneven author; not all of his collected edition has marks of permanence.

One can but make one's own suggestion:—

"The American," "French Poets and Novelists," "The Europeans," "Daisy Miller," "Eugene Pickering," "Washington Square," "A Bundle of Letters," "Portrait of a Lady," "Pandora," "The Pupil," "Brooksmith," "What Maisie Knew," and "The Awkward Age" (if one is "doing it all"), "Europe," "Four Meetings," "The Ambassadors," "The American Scene," "The Finer Grain" (all the volume, i.e., "The Velvet Glove," "Mona Montravers," "Round of Visits," "Crapey Cornelia," "Bench of Desolation"), "The Middle Years" (posthumous) and "The Ivory Tower" (notes first).

I "go easy" on the more cobwebby volumes; the most Jamesian are indubitably "The Wings of a Dove" and "The Golden Bowl"; upon them devotees will fasten, but the potential devotee may as well find his aptitude in the stories of "The Finer Grain" volume where certain exquisite titillations will come to him as readily as anywhere else. If he is to bask in Jamesian tickle, nothing will restrain him and no other author will to àny such extent afford him equal gratifications.

If, however, the reader does not find delectation in the list given above, I think it fairly useless for him to embark on the rest.

Part of James is a caviare, part I must reject according to my lights as bad writing; another part is a specialité, a pleasure for certain temperaments only; the part I have set together above seems to me maintainable as literature. One can definitely say: "this is good"; hold the argumentative field, suffer comparison with other writers; with, say, the De Goncourt, or De Maupassant. I am not impertinently throwing books on the scrap-heap; there are certain valid objections to James; there are certain standards which one may believe in, and having stated them, one is free to state that any author does not comply with them; granting always that there may be other standards with which he complies, or over which he charmingly or brilliantly triumphs.

James does not "feel" as solid as Flaubert; he does not give us "Everyman," but on the other hand, he was aware of things which Flaubert was not aware of, and in certain things supersedes the author of "Madame Bovary."

He appears at times to write around and around a thing and not always to emerge from the "amorous plan" of what he wanted to present, into definite presentation.

He does not seem to me at all times evenly skillful in catching the intonations of speech. He recalls the New England "a" in the "Lady's" small brothers "Ha-ard" (Haahr-d) but only if one is familiar with the phonetics described; but (vide the beginning of "The Birthplace") one is not convinced that he really knows (by any sure instinct) how people's voices would sound. Some remarks are in key, some obviously factitious.

He gives us more of his characters by description than he can by any attribution of conversation, save perhaps by the isolated and discreet remarks of Brooksmith.

His emotional centre is in being sensitive to the feel of the place or to the tonality of the person.

It is with his own so beautiful talk, his ability to hear his own voice in the rounded paragraph, that he is aptest to charm one. I find it often though not universally hard to "hear" his characters speaking. I have noted various places where the character notably stops speaking and the author interpolates words of his own; sentences that no one but Henry James could in any circumstances have made use of. Beyond which statements I see no great concision or any clarity to be gained by rearranging my perhaps too elliptical comments on individual books.

Honest criticism, as I conceive it, cannot get much further than saying to one's reader exactly what one would say to the friend who approaches one's bookshelf asking: "What the deuce shall I read?" Beyond this there is the "parlor game," the polite essay, and there is the official pronouncement, with neither of which we are concerned.

Of all exquisite writers James is the most colloquial, yet in the first edition of his "French Poets and Novelists," his style, save for a few scattered phrases, is so little unusual that most of the book seems, superficially, as if it might have been written by almost any one. It contains some surprising lapses . . . as bad as any in Mr. Hueffer or even in Mr. Mencken. It is interesting largely in that it shows us what our subject had to escape from.

Let us grant at once that his novels show him, all through his life, possessed of the worst possible taste in pictures, of an almost unpunctured ignorance of painting, of almost as great a lack of taste as that which he attributes to the hack-work and newspaper critiques of Théophile Gautier. Let us admit that "painting" to Henry James probably meant, to the end of his life, the worst possible late Renaissance conglomerations.

Let us admit that in 1876, or whenever it was, his

taste in poetry inclined to the swish of De Musset, that it very likely never got any further. By "poetry" he very possibly meant the "high-falutin" and he eschewed it in certain forms; himself taking still higher falutes in a to-be-developed mode of his own.

I doubt if he ever wholly outgrew that conception of the (by him so often invoked) Daughters of Memory. He arrived truly at a point from which he could look back upon people who "besought the deep blue sea to roll." Poetry to him began, perhaps, fullfledged, springing Minerva-like from the forehead of George Gordon, Lord Byron, and went pretty much to the bad in Charles Baudelaire; it did not require much divination by 1914 ("The Middle Years") to note that he had found Tennyson rather vacuous and that there "was something in" Browning.

James was so thoroughly a recorder of people, of their atmospheres, society, personality, setting; so wholly the artist of this particular genre, that it was impossible for him ever to hold a critical opinion of art out of key with the opinion about him—except possibly in so far as he might have ambitions for the novel, for his own particular métier. His critical opinions were simply an extension of his being in key with the nice people who "impressed" themselves on his gelatine "plate." (This is a theoretical generalization and must be taken *cum grano*.)

We may, perhaps, take his adjectives on De Musset as a desperate attempt to do "justice" to a man with whom he knew it impossible for him to sympathize. There is, however, nothing to hinder our supposing that he saw in De Musset's "gush" something for him impossible and that he wished to acknowledge it. Side by side

with this are the shreds of Back Bay or Buffalo, the
mid-week-prayer-meeting point of view.

His most egregious slip is in the essay on Baudelaire,
the sentence quoted by Hueffer.* Notwithstanding this,
he does effectively put his nippers on Baudelaire's weakness:—

"A good way to embrace Baudelaire at a glance is to
say that he was, in his treatment of evil, exactly what
Hawthorne was not—Hawthorne, who felt the thing at
its source, deep in the human consciousness. Baudelaire's infinitely slighter volume of genius apart, he was
a sort of Hawthorne reversed. It is the absence of
this metaphysical quality in his treatment of his favorite
subjects (Poe was his metaphysician, and his devotion
sustained him through a translation of 'Eureka!') that
exposes him to that class of accusations of which M.
Edmond Scherer's accusation of feeding upon *pourriture*
is an example; and, in fact, in his pages we never know
with what we are dealing. We encounter an inextricable
confusion of sad emotions and vile things, and we are at
a loss to know whether the subject pretends to appeal to
our conscience or—we were going to say—to our olfac-
tories. 'Le Mal?' we exclaim; 'you do yourself too much
honor. This is not Evil; it is not the wrong; it is simply
the nasty!' Our impatience is of the same order as that
which we should feel if a poet, pretending to pluck 'the
flowers of good,' should come and present us, as speci-
mens, a rhapsody on plum-cake and *eau de Cologne*."

Here as elsewhere his perception, apart from the read-
ability of the work, is worthy of notice.

* "For a poet to be realist is of course nonsense", and, as
Hueffer says, such a sentence from such a source is enough to
make one despair of human nature.

Hueffer says * that James belauds Balzac. I cannot
see it. I can but perceive Henry James wiping the floor
with the author of "Eugénie Grandet," pointing out all
his qualities, but almightily wiping the floor with him.
He complains that Gautier is lacking in a concern about
supernatural hocus-pocus and that Flaubert is lacking.
If Balzac takes him to any great extent in, James with
his inherited Swedenborgianism is perhaps thereby laid
open to Balzac.

It was natural that James should write more about
the bulky author of "La Comédie Humaine" than about
the others; here was his richest quarry, here was there
most to note and to emend and to apply so emended to
processes of his own. From De Maupassant, De Goncourt or Baudelaire there was nothing for him to acquire.

His dam'd fuss about furniture is foreshadowed in
Balzac, and all the paragraphs on Balzac's house-fur-
nishing propensities are of interest in proportion to our
interest in, or our boredom with, this part of Henry
James's work.

What, indeed, could he have written of the De Goncourts save that they were a little dull but tremendously
right in their aim? Indeed, but for these almost auto-
biographical details pointing to his growth out of Balzac,
all James would seem but a corollary to one passage in a
De Goncourt preface:—

"Le jour où l'analyse cruelle que mon ami, M. Zola,
et peutêtre moi-même avons apportée dans la peinture
du bas de la société sera reprise par un écrivain de talent,
et employée à la reproduction des hommes et des femmes
du monde, dans les milieux d'éducation et de distinction

* Ford Madox Hueffer's volume on Henry James.

—ce jour-là seulement le classicisme et sa queue seront
tués. . . .

"Le Réalisme n'a pas en effet l'unique mission de
décrire ce qui est bas, ce qui est répugnant. . . .

"Nous avons commencé, nous, par la canaille, parce
que la femme et l'homme du peuple, plus rapprochés de
la nature et de la sauvagerie, sont des créatures simples
et peu compliquées, tandis que le Parisien et la Parisienne
de la société, ces civilisés excessifs, dont l'originalité
tranchée est faite toute de nuances, toute de demi-teintes,
toute de ces riens insaisissables, pareils aux riens coquets
et neutres avec lesquels se façonne le caractère d'une
toilette distinguée de femme, demandent des années pour
qu'on les perce, pour qu'on les sache, pour qu'on les
attrape—et le romancier du plus grand génie, croyez-
le bien, ne les devinera jamais ces gens de salon, avec
les *racontars* d'amis qui vont pour lui à la découverte
dans le monde. . . .

"Ce projet de roman qui devait se passer dans le
grand monde, dans le monde le plus quintessencié, et
dont nous rassemblions lentement et minutieusement les
éléments délicats et fugaces, je l'abandonnais après la
mort de mon frère, convaincu de l'impossibilité de le
réussir tout seul."

But this particular paragraph could have had little
to do with the matter. "French Poets and Novelists"
was published in '78 and Edmond De Goncourt signed
the preface to "Les Frères Zemganno" in '79. The paragraphs quoted are interesting, however, as showing De
Goncourt's state of mind in that year. He had probably been preaching in this vein long before setting
the words on paper, before getting them printed.

If ever one man's career was foreshadowed in a few

sentences of another, Henry James's is to be found in this paragraph.

It is very much as if he said: I will not be a mega-therium botcher like Balzac; there is nothing to be said about these De Goncourts, but one must try to be rather more interesting than they are in, let us say, "Madame Gervaisais." *

Proceeding with the volume of criticism, we find that "Le Jeune H." simply didn't "get" Flaubert; that he was much alive to the solid parts of Turgenev. He shows himself very apt, as we said above, to judge the merits of a novelist on the ground that the people portrayed by the said novelist are or are not suited to reception into the household of Henry James senior; whether, in short, Emma Bovary or Frederic or M. Arnoux would have spoiled the so delicate atmosphere, have juggled the so fine susceptibilities of a refined 23rd Street family at the time of the Philadelphia "Centennial."

I find the book not so much a sign that Henry James was "disappointed," as Hueffer puts it, as that he was simply and horribly shocked by the literature of his continental forebears and contemporaries.

It is only when he gets to the Théâtre Français that he finds something which really suits him. Here there is order, tradition, perhaps a slight fustiness (but a quite pardonable fustiness, an arranged and suitable fustiness having its recompense in a sort of spiritual quiet) ; here, at any rate, was something decorous, something not to be found in Concord or in Albany. And it is easy to imagine the young James, not illuminated by De

* It is my personal feeling at the moment that *La Fille Elisa* is worth so much more than all Balzac that the things are as out of scale as a sapphire and a plum pudding, and that *Elisa,* despite the dull section, is worth most of James's writing. This is, however, aside from the question we are discussing.

Goncourt's possible conversation or writing, not even following the hint given in his essay on Balzac and Balzacian furniture, but sitting before Madame Nathalie in "Le Village" and resolving to be the Théâtre Français of the novel.

A resolution which he may be said to have carried out to the great enrichment of letters.

II

STRICTURES on the work of this period are no great detraction. "French Poets and Novelists" gives us a point from which to measure Henry James's advance. Genius showed itself partly in the escape from some of his original limitations, partly in acquirements. His art at length became "second nature," became perhaps half unconscious; or in part wholly unconscious; in other parts perhaps too highly conscious. At any rate in sunnier circumstances he talked exactly as he wrote, the same elaborate paragraph beautifully attaining its climax; the same sudden incision when a brief statement could dispose of a matter.

Be it said for his style: he is seldom or never involved when a direct bald statement will accurately convey his own meaning, *all of it*. He is not usually, for all his wide leisure, verbose. He may be highly and bewilderingly figurative in his language (vide Mr. Hueffer's remarks on this question).

Style apart, I take it that the hatred of tyrannies was as great a motive as any we can ascribe to Galileo or Leonardo or to any other great figure, to any other mythic Prometheus; for this driving force we may well overlook personal foibles, the early Bostonese bias, the heritage from his father's concern in commenting Swedenborg,

the later fusses about social caut?n and conservation of
furniture. Hueffer rather boasts about Henry James's
innocence of the classics. It is nothing to brag of, even
if a man struggling against natural medievalism have
entrenched himself in impressionist theory. If James
had read his classics, the better Latins especially, he
would not have so excessively cobwebbed, fussed, blathered, worried about minor mundanities. We may *con-
spuer* with all our vigor Henry James's concern with
furniture, the Spoils of Poynton, connoisseurship, Mrs.
Ward's tea-party atmosphere, the young Bostonian of
the immature works. We may relegate these things men-
tally to the same realm as the author's pyjamas and collar buttons, to his intellectual instead of his physical
valeting. There remains the capacious intelligence, the
searching analysis of things that cannot be so relegated
to the scrap-heap and to the wash-basket.

Let us say that English freedom legally and tradition-
ally has its basis in property. Let us say, à la Balzac,
that most modern existence is governed by, or at least
interfered with by, the necessity to earn money; let us
also say that a Frenchman is not an Englishman or a
German or an American, and that despite the remark
that the aristocracies of all people, the upper classes, are
the same everywhere, racial differences are *au fond* differences; they are likewise major subjects.

Writing, as I am, for the reader of good-will, for the
bewildered person who wants to know where to begin,
I need not apologize for the following elliptical notes.
James, in his prefaces, has written explanation to death
(with sometimes a very pleasant necrography). Leaving the "French Poets and Novelists," I take the novels
and stories as nearly as possible in their order of publi-

cation (as distinct from their order as rearranged and partially weeded out in the collected edition).

1875. (U. S. A.) "A Passionate Pilgrim and other Tales." "Eugene Pickering" is the best of this lot and most indicative of the future James. Contains also the title story and "Madame de Mauves." Other stories inferior.

1876. (U. S. A.) "Roderick Hudson," prentice work. First novel not up to the level of "Pickering."

1877. "The American"; essential James, part of the permanent work. "Watch and Ward," discarded by the author.

1878. "French Poets and Novelists," already discussed.

1878. "Daisy Miller." (The big hit and one of his best.) "An International Episode," "Four Meetings," good work.

1870. Short stories first printed in England with additions, but no important ones.

1880. "Confidence," not important.

1881. "Washington Square," one of his best, "putting America on the map," giving us a real past, a real background. "Pension Beaurepas" and "Bundle of Letters," especially the girls' letters, excellent, already mentioned.

1881. "The Portrait of a Lady," one of his best. Charming Venetian preface in the collected edition.

1884. "Tales of Three Cities," stories dropped from the collected edition, save "Lady Barbarina."

1884. "Lady Barbarina," a study in English blankness comparable to that exposed in the letters of the English young lady in "A Bundle of Letters." There is also New York of the period. "But if there was one thing Lady Barb disliked more than another it was describing Pasterns. She had always lived with people

who knew of themselves what such a place would be,
without demanding these pictorial effects, proper only,
as she vaguely felt, to persons belonging to the classes
whose trade was the arts of expression. Lady Barb of
course had never gone into it; but she knew that in her
own class the business was not to express but to enjoy,
not to represent but to be represented."

"Mrs. Lemon's recognition of this river, I should say,
was all it need have been; she held the Hudson existed
for the purpose of supplying New Yorkers with poetical
feelings, helping them to face comfortably occasions like
the present, and in general, meet foreigners with confidence. . . ."

"He believed, or tried to believe, the *salon* now possible in New York on condition of its being reserved entirely for adults; and in having taken a wife out of a
country in which social traditions were rich and ancient
he had done something toward qualifying his own house—
so splendidly qualified in all strictly material respects . . .
to be the scene of such an effort. A charming woman
accustomed only to the best on each side, as Lady Beau-
chemin said, what mightn't she achieve by being at home
—always to adults only—in an easy early inspiring comprehensive way and on the evening of the seven, when
worldly engagements were least numerous? He laid this
philosophy before Lady Barb in pursuance of a theory
that if she disliked New York on a short acquaintance
she couldn't fail to like it on a long. Jackson believed
in the New York mind—not so much indeed in its literary, artistic, philosophic or political achievements as
in its general quickness and nascent adaptability. He
clung to this belief, for it was an indispensable neat block
in the structure he was attempting to rear. The New
York mind would throw its glamour over Lady Barb if

she would only give it a chance; for it was thoroughly
bright, responsive and sympathetic. If she would only
set up by the turn of her hand a blest social centre, a
temple of interesting talk in which this charming organ
might expand and where she might inhale its fragrance
in the most convenient and luxurious way, without, as it
was, getting up from her chair; if she would only just
try this graceful good-natured experiment—which would
make every one like her so much too—he was sure all
the wrinkles in the gilded scroll of his fate would be
smoothed out. But Lady Barb didn't rise at all to his
conception and hadn't the least curiosity about the New
York mind. She thought it would be extremely disagreeable to have a lot of people tumbling in on Sunday evening without being invited, and altogether her husband's
sketch of the Anglo-American salon seemed to her to
suggest crude familiarity, high vociferation—she had already made a remark to him about 'screeching women'
—and random extravagant laughter. She didn't tell him
—for this somehow it wasn't in her power to express
and, strangely enough, he never completely guessed it—
that she was singularly deficient in any natural, or indeed, acquired understanding of what a salon might be.
She had never seen or dreamed of one—and for the
most part was incapable of imagining a thing she hadn't
seen. She had seen great dinners and balls and meets
and runs and races; she had seen garden-parties and
bunches of people, mainly women—who, however, didn't
screech—at dull stuffy teas, and distinguished companies
collected in splendid castles; but all this gave her no clew
to a train of conversation, to any idea of a social agreement that the interest of talk, its continuity, its accumulations from season to season shouldn't be lost. Conversation, in Lady Barb's experience, had never been

continuous; in such a case it would surely have been a
bore. It had been occasional and fragmentary, a trifle
jerky, with allusions that were never explained; it had
a dread of detail—it seldom pursued anything very far
or kept hold of it very long."

1885. "Stories Revived," adding to earlier tales "The
Author of Beltraffio," which opens with excess of the
treading-on-eggs manner, too much to be borne for twenty-four volumes. The pretense of extent of "people" interested in art and letters, sic: "It was the most complete
presentation that had yet been made of the gospel of art;
it was a kind of æsthetic war cry. 'People' had endeav-
ored to sail nearer 'to truth,' etc."

He implies too much of art smeared on limited multi-
tudes. One wonders if the eighties did in any great
aggregate gush up to this extent. Doesn't he try to
spread the special case out too wide?

The thinking is magnificently done from this passage
up to page sixteen or twenty, stated with great concision.
Compare it with "Madame Gervaisais" and we find
Henry James much more interesting when on the upper
reaches. Compare his expressiveness, the expressiveness
of his indirectness with that of constatation. The two
methods are curiously mixed in the opening of "Beltraffio." Such sentences as (page 30) "He said the most
interesting and inspiring things" are, however, pure
waste, pure "leaving the thing undone," unconcrete, un-
imagined; just simply bad writing or bad novelisting.
As for his special case he does say a deal about the author or express a deal by him, but one is bothered by the
fact that Pater, Burton, Hardy, Meredith were not, in
mere history, bundled into one; that Burton had been to
the East and the others had not; that no English novelist of that era would have taken the least notice of any-

thing going on in foreign countries, presumably European, as does the supreme author of "Beltraffio."

Doubtless he is in many ways the author Henry James
would have liked to meet and more illustrative of certain
English tones and limitations than any historical portrait
might have been. Still Henry James does lay it on . . .
more, I think, than the story absolutely requires. In
"Beltraffio" he certainly does present (not that he does
not comment to advantage) the two damn'd women ap-
pended to the gentlemanly hero of the tale. The most
violent post-Strindbergian school would perhaps have
called them bitches *tout bonnement,* but this word did
not belong to Henry James's vocabulary and besides it
is of too great an indistinctness. Author, same "bloody"
(in the English sense) author with his passion for
"form" appears in "Lesson of Master," and most of H.
J.'s stories of literary *milieux.* Perpetual Grandisonism
or Grandisonizing of this author with the passion for
form, all of 'em have it. *Ma ché!* There is, however,
great intensity in these same "be-deared" and be-"poor-
old"-ed pages. He has really got a main theme, a great
theme, he chooses to do it in silver point rather than in
the garish colors of,—well, of Cherbuliez, or the terms
of a religious maniac with three-foot long carving knife.

Novel of the gilded pill, an æsthetic or artistic message,
dogma, no better than a moral or ethic one, novel a
cumbrous camouflage substitute not for "that parlor
game" * the polite essay, but for the impolite essay or
conveyance of ideas; novel to do this should completely
incarnate the abstraction.

Finish of "Beltraffio" not perhaps up to the rest of it.
Not that one at all knows how else . . .

* T. S. Eliot.

Gush on page 42 * from both conversationalists. Still an adumbration of the search for the just word emerges on pages 43-44, real cut at barbarism and bigotry on the bottom of page 45 (of course not labeled by these monstrous and rhetorical brands, scorched on to their hides and rump sides). "Will it be a sin to make the most of that one too, so bad for the dear old novel?" Butler and James on the same side really chucking out the fake; Butler focused on Church of England; opposed to him the fakers booming the Bible "as literature" in a sort of last stand, a last ditch; seeing it pretty well had to go as history, cosmogony, etc., or the old tribal Daddy-slap-'em-with-slab of the Jews as anything like an ideal :—

"He told me more about his wife before we arrived at the gate of home, and if he be judged to have aired overmuch his grievance I'm afraid I must admit that he had some of the foibles as well as the gifts of the artistic temperament; adding, however, instantly that hitherto, to the best of my belief, he had rarely let this particular cat out of the bag. 'She thinks me immoral—that's the long and short of it,' he said, as we paused outside a moment and his hand rested on one of the bars of his gate; while his conscious, expressive, perceptive eyes—the eyes of a foreigner, I had begun to account them, much more than of the usual Englishman—viewing me now evidently as quite a familiar friend, took part in the declaration. 'It's very strange when one thinks it all over, and there's a grand comicality in it that I should like to bring out. She's a very nice woman, extraordinarily well-behaved, upright and clever and with a tremendous lot of good sense about a good many matters. Yet her conception of a novel—she has explained it to

* Page numbers in Collected Edition.

me once or twice, and she doesn't do it badly as exposition—is a thing so false that it makes me blush. It's a
thing so hollow, so dishonest, so lying, in which life is
so blinked and blinded, so dodged and disfigured, that it
makes my ears burn. It's two different ways of looking
at the whole affair,' he repeated, pushing open the gate.
'And they're irreconcilable!' he added with a sigh. We
went forward to the house, but on the walk, halfway
to the door, he stopped and said to me: 'If you're going
into this kind of thing there's a fact you should know
beforehand; it may save you some disappointment.
There's a hatred of art, there's a hatred of literature—I
mean of the genuine kinds. Oh, the shams—*those* they'll
swallow by the bucket!' I looked up at the charming house, with its genial color and crookedness, and I
answered with a smile that those evil passions might
exist, but that I should never have expected to find
them there. 'Ah, it doesn't matter, after all,' he a bit
nervously laughed; which I was glad to hear, for I was
reproaching myself with having worked him up."

Really literature in the XIXth and the beginning of
the XXth centuries is where science was in the days of
Galileo and the Inquisition. Henry James not blinking
it, neither can we. "Poor dears" and "dear olds" always
a little too plentiful.

1885. (continued) "Pandora," of the best. Let it
pass as a sop to America's virginal charm; as counter-
weight to "Daisy Miller," or to the lady of "The Portrait." Henry James alert to the German.

"The process of enquiry had already begun for him,
in spite of his having as yet spoken to none of his fellow
passengers; the case being that Vogelstein enquired not
only with his tongue, but with his eyes—that is with his
spectacles—with his ears, with his nose, with his palate,

with all his senses and organs. He was a highly upright young man, whose only fault was that his sense of comedy, or of the humor of things, had never been specifically disengaged from his several other senses. He vaguely felt that something should be done about this, and in a general manner proposed to do it, for he was on his way to explore a society abounding in comic aspects. This consciousness of a missing measure gave him a certain mistrust of what might be said of him; and if circumspection is the essence of diplomacy our young aspirant promised well. His mind contained several millions of facts, packed too closely together for the light breeze of the imagination to draw through the mass. He was impatient to report himself to his superior in Washington, and the loss of time in an English port could only incommode him, inasmuch as the study of English institutions was no part of his mission. On the other hand the day was charming; the blue sea, in Southampton Water, pricked all over with light, had no movement but that of its infinite shimmer. Moreover, he was by no means sure that he should be happy in the United States, where doubtless he should find himself soon enough disembarked. He knew that this was not an important question and that happiness was an unscientific term, such as a man of his education should be ashamed to use even in the silence of his thoughts. Lost none the less in the inconsiderate crowd and feeling himself neither in his own country nor in that to which he was in a manner accredited, he was reduced to his mere personality; so that during the hour, to save his importance, he cultivated such ground as lay in sight for a judgment of this delay to which the German steamer was subjected in English waters. Mightn't it be proved, facts, figures and documents—or at least

watch—in hand, considerably greater than the occasion
demanded?

"Count Vogelstein was still young enough in diplomacy
to think it necessary to have opinions. He had a good
many, indeed, which had been formed without difficulty;
they had been received ready-made from a line of ancestors who knew what they liked. This was of course
—and under pressure, being candid, he would have admitted it—an unscientific way of furnishing one's mind.
Our young man was a stiff conservative, a Junker of
Junkers; he thought modern democracy a temporary
phase and expected to find many arguments against it in
the great Republic. In regard to these things it was a
pleasure to him to feel that, with his complete training,
he had been taught thoroughly to appreciate the nature
of evidence. The ship was heavily laden with German
emigrants, whose mission in the United States differed
considerably from Count Otto's. They hung over the
bulwarks, densely grouped; they leaned forward on
their elbows for hours, their shoulders kept on a level
with their ears: the men in furred caps, smoking long-
bowled pipes, the women with babies hidden in remark-
ably ugly shawls. Some were yellow Germans and some
were black, and all looked greasy and matted with the
sea-damp. They were destined to swell still further
the huge current of the Western democracy; and Count
Vogelstein doubtless said to himself that they wouldn't
improve its quality. Their numbers, however, were
striking, and I know not what he thought of the nature
of this particular evidence."

For further style in vignette:

"He could see for himself that Mr. and Mrs. Day had
not at all her grand air. They were fat plain serious

people who sat side by side on the deck for hours and
looked straight before them. Mrs. Day had a white
face, large cheeks and small eyes; her forehead was surrounded with a multitude of little tight black curls; her
lips moved as if she had always a lozenge in her mouth.
She wore entwined about her head an article which Mrs.
Dangerfield spoke of as a 'nuby,' a knitted pink scarf
concealing her hair, encircling her neck and having
among its convolutions a hole for her perfectly expres-
sionless face. Her hands were folded on her stomach,
and in her still, swathed figure her bead-like eyes, which
occasionally changed their direction, alone represented
life. Her husband had a stiff gray beard on his chin
and a bare spacious upper lip, to which constant shaving
had imparted a hard glaze. His eyebrows were thick
and his nostrils wide, and when he was uncovered, in
the saloon, it was visible that his grizzled hair was dense
and perpendicular. He might have looked rather grim
and truculent hadn't it been for the mild familiar ac-
commodating gaze with which his large light-colored
pupils—the leisurely eyes of a silent man—appeared to
consider surrounding objects. He was evidently more
friendly than fierce, but he was more diffident than
friendly. He liked to have you in sight, but wouldn't
have pretended to understand you much or to classify
you, and would have been sorry it should put you under
an obligation. He and his wife spoke sometimes, but
seldom talked, and there was something vague and patient about them as if they had become victims of a
wrought spell. The spell, however, was of no sinister
cast; it was the fascination of prosperity, the confidence
of security, which sometimes makes people arrogant,
but which had had such a different effect on this simple

satisfied pair, in whom further development of every
kind appeared to have been happily arrested."

Pandora's approach to her parents :

"These little offices were usually performed deftly,
rapidly, with the minimum of words, and when their
daughter drew near them, Mr. and Mrs. Day closed their
eyes after the fashion of a pair of household dogs who
expect to be scratched."

The tale is another synthesis of some of the million
reasons why Germany will never conquer the world, why
the Hun is impossible, why "boche" is merely "bursch."
The imbecility of a certain Wellsian journalist in treating this gem is again proof that it is written for the
relatively-developed American, not for the island
écaillère. If Henry James, as Ford Madox Hueffer
says, set out to civilize the United States, it is at least
an easier job than raising British Suburbia to a bearable
level. From that milieu at least we have nothing of
value to learn ; we shall not take our tonality from that
niveau.

In describing "Pandora's" success as "purely personal,"
Henry James has hit on the secret of the Quattrocento,
1450 to 1550, the vital part of the Renaissance. Aristocracy decays when it ceases to be selective, when the
basis of selection is not personal. It is a critical acute-
ness, not a snobbism, which last is selection on some
other principle than that of a personal quality. It is
servility to rule-of-thumb criteria, and a dullness of perception, a timidity in acceptance. The whole force of
the Renaissance was in the personality of its selection.

There is no faking the amount of perceptive energy
concentrated in Henry James's vignettes in such phrases

as that on the parents like domestic dogs waiting to be
scratched, or in the ten thousand phrases of this sort
which abound in his writings.   If we were back in the
time of Bruyère, we could easily make a whole book of
"Characters" from Henry James's vignettes.* The
vein holds from beginning to end of his work; from
this writing of the eighties to "The Ivory Tower." As
for example, Gussie Braddon:

"Rosanna waited facing her, noting her extraordinary
perfection of neatness, of elegance, of arrangement, of
which it couldn't be said whether they most handed over
to you, as on some polished salver, the clear truth of her
essential commonness or transposed it into an element
that could please, that could even fascinate, as a supreme
attestation of care.   'Take her as an advertisement of all
the latest knowledges of how to "treat" every inch of
the human surface and where to "get" every scrap of
the personal envelope, so far as she *is* enveloped, and
she does achieve an effect sublime in itself and thereby
absolute in a wavering world.' "

We note no inconsiderable progress in the actual writing, in *maestria,* when we reach the ultimate volumes.

1886. "Bostonians."   Other stories in this collection
mostly rejected from collected edition.

"Princess Casamassima," inferior continuation of
"Roderick Hudson."   His original subject matter is beginning to go thin.

* Since writing the above I find that some such compilation
has been attempted; had ind d been planned by the anthologist.
and, in plan, approved by H. J.: "Pictures and Passages from
Henry James" selected by Ruth Head (Chatto and Windus,
1916), if not exactly the book to convince the rising generation
of H. J.'s powers of survival, is at any rate a most charming
tribute to our subject from one who had begun to read him
in "the eighties".

1888. "The Reverberator," process of fantasia beginning.

Fantasia of Americans vs. the "old aristocracy." "The American" with the sexes reversed. Possibly the theme shows as well in "Les Transatlantiques," the two methods, give one at least a certain pleasure of contrast.

1888. "Aspern Papers," inferior. "Louisa Pallant," a study in the maternal or abysmal relation, good James. "Modern Warning," rejected from collected edition.

1889. "A London Life." "The Patagonia."

"The Patagonia," not a masterpiece. Slow in opening, excellent in parts, but the sense of the finale intrudes all along. It seems true but there is no alternative ending. One doubts whether a story is really constructed with any mastery when the end, for the purpose of making it a story, is so unescapable. The effect of reality is produced, of course, by the reality of the people in the opening scene; there is no doubt about that part being "to the life."

"The Liar" is superb in its way, perhaps the best of the allegories, of the plots invented purely to be an exposition of impression. It is magnificent in its presentation of the people, both the old man and the Liar, who is masterly.

"Mrs. Temperly" is another such excellent delineation and shows James as an excellent hater, but G. S. Street expresses a concentration of annoyance with a greater polish and suavity in method; and neither explains, theorizes, nor comments

James never has De Maupassant's reality. His (H. J.'s) people almost always convince, i.e., we believe implicitly that they exist. We also think that Henry James has made up some sort of story as an excuse for writing his impression of the people.

One sees the slight vacancy of the stories of this period, the short clear sentence, the dallying with *jeu d'esprit*, with epigram no better than, though not inferior to, the run of epigram in the nineties. It all explains James's need of opacity, his reaching out for a chiaroscuro to distinguish himself from his contemporaries and in which he could put the whole of his much more complex apperception.

Then comes, roughly, the period of cobwebs and of excessive cobwebs and of furniture, finally justified in "The Finer Grain." a book of tales with no mis-fire, and the style so vindicated in the triumphs of the various books of Memoirs and "The American Scene."

Fantasias: "Dominic Ferrand," "Nona Vincent" (tales obviously aimed at the "Yellow Book," but seem to have missed it, a detour in James's career). All artists who discover anything make such detours and must, in the course of things (as in the cobwebs), push certain experiments beyond the right curve of their art. This is not so much the doom as the function of all "revolutionary" or experimental art, and I think masterwork is usually the result of the return from such excess. One does not know, simply does not know, the true curve until one has pushed one's method beyond it. Until then it is merely a frontier, not a chosen route. It is an open question, and there is no dogmatic answer, whether an artist should write and rewrite the same story (à la Flaubert) or whether he should take a new canvas.

"The Papers," a fantasia, diverting; "The Birthplace," fairy-godmother element mentioned above, excellent. "Edmund Orme," inferior; "Yellow Book" tale, not accepted by that periodical.

1889-1893. Period of this entoilment in the "Yellow

Book," short sentences, the epigrammatic. He reacts
from this into the allegorical. In general the work of
this period is not up to the mark. "The Chaperon," "The
Real Thing," fantasias of "wit." By fantasias I mean
sketches in which the people are "real" or convince one
of their verity, but where the story is utterly unconvinc-
ing, is not intended to convince, is merely a sort of exaggeration of the fitting situation or the situation which
ought to result in order to display some type at its apogee. "The Real Thing" rather better than other stories
in this volume.

Thus the lady and gentleman model in "The Real
Thing." London society is finely ladled in "The Chaperon," which is almost as a story, romanticism.

"Greville Fane" is a scandalous photograph from the
life about which the great blagueur scandalously lies in
his preface (collected edition). I have been too diverted
comparing it with *an* original to give a sane view of
its art.

1890. "The Tragic Muse." uneven, full of good
things but showing Henry James in the didactic role a
little too openly. He preaches, he also displays fine perception of the parochialism of the British political career. It is a readable novel with tracts interpolated.
(Excellent and commendable tracts arguing certainly for
the right thing, enjoyable, etc.) Excellent text-book for
young men with ambitions, etc.

1892. "Lesson of the Master" (cobweb). "The Pupil," a masterpiece, one of his best and keenest studies.
"Brooksmith" of the best.

1893. "The Private Life." Title story, waste verbiage
at the start, ridiculous to put all this camouflage over
something au fond merely an idea. Not life, not people, allegory, dated to "Yellow Book" era. Won't hold

against "Candide." H. J.'s tilting against the vacuity of
the public figure is, naturally, pleasing, i. e., it is pleasing
that he should tilt, but the amusement partakes of the
nature of seeing cocoanuts hurled at an aunt sally.

There are other stories, good enough to be carried by
H. J.'s best work, not detrimental, but not enough to have
"made him": "Europe" (Hawthorny), "Paste," "The
Middle Years," "Broken Wings," etc. Part of the great
man's work can perhaps only be criticized as "etc."

1895. "Terminations, Coxon Fund," perhaps best of
this lot, a disquisition, but entertaining, perhaps the germ
of Galsworthy to be found in it (to no glory of either
author) as perhaps a residuum of Dickens in Maisie's
Mrs. Wix. Verbalism, but delightful verbalism in
Coxon affair, sic:

"Already, at hungry twenty-six, Gravener looked as
blank and parliamentary as if he were fifty and popular,"

or

"a deeply wronged, justly resentful, quite irreproachable and insufferable person"

or (for the whole type)
"put such ignorance into her cleverness?"

Miss Anvoy's echo concerning "a crystal" is excellently introduced, but is possibly in the nature of a sleight
of hand trick (contemporary with "Lady Windemere's
Fan"). Does H. J.'s "politics" remind one of Dizzy's
scribbling, just a little? "Confidence, under the new
Ministry, was understood to be reviving," etc.

Perhaps one covers the ground by saying that the
James of this period is "light literature," entertaining if
one have nothing better to do. Neither "Terminations"
nor (1896) "Embarrassments" would have founded a
reputation.

1896-97. Improvement through "Other House" and

"Spoils of Poynton." I leave the appreciation of these, to me, detestable works to Mr. Hueffer. They seem to me full of a good deal of needless fuss, though I do not mean to deny any art that may be in them.

1897. The emergence in "What Maisie Knew." Problem of the adolescent female. Carried on in:

1899. "The Awkward Age," fairy godmother and spotless lamb and all the rest of it. Only real thing the impression of people, not observation or real knowledge. Action only to give reader the tone, symbolizing the tone of the people. Opening *tour de force*, a study in punks, a cheese *soufflé* of the leprous crust of society done to a turn and a niceness save where he puts on the *dulcissimo, vox humana,* stop. James was the dispassionate observer. He started with the moral obsession; before he had worked clear of it he was entoiled in the obsession of social tone. He has pages of clear depiction, even of satire, but the sentimentalist is always lurking just round the corner. This softens his edges. He has not the clear hardness, the cold satiric justness that G. S. Street has displayed in treating situations, certain struggles between certain idiocies and certain vulgarities. This book is a specialité of local interest. It is an étude in ephemera. If it contained any revelation in 1899, it no longer contains it. His characters are reduced to the status of *voyeurs*, elaborate analysis of the much too special cases, a bundle of swine and asses who cannot mind their own business, who do not know enough to mind their own business. James's lamentable lack of the classics is perhaps responsible for his absorption in bagatelles. . . . He has no real series of backgrounds of *moeurs du passé,* only the "sweet dim faded lavender" tune and in opposition to modernity, plush nickel-plated, to the disparagement, naturally, of the latter.

Kipling's "Bigod, now-I-know-all-about-this manner," is an annoyance, but one wonders if parts of Kipling by the sheer force of content, of tale to tell, will not outlast most of James's cobwebs. There is no substitute for narrative-sense, however many different and entrancing charms may be spread before us.

"The Awkward Age" might have been done, from one point of view, as satire, in one-fourth the space. On the other hand, James does give us the subtly graded atmospheres of his different houses most excellently. And indeed, this may be regarded as *his* subject.

If one were advocate instead of critic, one would definitely claim that these atmospheres, nuances, impressions of personal tone and quality *are his subject;* that in these he gets certain things that almost no one else had done before him. These timbres and tonalities are his stronghold, he is ignorant of nearly everything else. It is all very well to say that modern life is largely made up of velleities, atmospheres, timbres, nuances, etc., but if people really spent as much time fussing, to the extent of the Jamesian fuss about such normal trifling, age-old affairs, as slight inclinations to adultery, slight disinclinations to marry, to refrain from marrying, etc., etc., life would scarcely be worth the bother of keeping on with it. It is also contendable that one must depict such mush in order to abolish it.*

---

* Most good prose arises, perhaps, from an instinct of negation; is the detailed, convincing analysis of something detestable; of something which one wants to eliminate. Poetry is the assertion of a positive, *i. e.*, of desire, and endures for a longer period. Poetic satire is only an assertion of this positive, inversely, *i. e.*, as of an opposite hatred.

This is a highly untechnical, unimpressionist, in fact almost theological manner of statement; but is perhaps the root difference between the two arts of literature.

Most good poetry asserts something to be worth while, or

The main feeling in "The Awkward Age" is satiric. The dashes of sentiment do not help the work as literature. The acute observer is often referred to:

Page 131. "The ingenious observer just now suggested might even have detected . . ."

Page 133. "And it might have been apparent still to our sharp spectator . . ."

Page 310. "But the acute observer we are constantly taking for granted would perhaps have detected . . ."

Page 323. "A supposititious spectator would certainly have imagined . . ." (This also occurs in "Ivory Tower." Page 196.)

This scrutinous person wastes a great deal of time in pretending to conceal his contempt for Mrs. Brook, Vanderbank, the other punks, and lays it on so *thick* when presenting his old sentimentalist Longdon, who at the one critical moment behaves *with a stupidity,*

damns a contrary; at any rate asserts emotional values. The best prose is, has been a presentation (complicated and elaborate as you like) of circumstances, of conditions, for the most part abominable, or at the mildest, amendable. This assertion of the more or less objectionable only becomes doctrinaire and rotten art when the narrator mis-states from dogmatic bias, and when he suggests some quack remedy (prohibition, Christianity, social theory of one sort or another), the only cure being that humanity should display more intelligence and goodwill than humanity is capable of displaying.

Poetry = Emotional synthesis, quite as real, quite as realist as any prose (or intellectual) analysis.

Neither prose nor drama can attain poetic intensity save by construction. almost by scenario; by so arranging the circumstance that some perfectly simple speech, perception, dogmatic statement appears in abnormal vigor. Thus when Frederic in *L'Education* observes Mme. Arnoux's shoe-laces as she is descending the stair; or in Turgenev the statement, quotation of a Russian proverb about the "heart of another", or "Nothing but death is irrevocable" toward the end of *Nichée de Gentilshommes.*

with a lack of delicacy, since we are dealing with these refinements. Of course neither this stupidity of his action nor the tone of the other characters has anything to do with the question of *maestria*, if they *were* dispassionately or impartially rendered. The book is weak because all through it James is so manifestly carrying on a long *tenzone* so fiercely and loudly, a long argument *for* the old lavender. There is also the constant implication that Vanderbank ought to want Nanda, though why the devil he should be supposed to be even mildly under this obligation, is not made clear. A basis in the classics, castor oil, even Stevenson's "Virginibus Puerisque" might have helped matters. One's complaint is not that people of this sort don't exist, that they aren't like everything else a subject for literature, but that James doesn't anywhere in the book get down to bedrock. It is too much as if he were depicting stage scenery not *as* stage scenery, but as nature.

All this critique is very possibly an exaggeration. Take it at half its strength; I do not intend to defend it.

Epigrammatic manner in opening, compare Kipling; compare De Maupassant, superb ideas, verity, fantasia, fantasia group, reality, charming stories, poppycock. "Yellow Book" touches in "The Real Thing," general statements about their souls, near to bad writing, perfectly lucid.

"Nona Vincent," he writes like an adolescent, might be a person of eighteen doing first story.

Page 201. "Public interest in spiritual life of the army." ("The Real Thing.")

Page 201. German Invasion.

Loathsome prigs, stiff conventions, editor of cheap magazines ladled in Sir Wots-his-name.

1893. In the interim he had brought out "In the

Cage," excellent opening sentence, matter too much
talked around and around, and "The Two Magics." This
last a Freudian affair which seems to me to have attracted undue interest, i.e., interest out of proportion to the
importance as literature and *as part of* Henry James's
own work, because of this subject matter. The obscen-
ity of "The Turn of the Screw" has given it undue prom-
inence. People now "drawn" to obscene as were people
of Milton's period by an equally disgusting bigotry; one
unconscious on author's part; the other, a surgical treatment of a disease. Thus much for progress on part of
authors if public has not progressed. The point of my
remarks is that an extraneous criterion comes in. One
must keep to the question of literature, not of irrelevan-
cies. Galdos' "Lo Prohibido" does Freud long before the
sex crank got to it. Kipling really does the psychic,
ghosts, etc., to say nothing of his having the "sense of
story."

1900. "The Soft Side," collection containing: "The
Abasement of the Northmores," good: again the motif
of the vacuity of the public man, the "figure"; he has
tried it again in "The Private Life," which, however, falls
into the allegorical. A rotten fall it is too, and Henry
James at his worst in it, i.e., the allegorical. "Fordham's
Castle" appears in the collected edition only—it may belong to this period but is probably earlier, comedietta,
excellently, perhaps flawlessly done. Here, as so often,
the circumstances are mostly a description of the character of the personal tone of the "sitters"; for his people
are so much more, or so much more often, "sitters" than
actors. Protagonists it may be. When they act, they
are apt to stage-act, which reduces their action again to
being a mere attempt at description. ("The Liar," for

example.) Compare Maupassant's "Toine" for treatment of case similar to "Fordham Castle."

1902-05. "The Sacred Fount," "Wings of a Dove," "Golden Bowl" period.

"Dove" and "Bowl" certainly not models for other writers, a caviare not part of the canon (metaphors be hanged for the moment).

Henry James is certainly not a model for narrative novelists, for young writers of fiction; perhaps not even a subject of study till they have attained some sublimity of the critical sense or are at least ready to be constantly alert, constantly on guard.

I cannot see that he will harm a critic or a describer of places, a recorder of impressions, whether they be people, places, music.

1903. "Better Sort," mildish.

1903. "The Ambassadors," rather clearer than the other work. Etude of Paris vs. Woollett. Exhortation to the idle, well-to-do, to leave home.

1907. "The American Scene," triumph of the author's long practice. A creation of America. A book no "serious American" will neglect. How many Americans make any attempt toward a realization of that country is of course beyond our power to compute. The desire to see the national face in a mirror may be in itself an exotic. I know of no such grave record, of no such attempt at faithful portrayal, as "The American Scene." Thus America is to the careful observer; this volume and the American scenes in the fiction and memoirs, in "The Europeans," "The Patagonia," "Washington Square," etc., bulk large in the very small amount of writing which can be counted as history of *moeurs contemporaines*, of national habit of our time and of the two or three generations preceding us. Newport, the standardized face, the Capitol, Independence Hall, the absence of penetralia, innocence, essential vagueness, etc., language "only definable as not in *intention* Yiddish," the tabernacle of Grant's ashes, the public collapse of the individual, the St. Gaudens statue. There is nothing to be gained by making excerpts; the volume is large, but one should in time drift through it. I mean any American with pretenses to an intellectual life should drift through it. It is not enough to have perused "The Constitution" and to have "heerd tell" of the national founders.

1910. "The Finer Grain," collection of short stories without a slip. "The Velvet Glove," "Mona Montravers," "A Round of Visits" (the old New York versus the new), "Crapey Cornelia," "The Bench of Desolation."

It is by beginning on this collection, or perhaps taking it after such stories as "The Pupil" and "Brooksmith," that the general literate reader will best come to James, must in brief be convinced of him and can tell whether or not the "marginal" James is for him. Whether or no the involutions of the "Golden Bowl" will titillate his arcane sensibilities. If the reader does not "get" "The Finer Grain" there is no sense in his trying the more elaborate "Wings of a Dove," "Sacred Fount," "Golden Bowl." If, on the contrary, he does feel the peculiar, unclassic attraction of the author he may or may not enjoy the uncanonical books.

1911. "The Outcry," a relapse. Connoisseurship fad again, inferior work.

1913. "A Small Boy and Others," the beginning of the memoirs. Beginning of this volume disgusting. First three pages enough to put one off Henry James once and for all, damn badly written, atrocious vocabulary. Page 33, a few lines of good writing. Reader might start about here, any reader, that is, to whom New York of that period is of interest. New York of the fifties is significant, in so far as it is typical of what a hundred smaller American cities have been since. The tone of the work shows in excerpts:

"The special shade of its identity was thus that it was not conscious—really not conscious of anything in the world; or was conscious of so few possibilities at least, and these so immediate and so a matter of course, that it came almost to the same thing. That was the testimony that the slight subjects in question strike me as having borne to their surrounding medium—the fact that their unconsciousnes could be so preserved . . ."

Or later, when dealing with a pre-Y.-M.-C.-A. America.

"Infinitely queer and quaint, almost incongruously droll, the sense somehow begotten in ourselves, as very young persons, of our being surrounded by a slightly remote, yet dimly rich, outer and quite kindred circle of the tipsy. I remember how, once, as a very small boy, after meeting in the hall a most amiable and irreproachable gentleman, all but closely consanguineous, who had come to call on my mother, I anticipated his further entrance by slipping in to report to that parent that I thought *he* must be tipsy. And I was to recall perfectly afterwards the impression I so made on her—in which the general proposition that the gentlemen of a certain group or connection might on occasion be best described by the term I had used, sought to destroy the particular presumption that our visitor wouldn't, by his ordinary measure, show himself for one of these. He didn't to all appearance, for I was afterwards disappointed at the lapse of lurid evidence: that memory

remained with me, as well as a considerable subsequent
wonder at my having leaped to so baseless a view . . ."

"The grim little generalization remained, none the less,
and I may speak of it—since I speak of everything—as
still standing: the striking evidence that scarce aught but
disaster *could,* in that so unformed and unseasoned
society, overtake young men who were in the least exposed. Not to have been immediately launched in business of a rigorous sort was to *be* exposed— in the absence, I mean, of some fairly abnormal predisposition
to virtue; since it was a world so simply constituted
that whatever wasn't business, or exactly an office or a
"store," places in which people sat close and made
money, was just simply pleasure, sought, and sought
only, in places in which people got tipsy. There was
clearly no mean, least of all the golden one, for it was
just the ready, even when the moderate, possession of
gold that determined, that hurried on disaster. There
were whole sets and groups, there were 'sympathetic,'
though too susceptible, races, that seemed scarce to
recognize or to find possible any practical application of
moneyed, that is, of transmitted ease, however limited,
but to go more or less rapidly to the bad with it—
which meant even then going as often as possible to
Paris . . ."

"The field was strictly covered, to my young eyes, I
make out, by three classes, the busy, the tipsy, and
Daniel Webster. . . ."

"It has carried me far from my rather evident proposition that if we saw the 'natural' so happily embodied
about us—and in female maturity, or comparative maturity, scarce less than in female adolescence—this was
because the artificial, or in other words the complicated,
was so little there to threaten it. . . ."

On page 72 he quotes his father on "flagrant morality."
In Chapter X we have a remarkable portrayal of a
character by almost nothing save vacuums, "timorous
philistine in a world of dangers." Our author notes the
"finer civility" but does not see that it is a thing of no
period. It is the property of a few individuals, personally transmitted. Henry James had a mania for
setting these things in an era or a "faubourg," despite
the continued testimony that the worst manners have
constantly impinged upon the most brilliant societies;
that decent detail of conduct is a personal talent.

The production of "Il Corteggiano" proves perhaps
nothing more than the degree in which Castiglione's
contemporaries "needed to be told." On page 236
("Small Boy and Others") the phrase "presence without
type." On page 286, the people "who cultivated for
years the highest instructional, social and moral possibilities of Geneva." Page 283, "discussion of a work
of art mainly hung in those days on that issue of the
producible *name*." Page 304, "For even in those days
some Americans were rich and several sophisticated."
Page 313, The real give away of W. J. Page 341,
Scarification of Ste-Beuve. Page 179, Crystal Palace.
Page 214, Social relativity.

One is impatient for Henry James to do people.

A LITTLE TOUR IN FRANCE. The disadvantage of giving impressions of real instead of imaginary places is
that they conflict with other people's impressions. I do
not see Angoulême viâ Balzac, nor do I feel Henry
James's contacts with the places where our tracks have
crossed very remarkable. I dare say it is a good enough
guide for people more meagrely furnished with associations or perceptions. Allow me my *piéton's* shrug for
the man who has gone only by train.

Henry James is not very deep in ancient associations. The American's enjoyment of England in "The Passionate Pilgrim" is more searching than anything continental. Windy generality in "Tour in France," and perhaps indication of how little Henry James's tentacles penetrated into any era before 1600, or perhaps before 1780.

Vignette bottom of page 337-8 ("Passionate Pilgrim"). "full of glimpses and responses, of deserts and desolations." "His perceptions would be fine and his opinions pathetic." Commiseration of Searle vs. detachment, in "Four Meetings."

Of the posthumous work, "The Middle Years" is perhaps the most charming. "The Ivory Tower," full of accumulated perceptions, swift illuminating phrases, perhaps part of a masterpiece. "The Sense of the Past," less important. I leave my comment of "The Middle Years" as I wrote it, but have recast the analysis of notes to "The Ivory Tower."

Flaubert is in six volumes, four or five of which every literate man must at one time or another assault. James is strewn over about forty—part of which must go into desuetude, have perhaps done so already.

I have not in these notes attempted the Paterine art of appreciation, e.g., as in taking the perhaps sole readable paragraph of Pico Mirandola and writing an empurpled descant.

The problem—discussion of which is about as "artistic" as a street map—is: can we conceive a five or six volume edition of James so selected as to hold its own internationally? My contention is for this possibility.

My notes are no more than a tentative suggestion, to wit: that some such compact edition might be, to advantage, tried on the less patient public. I have been, alas, no more fortunate than our subject in keeping out

irrelevant, non-esthetic, non-literary, non-technical vistas
and strictures.

"THE MIDDLE YEARS"

THE MIDDLE YEARS is a tale of the great adventure;
for, putting aside a few simple adventures, sentimental,
phallic, Nimrodic, the remaining great adventure is precisely the approach to the Metropolis; for the provincial
of our race the specific approach to London, and no
subject surely could more heighten the pitch of writing
than that the treated approach should be that of the
greatest writer of our time and own particular language.
We may, I think, set aside Thomas Hardy as of an
age not our own; of perhaps Walter Scott's or of L'Abbé
Prévost's, but remote from us and things familiarly
under our hand; and we skip over the next few crops of
writers as lacking in any comparative interest, interest
in a writer being primarily in his degree of sensitization; and on this count we may throw out the whole
Wells-Bennett period, for what interest can we take in
instruments which must of nature miss two-thirds of
the vibrations in any conceivable situation? In James
the maximum sensibility compatible with efficient writing was present. Indeed, in reading these pages one
can but despair over the inadequacy of one's own literary
sensitization, one's so utterly inferior state of awareness; even allowing for what the author himself allows:
his not really, perhaps, having felt at twenty-six, all that
at seventy he more or less read into the memory of his
feeling. The point is that with the exception of exceptional moments in Hueffer, we find no trace of such
degree of awareness in the next lot of writers, or until
the first novels of Lewis and Joyce, whose awareness
is, without saying, of a nature greatly different in kind.

It is not the book for any reader to tackle who has
not read a good deal of James, or who has not, in
default of that reading, been endowed with a natural
Jamesian sensibility (a case almost negligible by any
likelihood) ; neither is it a book of memoirs, I mean
one does not turn to it seeking information about Victorian worthies; any more than one did, when the old
man himself was talking, want to be told anything; there
are encyclopedias in sufficiency, and statistics, and human
mines of information, boring sufficiency; one asked and
asks only that the slow voice should continue—evaluat-
ing, or perhaps only tying up the strands of a sentence:
"And how my old friend . . . *Howells* . . ." etc

The effects of H. J.'s first breakfasts in Liverpool,
invited upstairs at Half Moon Street, are of infinitely
more value than any anecdotes of the Laureate (even
though H. J.'s inability not to see all through the Laureate is compensated by a quip melting one's personal
objection to anything Tennyson touched, by making him
merely an old gentleman whatsoever with a gleam of fun
in his make-up).

All comers to the contrary, and the proportionate sale
of his works, and statistics whatsoever to the contrary,
only an American who has come abroad will ever draw
all the succulence from Henry James's writings; the
denizen of Manchester or Wellington may know what
it feels like to reach London, the Londoner born will
not be able quite to reconstruct even this part of the
book; and if for intimacy H. J. might have stayed at
the same hotel on the same day as one's grandfather;
and if the same American names had part in one's own
inceptions in London, one's own so wholly different and
less padded inceptions; one has perhaps a purely personal, selfish, unliterary sense of intimacy: with, in my

own case, the vast unbridgeable difference of settling-in
and escape.

The essence of James is that he is always "settling-in,"
it is the ground-tone of his genius.

Apart from the state of James's sensibility on arrival
nothing else matters, the "mildness of the critical air,"
the fatuity of George Eliot's husband, the illustrational
and accomplished lady, even the faculty for a portrait
in a paragraph, not to be matched by contemporary
effects in half-metric, are indeed all subordinate to one's
curiosity as to what Henry James knew, and what he
did not know on landing. The portrait of the author on
the cover showing him bearded, and looking rather like
a cross between a bishop and a Cape Cod longshoreman,
is an incident gratuitous, interesting, but in no way con-
nected with the young man of the text.

The England of a still rather whiskered age, never
looking inward, in short, the Victorian, is exquisitely embalmed, and "mounted," as is, I think, the term for
microscopy. The book is just the right length as a
volume, but one mourns there not being twenty more,
for here is the unfinished work . . . not in "The Sense
of the Past," for there the pen was weary, as it had
been in "The Outcry," and the talent that was never most
worth its own while when gone off on connoisseurship,
was, conceivably, finished; but here in his depiction of
his earlier self the verve returned in full vigor.

THE NOTES TO "THE IVORY TOWER" *

THE great artists among men of letters have occasionally and by tradition burst into an *Ars Poetica* or an
Arte nuevo de hacer Comedias, and it should come as no

* Recast from an article in *The Future.*

surprise that Henry James has left us some sort of
treatise on novel-writing—no surprise, that is, to the
discriminating reader who is *not*, for the most part, a
writer of English novels. Various reviewers have
hinted obscurely that some such treatise is either adumbrated or concealed in the Notes for "The Ivory Tower"
and for "The Sense of the Past"; they have said, indeed, that novelists will "profit greatly," etc., but no one
has set forth the gist or the generalities which are to be
found in these notes.

Divested of its fine verbiage, of its clichés, of its pro-
vincialisms of American phrase, and of the special details relating to the particular book in his mind, the
formula for building a novel (any novel, not merely any
"psychological" novel); the things to have clearly in
mind before starting to write it are enumerated in "The
Ivory Tower" notes somewhat as follows:—

1. Choice of names for characters; names that will
"fit" their owners, and that will not "joggle" or be
cacophonic when in juxtaposition on the page.

2. Exposition of one group of characters and of the
"situation." (In "The Ivory Tower" this was to be done
in three subdivisions. "Book I" was to give the "Immediate Facts.")

3. One character at least is hitched to his "characteristic." We are to have one character's impression on
another.

4. (Book III.) Various reactions and interactions of
characters.

5. The character, i.e., the main character, is "faced
with the situation."

6. For "The Ivory Tower" and probably for any novel,
there is now need to show clearly and definitely the
"antecedents," i.e., anything that had happened before

the story started. And we find Henry James making
up his mind which characters have interacted before this
story opens, and which things are to be due to fresh
impacts of one character on another.

7. Particular consideration of the special case in hand.
The working-free from incongruities inherent in the first
vague preconceptions of the plot. Thus:

(a) The hinge of the thing is not to be the effect of
A. on B. or of B. on A.; nor of A. on C. or
of C. on B.; but is to be due to an effect all
round, of A. and B. and C. working on each
other.

(b) James's care not to repeat figures from earlier
novels. Not a categoric prohibition, but a caution not to sail too near the wind in this matter.

(c) A care not to get too many "personally remarkable" people, and not enough stupid ones into
the story.

(d) Care for the relative "weight" as well as the
varied "tone" of the characters.

(We observe, in all this, the peculiarly American passion for "art"; for having a system in things, cf.
Whistler.)

(e) Consideration how far one character "faces" the
problem of another character's "character."

(This and section "d" continue the preoccupation with
"moral values" shown in James's early criticism in
"French Poets and Novelists.")

8. Definite *"joints";* or relations of one character to
another finally fitted and settled.

This brings us again to point 5. The character, i.e.,
the main character definitely "faced" with the situation.

9. The consequences.

10. (a) Further consideration of the state of character C. before contact with B., etc.

(b) The effect of further characters on the mind, and thence on the action of A.

(c) Considerations of the effect of a fourth main character: of introducing a subsidiary character, and its effect, i.e., that of having an extra character for a particular function.

11. The great "*coup*" foreshadowed.

(In this case the mild Othello, more and more drifting consciously into the grip of the mild Iago—I use the terms "Othello" and "Iago" merely to avoid, if not "hero," at least "villain"; the sensitive temperament allowing the rapacious temperament to become effective.)

(a) The main character in perplexity as to how far he shall combat the drift of things.

(b) The opposed character's perception of this.

(These sub-sections are, of course, sub-sections for a psychological novel; one would have different but equivalent "joints" in a novel of action.)

(c) Effect of all this on third character. (In this case female, attracted to "man-of-action" quality).

(d) A.'s general perception of these things and his weighing of values, a phase solely for the psychological novel.

(e) Weighing of how much A.'s perception of the relations between B. and C. is to be dénouement, and how much, more or less, known.

12. Main character's "solution" or vision of what course he will take.

13. The fourth character's "break into" things, or into a perception of things.

(a) Actions of an auxiliary character, of what would

have been low life in old Spanish or Elizabethan drama. This character affects the main action (as sometimes a *"gracioso"* [servant, buffoon, Sancho Panza] affects the main action in a play, for example, of Lope de Vega's).

(b) Caution not to let author's interest in fascinating auxiliary character run away with his whole plan and design.

(This kind of restraint is precisely what leaves a reader "wanting more"; which gives a novel the "feel" of being full of life; convinces the reader of an abundant energy, an abundant sense of life in an author.)

14. Effects of course of the action on fourth main character and on the others. The scale being kept by the relation here not being between main character and *one* antagonist, but with a group of three people, relations "different" though their "point" is the same; *cf.* a main character vs. a Rosenkrantz and Guildenstern, or "attendant lords." James always has half an eye on play construction; the scene.

(a) The second auxiliary character brought out more definitely. (This is accidental. It might happen at any suitable point in a story wherever needed.)

(b) Act of this auxiliary person reaches through to main action.

15. We see the author determining just how bad a case he is going to make his villain.

(a) Further determination of his hero. (In this case an absolute non-producer, non-accumulator.)

(b) Care not to get an unmixed "bad" in his "villain," but to keep a right balance, a dependency, in this case, on the main character's weakness or easiness.

(c) Decision how the main "coup" or transfer shall slide through.

16. Effect upon C. Effect upon main characters' relations to D., E. and F.

At this point, in the consideration of eight of the ten "books" of his novel, we see the author most intent on his composition or architecture, most anxious to get all the sections fitted in with the greatest economy, a sort of crux of his excitement and anxiety, a fullness of his perception that the thing must be so tightly packed that no sentence can afford to be out of place.

17. Climax. The *Deus* or, in this case, *Dea, ex machina*. Devices for prolonging climax. The fourth main character having been, as it were, held back for a sort of weight or balance here, and as a "resolution" of the tangles.

Finis.

18. Author's final considerations of time scheme, i.e., fitting the action into time not too great for unity, and great enough to allow for needed complexity. Slighter consideration of place scheme; where final scenes shall be laid, etc.

Here in a few paragraphs are the bare bones of the plan described in eighty of Henry James's pages. The detailed thoroughness of this plan, the complicated consciousness displayed in it, gives us the measure of this author's superiority, as conscious artist, over the "normal" British novelist, i.e., over the sort of person who tells you that when he did his first book he "just sat down and wrote the first paragraph," and then found he "couldn't stop." This he tells you in a manner clearly implying that, from that humble beginning to the shining hour of the present, he has given the matter no further thought, and that his succeeding works were all knocked off with equal simplicity.

I give this outline with such fullness because it is a landmark in the history of the novel as written in English. It is inconceivable that Fielding or Richardson should have left, or that Thomas Hardy should leave, such testimony to a comprehension of the novel as a "form." The Notes are, on the other hand, quite distinct from the voluminous prefaces which so many French poets write before they have done anything else. James, we note, wrote no prefaces until there were twenty-four volumes of his novels and stories waiting to be collected and republished. The Notes are simply the accumulation of his craftsman's knowledge, they are, in all their length, the summary of the things he would have, as a matter of habit, in his mind before embarking on composition.

I take it rather as a sign of editorial woodenheadedness that these Notes are printed at the *end* of "The Ivory Tower"; if one have sense enough to suspect that the typical mentality of the elderly heavy reviewer has been shown, one will for oneself reverse the order; read the notes with interest and turn to the text already with the excitement of the sport or with the zest to see if, with this chance of creating the masterpiece so outlined, the distinguished author is going to make good. If on the other hand one reads the unfinished text, there is no escaping the boredom of re-reading in skeleton, with tentative and confusing names, the bare statement of what has been, in the text, more fully set before us.

The text is attestation of the rich, banked-up perception of the author. I dare say the snap and rattle of the fun, or much of it, will be only half perceptible to those who do not know both banks of the Atlantic; but enough remains to show the author at his best; despite the fact that occasionally he puts in the mouths of his characters sentences or phrases that no one but he himself could have used. I cannot attribute this to the unfinished state of the manuscript. These oversights are few, but they are the kind of slip which occurs in his earlier work. We note also that his novel is a descriptive novel, not a novel that simply depicts people speaking and moving. There is a constant dissertation going on, and in it is our major enjoyment. The Notes to "The Sense of the Past" are not so fine a specimen of method, as they are the plan not of a whole book, but only of the latter section. The editor is quite right to print them at the end of the volume.

Of the actual writing in the three posthumous books, far the most charming is to be found in "The Middle Years." Here again one is not much concerned with Mr. James's mildly ironic reminiscences of Tennyson and the Victorians, but rather with James's own temperament, and with his recording of inn-rooms, breakfasts, butlers, etc., very much as he had done in his fiction. There is no need for its being "memoirs" at all; call the protagonist Mr. Ponsonby or Mr. Hampton, obliterate the known names of celebrities and half celebrities, and the whole thing becomes a James novel, and, so far as it goes, a mate to the best of them.

Retaining the name of the author, any faithful reader of James, or at any rate the attentive student, finds a good deal of amusement in deciphering the young James, his temperament as mellowed by recollection and here recorded forty years later, and then in contrasting it with the young James as revealed or even "betrayed" in his own early criticisms, "French Poets and Novelists,"

a much cruder and more savagely puritanical and plainly
New England product with, however, certain permanent
traits of his character already in evidence, and with a
critical faculty keen enough to hit on certain weaknesses
in the authors analyzed, often with profundity, and
with often a "rightness" in his mistakes. I mean that
apparent errors are at times only an excess of zeal and
overshooting of his mark, which was to make for an
improvement, by him, of certain defects.

III

REMY DE GOURMONT

A DISTINCTION

followed by notes

THE mind of Rémy de Gourmont was less like the mind of Henry James than any contemporary mind I can think of. James' drawing of *mœurs contemporaines* was so circumstantial, so concerned with the setting, with detail, nuance, social aroma, that his transcripts were "out of date" almost before his books had gone into a second edition; out of date that is, in the sense that his interpretations of society could never serve as a guide to such supposititious utilitarian members of the next generation as might so desire to use them.

He has left his scene and his characters, unalterable as the little paper flowers permanently visible inside the lumpy glass paperweights. He was a great man of letters, a great artist in portrayal; he was concerned with mental temperatures, circumvolvulous social pressures, the clash of contending conventions, as Hogarth with the cut of contemporary coats.

On no occasion would any man of my generation have broached an intimate idea to H. J., or to Thomas Hardy, O.M., or, years since, to Swinburne, or even to Mr. Yeats with any feeling that the said idea was likely to be received, grasped, comprehended. However much one may have admired Yeats' poetry; however much one may have been admonished by Henry James' prose works, one has never thought of agreeing with either.

You could, on the other hand, have said to De Gourmont anything that came into your head; you could have sent him anything you had written with a reasonable assurance that he would have known what you were driving at. If this distinction is purely my own, and subjective, and even if it be wholly untrue, one will be very hard pressed to find any other man born in the "fifties" of whom it is even suggestible.

De Gourmont prepared our era; behind him there stretches a limitless darkness; there *was* the counter-reformation, still extant in the English printer; there *was* the restoration of the Inquisition by the Catholic Roman Church, holy and apostolic, in the year of grace 1824; there was the Mephistopheles period, morals of the opera left over from the Spanish XVIIth century plays of "capa y espada"; Don Juan for subject matter, etc.; there was the period of English Christian bigotry, Saml. Smiles, exhibition of '51 ("Centennial of '76"), machine-made building "ornament," etc., enduring in the people who did not read Saml. Butler; there was the Emerson-Tennysonian plus optimism period; there was the "æsthetic" era during which people "wrought" as the impeccable Beerbohm has noted; there was the period of funny symboliste trappings, "sin," satanism, rosy cross, heavy lilies, Jersey Lilies, etc.,

"Ch'hanno perduto il ben del intelletto"
all these periods had mislaid the light of the XVIIIth century; though in the symbolistes Gourmont had his beginning.

II.

In contradiction to, in wholly antipodal distinction from, Henry James, De Gourmont was an artist of the nude. He was an intelligence almost more than an artist; when he portrays, he is concerned with hardly more than the permanent human elements. His people are only by accident of any particular era. He is poet, more by possessing a certain quality of mind than by virtue of having written fine poems; you could scarcely contend that he was a novelist.

He was intensely aware of the differences of emotional timbre; and as a man's message is precisely his *façon de voir*, his modality of apperception, this particular awareness was his "message."

Where James is concerned with the social tone of his subjects, with their entourage, with their *superstes* of dogmatized "form," ethic, etc., De Gourmont is concerned with their modality and resonance in emotion.

Mauve, Fanette, Neobelle, La Vierge aux Platres, are all studies in different *permanent* kinds of people; they are not the results of environments or of "social causes," their circumstance is an accident and is on the whole scarcely alluded to. Gourmont differentiates his characters by the modes of their sensibility, not by sub-degrees of their state of civilization.

He recognizes the right of individuals to *feel* differently. Confucian, Epicurean, a considerer and entertainer of ideas, this complicated sensuous wisdom is almost the one ubiquitous element, the "self" which keeps his superficially heterogeneous work vaguely "unified."

The study of emotion does not follow a set chronological arc; it extends from the "Physique de l'Amour"

to "Le Latin Mystique"; from the condensation of
Fabre's knowledge of insects to
"Amas ut facias pulchram"
in the Sequaire of Goddeschalk
(in "Le Latin Mystique").

He had passed the point where people take abstract
statement of dogma for "enlightenment." An "idea" has
little value apart from the modality of the mind which
receives it. It is a railway from one state to another,
and as dull as steel rails in a desert.

The emotions are equal before the æsthetic judgment.
He does not grant the duality of body and soul, or at
least suggests that this mediæval duality is unsatisfactory; there is an interpenetration, an osmosis of body
and soul, at least for hypothesis. "My words are the unspoken words of my body."

And in all his exquisite treatment of all emotion he
will satisfy many whom August Strindberg, for egregious example, will not. From the studies of insects to
Christine evoked from the thoughts of Diomède, sex is
not a monstrosity or an exclusively German study.* And
the entire race is not bound to the habits of the *mantis*
or of other insects equally melodramatic. Sex, in so far
as it is not a purely physiological reproductive mechanism, lies in the domain of æsthetics, the junction of tactile
and magnetic senses; as some people have accurate ears
both for rhythm and for pitch, and as some are tone deaf,
some impervious to rhythmic subtlety and variety, so in
this other field of the senses some desire the trivial, some
the processional, the stately, the master-work.

As some people are good judges of music, and insen-
sible to painting and sculpture, so the fineness ot one

* "A German study;" Hobson; "A German study." Tarr.

sense entails no corresponding fineness in another, or at
least no corresponding critical perception of differences.

III.

Emotions to Henry James were more or less things
that other people had and that one didn't go into; at any
rate not in drawing rooms. The gods had not visited
James, and the Muse, whom he so frequently mentions,
appeared doubtless in corsage, the narrow waist, the
sleeves puffed at the shoulders, à la mode 1890-2.

De Gourmont is interested in hardly anything save
emotions, and the ideas that will go into them, or take
life in emotional application. (Apperceptive rather than
active.)

One reads LES CHEVAUX DE DIOMÈDE (1897) as one
would have listened to incense in the old Imperial court.
There are many spirits incapable. De Gourmont calls
it a "romance of possible adventures"; it might be called
equally an aroma, the fragrance of roses and poplars,
the savor of wisdoms, not part of the canon of literature,
a book like "Daphnis and Chloe" or like Marcel
Schwob's "Livre de Monelle"; not a solidarity like Flaubert; but an osmosis, a pervasion.

"My true life is in the unspoken words of my body."

In "UNE NUIT AU LUXEMBOURG," the characters talk
at more length, and the movement is less convincing.
"Diomède" was De Gourmont's own favorite and we
may take it as the best of his art, as the most complete
expression of his particular "façon d'apercevoir"; if,
even in it, the characters do little but talk philosophy, or
rather drift into philosophic expression out of a haze of
images, they are for all that very real. It is the climax

of his method of presenting characters differentiated by emotional timbre, a process which had begun in "His-toires Magiques" (1895) ; and in "D'un Pays Loin-tain" (published 1898, in reprint from periodicals of 1892-4).

"Songe d'une Femme" (1899) is a novel of modern life, De Gourmont's sexual intelligence, as contrasted to Strindberg's sexual stupidity well in evidence. The work is untranslatable into English, but should be used before 30 by young men who have been during their undergrad-uate days too deeply inebriated with the Vita Nuova.

"Tout ce qui se passe dans la vie, c'est de la mauvaise littérature."

"La vraie terre natale est celle où on a eu sa première émotion forte."

"La virginité n'est pas une vertu, c'est un état; c'est une sous-division des couleurs."

Livres de chevet for those whom the Strindbergian school will always leave aloof.

"Les imbéciles ont choisi le beau comme les oiseaux choisissent ce qui est gras. La bêtise leur sert de cornes."

"Coeur Virginal" (1907) is a light novel, amusing, and accurate in its psychology.

I do not think it possible to overemphasize Gourmont's sense of beauty. The mist clings to the lacquer. His spirit was the spirit of Omakitsu; his *pays natal* was near to the peach-blossom-fountain of the untranslatable poem. If the life of Diomède is overdone and done badly in modern Paris, the wisdom of the book is not thereby invalidated. It may be that Paris has need of some more Spartan corrective, but for the descendants of witch-burners Diomède is a needful communication.

IV.

As Voltaire was a needed light in the 18th century, so in our time Fabre and Frazer have been essentials in the mental furnishings of any contemporary mind qualified to write of ethics or philosophy or that mixed molasses religion. "The Golden Bough" has supplied the data which Voltaire's-incisions had shown to be lacking. It has been a positive succeeding his negative. It is not necessary perhaps to read Fabre and Frazer entire, but one must be aware of them; people unaware of them invalidate all their own writing by simple ignorance, and their work goes ultimately to the scrap heap.

"Physique de l'Amour" (1903) should be used as a text book of biology. Between this biological basis in instinct, and the "Sequaire of Goddeschalk" in "Le Latin Mystique" (1892) stretch Gourmont's studies of amour and æsthetics. If in Diomède we find an Epicurean receptivity, a certain aloofness, an observation of contacts and auditions, in contrast to the Propertian attitude:

> Ingenium nobis ipsa puella facit,

this is perhaps balanced by

> "Sans vous, je crois bien que je n'aimerais plus beaucoup et que je n'aurais plus une extrême confiance ni dans la vie ni moi-même." (In "Lettres à l'Amazone.")

But there is nothing more unsatisfactory than saying that De Gourmont "had such and such ideas" or held "such and such views," the thing is that he held ideas, in-

tuitions, perceptions in a certain personal exquisite manner. In a criticism of him, "criticism" being an over
violent word, in, let us say, an indication of him, one
wants merely to show that one has oneself made certain
dissociations; as here, between the æsthetic receptivity
of tactile and magnetic values, of the perception of
beauty in these relationships, and the conception of love,
passion, emotion as an intellectual instigation; such as
Propertius claims it; such as we find it declared in the
King of Navarre's

"De fine amor vient science et beauté";

and constantly in the troubadours.

(I cannot repeat too often that there was a profound
psychological knowledge in mediæval Provence, however Gothic its expression; that men, concentrated on
certain validities, attaining an exact and diversified terminology, have there displayed considerable penetration;
that this was carried into early Italian poetry; and faded
from it when metaphors became decorative instead of
interpretative; and that the age of Aquinas would not
have tolerated sloppy expression of psychology concurrent with the exact expression of "mysticism." There
is also great wisdom in Ovid. *Passons!*)

De Gourmont's wisdom is not wholly unlike the wisdom which those ignorant of Latin may, if the gods
favor their understanding, derive from Golding's "Metamorphoses."

V.

Barbarian ethics proceed by general taboos. Gourmont's essays collected into various volumes, "Promenades," "Epilogues," etc., are perhaps the best intro-

duction to the ideas of our time that any unfortunate,
suddenly emerging from Peru, Peoria, Oshkosh, Ice-
land, Kochin, or other out-of-the-way lost continent could
desire. A set of Landor's collected works will go further towards civilizing a man than any university education now on the market. Montaigne condensed Renaissance awareness. Even so small a collection as Lionel
Johnson's "Post Liminium" might save a man from utter
barbarity.

But if, for example, a raw graduate were contemplat-
ing a burst into intellectual company, he would be less
likely to utter unutterable *bêtisses, gaffes,* etc., after reading Gourmont than before. One cannot of course create intelligence in a numbskull.

Needless to say, Gourmont's essays are of uneven
value as the necessary subject matter is of uneven value.
Taken together, proportionately placed in his work, they
are a portrait of the civilized mind. I incline to think
them the best portrait available, the best record that is,
of the civilized mind from 1885-1915.

There are plenty of people who do not know what the
civilized mind is like, just as there were plenty of mules
in England who did not read Landor contemporaneously,
or who did not in his day read Montaigne. Civilization
is individual.

Gourmont arouses the senses of the imagination, pre-
paring the mind for receptivities. His wisdom, if not
of the senses, is at any rate viâ the senses. We base our
"science" on perceptions, but our ethics have not yet attained this palpable basis.

In 1898, "PAYS LOINTAIN" (reprinted from magazine
publication of 1892-4), De Gourmont was beginning his
method:

"Douze crimes pour l'honneur de l'infini."

He treats the special case, cases as special as any of
James', but segregated on different demarcative lines.
His style had attained the vividness of
"Sa vocation était de parâitre malheureuse, de passer
dans la vie comme une ombre gémissante, d'inspirer de
la pitié, du doute et de l'inquiétude.   Elle avait toujours
l'air de porter des fleurs vers une tombe abandonnée."
La Femme en Noir.
In "HISTOIRES MAGIQUES" (1894): "La Robe
Blanche," "Yeux d'eau," "Marguerite Rouge," "Soeur de
Sylvie," "Danaette," are all of them special cases, already
showing his perception of nevrosis, of hyperæsthesia.
His mind is still running on tonal variations in "Les
Litanies de la Rose."

"Pourtant il y a des yeux au bout des doigts."
"Femmes, conservatrices des traditions milésiennes."

"EPILOGUES" (1895-98).   Pleasant rereading, a book
to leave lying about, to look back into at odd half hours.
A book of accumulations.   Full of meat as a good
walnut.
Heterogeneous as the following paragraphs:
"Ni la croyance en un seul Dieu, ni la morale ne sont
les fondements vrais de la religion.   Une religion, même
le Christianisme, n'eut jamais sur les moeurs qu'une influence dilatoire, l'influence d'un bras levé; elle doit re-
commencer son prêche, non pas seulement avec chaque
génération humaine, mais avec chaque phase d'une vie
individuelle.   N'apportant pas des vérités évidentes en
soi, son enseignement oublié, elle ne laisse rien dans les

âmes que l'effroi du peut-être et la honte d'être asservi à une peur ou à une espérance dont les chaînes fantômales entravent non pas nos actes mais nos désirs.

. . . . . .

"L'essence d'une religion, c'est sa littérature. Or la littérature religieuse est morte." *Religions.*

"Je veux bien que l'on me protège contre des ennemis inconnus, l'escarpe ou le cambrioleur,—mais contre moi-même, vices ou passions, non." *Madame Boulton.*

"Si le cosmopolitisme littéraire gagnait encore et qu'il réussît à éteindre ce que les différences de race ont allumé de haine de sang parmi les hommes, j'y verrais un gain pour la civilisation et pour l'humanité tout entière." *Cosmopolitisme.*

"Augier! Tous les lucratifs rêves de la bourgeoise économe ; tous les soupirs des vierges confortables ; toutes les réticences des consciences soignées ; toutes les joies permises aux ventres prudents ; toutes les veuleries des bourses craintives ; tous les siphons conjugaux ; toutes les envies de la robe montante contre les épaules nues ; toutes les haines du waterproof contre la grâce et contre la beauté! Augier, crinoline, parapluie, bec-de-corbin, bonnet grec . . ." *Augier.*

"Dieu aime la mélodie grégorienne, mais avec modération. Il a soin de varier le programme quotidien des concerts célestes, dont le fond reste le plain-chant lithurgique, par des auditions de Bach, Mozart, Haendel, Haydn, 'et même Gounod.' Dieu ignore Wagner, mais il aime la variété." *Le Dieu des Belges.*

"La propriété n'est pas sacrée ; elle n'est qu'un fait acceptable comme nécessaire au developpement de la liberté individuelle . . .

. . . . . .

"L'abominable loi des cinquantes ans—contre laquelle

Proudhon lutta en vain si courageusement—commence à faire sentir sa tyrannie. La veuve de M. Dumas a fait interdire la reprise d'Antony. Motif: son bon plaisir. Des caprices d'héritiers peuvent d'un jour à l'autre nous priver pendant cinquante ans de toute une oeuvre.

.   .   .   .   .   .

"Demain les oeuvres de Renan, de Taine, de Verlaine, de Villiers peuvent appartenir à un curé fanatique ou à une dévote stupide." *La Propriété Littéraire.*

"M. Desjardins, plus modeste, inaugure la morale artistique et murale, secondé par l'excellent M. Puvis de Chavannes qui n'y comprend rien, mais s'avoue tout de même bien content de figurer sur les murs." *U. P. A. M.*

"Les auteurs, 'avertis par le Public . . .' Il y a dans ces mots toute une esthétique, non seulement dramatique, mais démocratique. Plus d'insuccès. Plus de fours. Admirable invention par laquelle, sans doute, le peuple trouvera enfin l'art qui lui convient et les auteurs qu'il mérite." *Conscience Littéraire.*

"Le citoyen est une variété de l'homme; variété dégénérée ou primitive il est à l'homme ce que le chat de goutière est au chat sauvage.

.   .   .   .   .   .

"Comme toutes les créations vraiment belles et noblement utiles, la sociologie fut l'oeuvre d'un homme de génie, M. Herbert Spencer, et le principe de sa gloire.

.   .   .   .   .   .

"La saine Sociologie traite de l'évolution à travers les âges d'un groupe de métaphores, Famille, Patrie, Etat, Société, etc. Ces mots sont de ceux que l'on dit collectifs et qui n'ont en soi aucune signification, l'histoire les a employés de tous temps, mais la Sociologie, par d'astucieuses définitions précise leur néant tout en propageant leur culte.

"Car tout mot collectif, et d'abord ceux du vocabulaire sociologique sont l'objet d'un culte. A la Famille, à la Patrie, à l'Etat, à la Société, on sacrifie des citoyens mâles et des citoyens femelles; les mâles en plus grand nombre; ce n'est que par intermède, en temps de grève ou d'émeute, pour essayer un nouveau fusil que l'on perfore des femelles; elles offrent au coup une cible moins défiante et plus plaisante; ce sont là d'inévitables petits incidents de la vie politique. Le mâle est l'hostie ordinaire.

. . . . . .

"Le caractère fondamental du citoyen est donc le dévouement, la résignation et la stupidité; il exerce principalement ces qualités selon trois fonctions physiologiques, comme animal reproducteur, comme animal électoral, comme animal contribuable.

. . . . . .

"Devenu animal électoral, le citoyen n'est pas dépourvu de subtilité. Ayant flairé, il distingue hardiment entre un opportuniste et un radical. Son ingéniosité va jusqu'à la méfiance: le mot Liberté le fait aboyer, tel un chien perdu. A l'idée qu'on va le laisser seul dans les ténèbres de sa volonté, il pleure, il appelle sa mère, la République, son père, l'Etat.

. . . . . .

"Du fond de sa grange ou de son atelier, il entretient volontiers ceux qui le protègent contre lui-même.

. . . . . .

"Et puis songe: si tu te révoltais, il n'y aurait plus de lois, et quand tu voudrais mourir, comment ferais-tu, si le registre n'était plus là pour accueillir ton nome?" *Paradoxes sur le Citoyen.*

"Si l'on est porté à souhaiter un déraillement, il faut parler, il faut écrire, il faut sourire, il faut s'abstenir—

c'est le grand point de toute vie civique. Les actuelles organisations sociales ont cette tare fondamentale que l'abstention légale et silencieuse les rend inermes et ridicules. Il faut empoisonner l'Autorité, lentement, en jouant. C'est si charmant de jouer et si utile au bon fonctionnement humain! Il faut se moquer. Il faut passer, l'ironie dans les yeux, à travers les mailles des lois anti-libérales, et quand on promène à travers nos vignes, gens de France, l'idole gouvernementale, gardez-vous d'aucun acte vilain, des gros mots, des violences— rentrez chez vous, et mettez les volets. Sans avoir rien fait que de très simple et de très innocent vous vous réveillerez plus libres le lendemain." *Les Faiseurs de Statues.*

"Charmant Tzar, tu la verras chez toi, la Révolution, stupide comme le peuple et féroce comme la bourgeoisie; tu la verras, dépassant en animalité et en rapacité sanglante tout ce qu'on t'a permis de lire dans les tomes ex-purgés qui firent ton éducation." *Le Délire Russe.*

"Or un écrivain, un poète, un philosophe, un homme des régions intellectuelles n'a qu'une patrie: sa langue." *Querelles de Belgique.*

"Il faut encore, pour en revenir aux assassins, noter que le crime, sauf en des rares cas passionnels, est le moyen et non le but." *Crîmes.*

"Le vers traditionnel est patriotique et national; le vers nouveau est anarchiste et sans patrie. Il semble que la rime riche fasse partie vraiment de la richesse nationale: on vole quelquechose à l'Etat en adoucissant la sonorité des ronrons: 'La France, Messieurs, manque de con-sonnes d'appui!' D'autre part, l'emploi de l'assonance a quelquechose de rétrograde qui froisse les vrais démo-crates.

"Il est amusant de voir des gens qui ne doivent leur état 'd'hommes modernes' qu'à la fauchaison brutale de toutes les traditions Françaises, protester aussi sottement contre des innovations non seulement logiques, mais inévitables. Ce qui donne quelque valeur à leur acrimonie, c'est qu'ils ignorent tout de cette question si complexe; de là leur liberté critique, n'ayant lu ni Gaston Paris, ni Darmesteter, ni aucun des écrivains récents qui étudièrent avec prudence tant de points obscurs de la phonétique et de la rythmique, ils tirent une autorité évidente de leur incompétence même." *Le Vers Libre et les Prochaines Elections.*

"PELERIN DU SILENCE" (1896) contains "Fleurs de Jadis" (1893), "Château Singulier" (1894), "Livres des Litanies," "Litanie de la Rose" * (1892), Théâtre Muet, "Le Fantôme" (1893).

"LIVRE DES MASQUES" (1896), not particularly important, though the preface contains a good reformulation: as, for example,

"Le crime capital pour un écrivain, c'est le conformisme, l'imitativité, la soumission aux règles et aux enseignements. L'oeuvre d'un écrivain doit être non seulement le reflet, mais le reflet grossi de sa personnalité. La seule excuse qu'un homme ait d'ècrire c'est de s'écrire luimême, de dévoiler aux autres la sort de monde qui se mire en son miroir individuel; Sa seule excuse est d'être original; il doit dire des choses non encore dites, et les dire en une forme non encore formulée. Il doit se créer sa propre esthétique—et nous devrons admettre autant d'esthétiques qu'il y a d'esprits originaux et les juger d'après ce qu'elles sont, et non d'après ce qu'elles ne sont pas.

* * * * * *

* Quoted in *L. R.*, February, 1918.

"L'esthétique est devenue elle aussi, un talent personnel." * *Préface.*

"Comme tous les écrivains qui sont parvenus à comprendre la vie, c'est-à-dire son inutilité immédiate, M. Francis Poictevin, bien que né romancier, a promptement renoncé au roman.

. . . . .

"Il est très difficile de persuader à de certains vieillards —vieux ou jeunes—qu'il n'y a pas de sujets; il n'y a en littérature qu'un sujet, celui qui écrit, et toute la littérature, c'est-à-dire toute la philosophie, peut surgir aussi bien à l'appel d'un chien écrasé qu'aux acclamations de Faust· interpellant la Nature: 'Où te saisir, ô Nature infinie? Et vous, mamelles?'" *Francis Poictevin.*

This book is of the '90s, of temporary interest, judgment in mid-career, less interesting now that the complete works of the subjects are available, or have faded from interest. This sort of criticism is a duty imposed on a man by his intelligence. The doing it a duty, a price exacted for his possession of intelligence.

In places the careless phrase, phrases careless of sense, in places the thing bien dit as in Verlaine. Here and there a sharp sentence, as

"M. Moréas ne comprendra jamais combien il est ridicule d'appeler Racine le Sophocle de la Ferté Milon."

or:

"Parti de la chanson de Saint Léger, il en est, dit-on, arrivé au XVIIème. siècle, et cela en moins de dix années; ce n'est pas si décourageant qu'on l'a cru. Et maintenant que les textes se font plus familiers, la route s'abrège; d'ici peu de haltes, M. Moréas campera sous le vieux chêne Hugo et, s'il persévère, nous le verrons at-

* Each of the senses has its own particular eunuchs.

teindre le but de son voyage, qui est sans doute de se re-
joindre lui-même." *Jean Moréas.*

This first "Livre des Masques" is of historical interest,
as a list of men interesting at their time. It is work done
in establishing good work, a necessary scaffolding, the
debt to De Gourmont, because of it, is ethical rather than
artistic. It is a worthy thing to have done. One should
not reproach flaws, even if it appears that the author
wastes time in this criticism, although this particular sort
of half energy probably wouldn't have been any use for
more creative or even more formulative writing. It is
not a carving of statues, but only holding a torch for the
public; ancillary writing. Local and temporal, introducing some men now better known and some, thank
Heaven, unknown or forgotten.

"DEUXIÈME LIVRE DES MASQUES" (1898), rather more
important, longer essays, subjects apparently chosen
more freely, leaves one perhaps more eager to read Alfred Valette's "Le Vierge" than any other book mentioned.

"Etre nul arrête dans son développement vers une
nullité équilibrée."

We find typical Gourmont in the essay on Rictus:

"Ici c'est l'idée de la résignation qui trouble le Pauvre:
comme tant d'autres, il la confond avec l'idée bouddhiste
de non-activité. Cela n'a pas d'autre importance en un
temps où l'on confond tout, et où un cerveau capable
d'associer et de dissocier logiquement les idées doit être
considéré comme une production miraculeuse de la
Nature.

.   .   .   .

"Or l'art ne joue pas; il est grave, même quand il rit,
même quand il danse. Il faut encore comprendre qu'en

art tout ce qui n'est pas nécessaire est inutile; et tout ce
qui est inutile est mauvais." *Jehan Rictus.*
He almost convinces one of Ephraim Mikhail's poetry,
by his skillful leading up to quotation of:
  "Mais le ciel gris est plein de tristesse caline
  Inéffablement douce aux coeurs chargés d'ennuis."
The essay on the Goncourt is important, and we find in
it typical dissociation.

  "Avec de la patience, on atteint quelquefois l'exactitude, et avec de la conscience, la véracité; ce sont les
qualités fondamentales de l'histoire.

      .   .   .   .   .   .

  "Quand on a gouté à ce vin on ne veut plus boire l'ordinaire vinasse des bas littérateurs. Si les Goncourt
étaient devenus populaires, si la notion du style pouvait
pénétrer dans les cerveaux moyens! On dit que le peuple d'Athêne avait cette notion.

      .   .   .   .   .   .

  "Et surtout quel memorable désintéressement! En
tout autre temps nul n'aurait songé à louer Edmond de
Goncourt pour ce dédain de l'argent et de la basse popu-
larité, car l'amour est exclusif et celui qui aime l'art
n'aime que l'art: mais après les exemples de toutes les
avidités qui nous ont été donnés depuis vingt ans par les
boursiers des lettres, par la coulisse de la littérature, il
est juste et nécessaire de glorifier, en face de ceux qui
vivent pour l'argent, ceux qui vécurent pour l'idée et
pour l'art.

      .   .   .   .   .   .

  "La place des Goncourt dans l'histoire littéraire de ce
siècle sera peut-être même aussi grande que celle de
Flaubert, et ils la devront à leur souci si nouveau, si
scandaleux, en une littérature alors encore toute rhétori-
cienne, de la 'non-imitation'; cela a revolutionné le

monde de l'écriture. Flaubert devait beaucoup à Chateaubriand: il serait difficile de nommer le maître des Goncourt. Ils conquirent pour eux, ensuite pour tous les talents, le droit à la personnalité stricte, le droit pour un écrivain de s'avouer tel quel, et rien qu'ainsi, sans s'inquiéter des modèles, des règles, de tout le pédantisme universitaire et cénaculaire, le droit de se mettre face-à-face avec la vie, avec la sensation, avec le rêve, avec l'idée, de créer sa phrase—et même, dans les limites du génie de la langue, sa syntaxe." *Les Goncourt.*

One is rather glad M. Hello is dead. Ghil is mentionable, and the introductory note on Felix Fénéon is of interest.

Small reviews are praised in the notes on Dujardins and Alfred Vallette.

"Il n'y a rien de plus utile que ces revues spéciales dont le public élu parmi les vrais fidèles admet les discussions minutieuses, les admirations franches." *On Edouard Dujardins.*

"Il arrive dans l'ordre littéraire qu'une revue fondée avec quinze louis a plus d'influence sur la marche des idées et par conséquent, sur la marche du monde (et peut-être sur la rotation des planètes) que les orgueilleux recueils de capitaux académiques et de dissertations commerciales." *On Alfred Vallette.*

"Promenades Philosophiques" (1905-8). One cannot brief such work as the Promenades. The sole result is a series of aphorisms, excellent perhaps, but without cohesion; a dozen or so will show an intelligence, but convey neither style nor personality of the author:

"Sans doute la religion n'est pas vraie, mais l'anti-religion n'est pas vraie non plus: la vérité réside dans un état parfait d'indifférence.

"Peu importe qu'on me sollicite par des écrits ou par des paroles; le mal ne commence qu'au moment où on m'y plie par la force." *Autre Point de Vue.*

"L'argent est le signe de la liberté. Maudire l'argent, c'est maudire la liberté, c'est maudire la vie qui est nulle si elle n'est libre." *L'Argent.*

"Quand on voudra définir la philosophie du XIXème siècle, on s'apercevra qu'il n'a fait que de la théologie.

.   .   .   .

"Apprendre pour apprendre est peut-être aussi grossier que manger pour manger.

.   .   .   .

"C'est singulier en littérature, quand la forme n'est pas nouvelle, le fond ne l'est pas non plus.

.   .   .   .

"Le nu de l'art contemporain est un nu d'hydrothérapie.

.   .   .   .

"L'art doit être à la mode ou créer la mode.

.   .   .   .

"Les pacifistes, de braves gens à genoux, près d'une balance et priant le ciel qu'elle s'incline, non pas selon les lois de la pesanteur, mais selon leurs voeux.

.   .   .   .

"La propriété est nécessaire, mais il ne l'est pas qu'elle reste toujours dans les mêmes mains.

.   .   .   .

"Il y a une simulation de l'intelligence comme il y a une simulation de la vertu.

.   .   .   .

"Le roman historique. Il y a aussi la peinture his-

torique, l'architecture historique, et, à la mi-carême, le
costume historique.

. . . . . .

"Etre impersonnel c'est être personnel selon un mode
particulier : Voyez Flaubert. On dirait en jargon : l'ob-
jectif est une des formes du subjectif.

. . . . . .

"La maternité, c'est beau, tant qu'on n'y fait pas attention. C'est vulgaire dès qu'on admire.

. . . . . .

"L'excuse du christianisme, ça a été son impuissance
sur la réalité. Il a corrompu l'esprit bien plus que la vie.

"Je ne garantis pas qu'aucune de ces notes ne se trouve
déjà dans un de mes écrits, ou qu'elle ne figurera pas
dans un écrit futur. On les retrouvera peut-être même
dans des écrits qui ne seront pas les miens." *Des Pas sur
le Sable.*

Those interested in the subject will take "LE PROB-
LÈME DU STYLE" (1902) entire ; the general position may
perhaps be indicated very vaguely by the following quo-
tations :

"Quant à la peur de se gâter le style, c'est bon pour un
Bemho, qui use d'une langue factice. Le style peut se
fatiguer comme l'homme même ; il vieillira de même que
l'intelligence et la sensibilité dont il est le signe ; mais pas
plus que l'individu, il ne changera de personnalité, à
moins d'un cataclysme psychologique. Le régime ali-
mentaire, le séjour à la campagne ou à Paris, les occupa-
tions sentimentales et leurs suites, les maladies ont bien
plus d'influence sur un style vrai que les mauvaises lectures. Le style est un produit physiologique, et l'un des
plus constants ; quoique dans la dépendance des diverses
fonctions vitales.

. . . . . .

"Les Etats-Unis tomberaient en langueur, sans les

voyages en Europe de leur aristocratie, sans la diversité extrême des climats, des sols et par conséquent des races en évolution dans ce vaste empire. Les échanges entre peuples sont aussi nécessaires à la révigoration de chaque peuple que le commerce social à l'exaltation de l'énergie individuelle. On n'a pas pris garde à cette necessite quand on parle avec regret de l'influence des littératures étrangères sur notre littérature.

. . . . . .

"Aujourd'hui l'influence d'Euripide pourrait encore déterminer en un esprit original d'intéressantes oeuvres; l'imitateur de Racine dépasserait à peine le comique involontaire. L'étude de Racine ne deviendra profitable que dans plusieurs siècles et seulement à condition que, complètement oublié, il semble entièrement nouveau, entièrement étranger, tel que le sont devenus pour le public d'aujourd'hui Adenès li Rois ou Jean de Meung. Euripide était nouveau au XVIIème siècle. Théocrite l'était alors que Chénier le transposait. 'Quand je fais des vers, insinuait Racine, je songe toujours à dire ce qui ne s'est point encore dit dans notre langue.' André Chénier a voulu exprimer célà aussi dans une phrase maladroite; et s'il ne l'a dit il l'a fait. Horace a bafoué les serviles imitateurs; il n'imitait pas les Grecs, il les étudiait.

. . . . . .

" 'Le style est l'homme même' est un propos de naturaliste, qui sait que le chant des oiseaux est déterminé par la forme de leur bec, l'attache de leur langue, le diamètre de leur gorge, la capacité de leurs poumons.

. . . . . .

"Le style, c'est de sentir, de voir, de penser, et rien plus.

. . . . . .

"Le style est une spécialisation de la sensibilité.

. . . . . .

INSTIGATIONS

"Une idée n'est qu'une sensation défraîchie, une image effacée.

. . . . . .

"La vie est un dépouillement. Le but de l'activité propre d'un homme est de nettoyer sa personnalité, de la laver de toutes les souillures qu'y déposa l'éducation, de la dégager de toutes les empreintes qu'y laissèrent nos admirations adolescentes.

. . . . . .

"Depuis un siècle et demi, les connaissances scientifiques ont augmenté énormément ; l'esprit scientifique a rétrogradé ; il n'y a plus de contact immédiat entre ceux qui lisent et ceux qui créent la science, et (je cite pour la seconde fois la réflexion capitale de Buffon) : 'On n'acquiert aucune connaissance transmissible qu'en voyant par soi-même' : Les ouvrages de seconde main amusent l'intelligence et ne stimulent pas son activité.

. . . . . .

"Rien ne pousse à la concision comme l'abondance des idées." *Le Problème du Style,* 1902.

Christianity lends itself to fanaticism. Barbarian ethics proceed by general taboos. The relation of two individuals in relation is so complex that no third person can pass judgment upon it. Civilization is individual. The truth is the individual. The light of the Renaissance shines in Varchi when he declines to pass judgment on Lorenzaccio.

One might make an index of, but one cannot write an essay upon, the dozen volumes of Gourmont's collected discussions. There was weariness towards the end of his life. It shows in even the leisurely charm of "Lettres à l'Amazone." There was a final flash in his drawing of M. Croquant.

The list of his chief works published by the Mercure de France, 26 Rue de Condé, Paris, is as follows:

"Sixtine."
"Le Pèlerin du Silence."
"Les Chevaux de Diomède."
"D'un Pays Lointain."
"Le Songe d'une Femme."
"Lilith, suivi de Théodat."
"Une Nuit au Luxembourg."
"Un Coeur Virginal."
"Couleurs, suivi de Choses Anciennes."
"Histoires Magiques."
"Lettres d'un Satyre."
"Le Chat de Misère.
"Simone."

CRITIQUE

"Le Latin Mystique."
"Le Livre des Masques" (Ier. et IIème).
"La Culture des Idées."
"Le Chemin de Velours."
"Le Problème du Style."
"Physique de l'Amour."
"Epilogues."
"Esthétique de la Langue Française."
"Promenades Littéraires."
"Promenades Philosophiques."
"Dialogue des Amateurs sur les Choses du Temps."
"Nouveaux Dialogues des Amateurs sur les Choses du
    Temps."
"Dante, Béatrice et la Poèsie Amoureuse."
"Pendant l'Orage."

De Gourmont's readiness to coöperate in my first plans for establishing some sort of periodical to maintain communications between New York, London and Paris, was graciously shown in the following (post-mark June 13, '15):

Dimanche.

Cher Monsieur:

J'ai lu avec plaisir votre longue lettre, qui m'expose si clairement la nécessité d'une revue unissant les efforts des Americains, des Anglais, et des Français. Pour cela, je vous servirai autant qu'il sera en mon pouvoir. Je ne crois pas que je puisse beaucoup. J'ai une mauvaise santé et je suis extrêmement fatigué; je ne pourrai vous donner que des choses très courtes, des indications d'idées plutôt que des pages accomplies, mais je ferai de mon mieux. J'espère que vous réussirez à mettre debout cette petite affaire littéraire et que vous trouverez parmi nous des concours utiles. Evidemment si nous pourions amener les Américains à mieux sentir la vraie littérature française et surtout à ne pas la confondre avec tant d'oeuvres courantes si médiocres, cela serait un résultat très heureux. Sont-ils capables d'assez de liberté d'esprit pour lire, sans être choqués, mes livres par example, elle est bien douteux et il faudrait pour cela un long travail de préparation. Mais pourquoi ne pas l'entreprendre? En tous les pays, il y a un noyau de bons esprits, d'esprits libres, il faut leur donner quelque chose qui les change de la fadeur des magazines, quelque chose qui leur donne ·confiance en eux-mêmes et leur soit un point d'appui. Comme vous le dites, il faudra pour commencer les amener à respecter l'individualisme français, le sens de la liberté que quelques uns d'entre nous possèdent à un si haut point. Ils comprennent cela en théologie. Pourquoi ne le comprendraient-ils pas en art, en poésie, en littérature, en philosophie. Il faut leur faire voir—s'ils ne le voient pas déjà—que l'individualisme français peut, quand il le faut, se plier aux plus dures disciplines.

Conquérir l'Américain n'est pas sans doute votre seul but. Le but du *Mercure* a été de permettre à ceux qui en valent la peine d'écrire franchement ce qu'il pense— seul plaisir d'un écrivain. Cela doit aussi être le vôtre.

Votre bien dévoué,

Remy de Gourmont.

"The aim of the *Mercure* has been to permit any man, who is worth it, to write down his thought frankly— this is a writer's sole pleasure. And this aim should be yours."

"Are they capable of enough mental liberty to read my books, for example, without being horrified? I think this very doubtful, and it will need long preparation. But why not try it? There are in all countries knots of intelligent people, open-minded; one must give something to relieve them from the staleness of magazines, something which will give them confidence in themselves and serve as a rallying point. As you say, one must begin by getting them to respect French individualism; the sense of liberty which some of us have in so great degree. They understand this in theology, why should they not understand it in art, poetry, literature?"

If only my great correspondent could have seen letters I received about this time from English alleged intellectuals !!!!!!! The incredible stupidity, the ingrained refusal of thought !!!!! Of which more anon, if I can bring myself to it. Or let it pass? Let us say simply that De Gourmont's words form an interesting contrast with the methods employed by the British literary episcopacy to keep one from writing what one thinks, or to punish one (financially) for having done so.

Perhaps as a warning to young writers who can not afford the loss, one would be justified in printing the following:

                    50a. Albermarle Street, London W.
22 October, '14.
Dear Mr. Pound:

Many thanks for your letter of the other day. I am afraid I must say frankly that I do not think I can open the columns of the *Q. R.*—at any rate, at present—to any one associated publicly with such a publication as *Blast*. It stamps a man too disadvantageously.

                              Yours truly,
                              G. W. Prothero.

Of course, having accepted your paper on the *Noh,* I could not refrain from publishing it. But other things would be in a different category.

I need scarcely say that *The Quarterly Review* is one of the most profitable periodicals in England, and one of one's best "connections," or sources of income. It has, of course, a tradition.

"It is not that Mr. Keats (if that be his real name, for we almost doubt that any man in his senses would put his real name to such a rhapsody)"—

write their Gifford of Keats' "Endymion." My only comment is that the *Quarterly* has done it again. Their Mr. A. Waugh is a lineal descendant of Gifford, by way of mentality. A century has not taught them manners. In the eighteen forties they were still defending the review of Keats. And more recently Waugh has lifted up his senile slobber against Mr. Eliot. It is indeed time that the functions of both English and American literature were taken over by younger and better men.

As for their laying the birch on my pocket. I compute that my support of Lewis and Brzeska has cost me at the lowest estimate about £20 per year, from one source alone since that regrettable occurrence, since I dared to discern a great sculptor and a great painter in the midst of England's artistic desolation.   ("European and Asiatic papers please copy.")

Young men, desirous of finding before all things smooth berths and elderly consolations, are cautioned to behave more circumspectly.

The generation that preceded us does not care much whether we understand French individualism, or the difference between the good and bad in French literature. Nor is it conceivable that any of them would write to a foreigner: "indications of ideas, rather than work accomplished, but I will send you my best."

De Gourmont's next communication to me was an inquiry about Gaudier-Brzeska's sculpture.

IV

IN THE VORTEX

Eliot
Joyce
Lewis
An historical essayist
The new poetry
Breviora

T. S. ELIOT

*Il n'y a de livres que ceux où un écrivain s'est raconté
lui-même en racontant les moeurs de ses contemporains—
leurs rêves, leurs vanités, leurs amours, et leurs folies.—*
Remy de Gourmont.

De Gourmont uses this sentence in writing of the incontestable superiority of "Madame Bovary," "L'Éducation Sentimentale" and "Bouvard et Pécuchet" to "Sa-
lammbo" and "La Tentation de St. Antoine." A casual
thought convinces one that it is true for all prose. Is it
true also for poetry? One may give latitude to the interpretation of *rêves;* the gross public would have the
poet write little else, but De Gourmont keeps a proportion. The vision should have its place in due setting if
we are to believe its reality.

* *Prufrock and Other Observations,* by T. S. Eliot. *The
Egoist,* London. Essay first published in *Poetry,* 1917.

The few poems which Mr. Eliot has given us maintain
this proportion, as they maintain other proportions of art.
After much contemporary work that is merely factitious,
much that is good in intention but impotently unfinished
and incomplete; much whose flaws are due to sheer ignorance which a year's study or thought might have reme-
died, it is a comfort to come upon complete art, naïve
despite its intellectual subtlety, lacking all pretense.

It is quite safe to compare Mr. Eliot's work with anything written in French, English or American since the
death of Jules Laforgue. The reader will find nothing
better, and he will be extremely fortunate if he finds
much half as good.

The necessity, or at least the advisability of comparing
English or American work with French work is not
readily granted by the usual English or American writer.
If you suggest it, the Englishman answers that he has
not thought about it—he does not see why he should
bother himself about what goes on south of the channel;
the American replies by stating that you are "no longer
American." This is the bitterest jibe in his vocabulary.
The net result is that it is extremely difficult to read one's
contemporaries. After a time one tires of "promise."

I should like the reader to note how complete is Mr.
Eliot's depiction of our contemporary condition. He has
not confined himself to genre nor to society portraiture.
His

    lonely men in shirt-sleeves leaning out of windows
are as real as his ladies who

                     come and go
  Talking of Michelangelo.

His "one night cheap hotels" are as much "there" as are
his

four wax candles in the darkened room,
Four rings of light upon the ceiling overhead,
An atmosphere of Juliet's tomb.

And, above all, there is no rhetoric, although there is
Elizabethan reading in the background.   Were I a French
critic, skilled in their elaborate art of writing books about
books, I should probably go to some length discussing
Mr. Eliot's two sorts of metaphor: his wholly unrealiz-
able, always apt, half ironic suggestion, and his precise
realizable picture.   It would be possible to point out his
method of conveying a whole situation and half a character by three words of a quoted phrase; his constant
aliveness, his mingling of very subtle observation with
the unexpectedness of a backhanded cliché.   It is, however, extremely dangerous to point out such devices.   The
method is Mr. Eliot's own, but as soon as one has reduced even a fragment of it to formula, some one else,
not Mr. Eliot, some one else wholly lacking in his apti-
tudes, will at once try to make poetry by mimicking his
external procedure.   And this indefinite "some one" will,
needless to say, make a botch of it.

For what the statement is worth, Mr. Eliot's work interests me more than that of any other poet now writing
in English.*   The most interesting poems in Victorian
English are Browning's "Men and Women," or, if that
statement is too absolute, let me contend that the form
of these poems is the most vital form of that period of
English, and that the poems written in that form are the
least like each other in content.   Antiquity gave us Ovid's
"Heroides" and Theocritus' woman using magic.   The
form of Browning's "Men and Women" is more alive

* A. D. 1917.

than the epistolary form of the "Heroides." Browning
included a certain amount of ratiocination and of purely
intellectual comment, and in just that proportion he lost
intensity. Since Browning there have been very few good
poems of this sort. Mr. Eliot has made two notable additions to the list. And he has placed his people in contemporary settings, which is much more difficult than to
render them with mediæval romantic trappings. If it
is permitted to make comparison with a different art, let
me say that he has used contemporary detail very much
as Velasquez used contemporary detail in "Las Meninas";
the cold gray-green tones of the Spanish painter have, it
seems to me, an emotional value not unlike the emotional
value of Mr. Eliot's rhythms, and of his vocabulary.

James Joyce has written the best novel of my decade,
and perhaps the best criticism of it has come from a Bel-
gian who said, "All this is as true of my country as of
Ireland." Eliot has a like ubiquity of application. Art
does not avoid universals, it strikes at them all the harder
in that it strikes through particulars. Eliot's work rests
apart from that of the many new writers who have used
the present freedoms to no advantage, who have gained
no new precisions of language, and no variety in their
cadence. His men in shirt-sleeves, and his society ladies,
are not a local manifestation; they are the stuff of our
modern world, and true of more countries than one. I
would praise the work for its fine tone, its humanity, and
its realism; for all good art is realism of one sort or another.

It is complained that Eliot is lacking in emotion. "La
Figlia che Piange" is an adequate confutation.

If the reader wishes mastery of "regular form," the
"Conversation Galante" is sufficient to show that symmet-
rical form is within Mr. Eliot's grasp. You will hardly

find such neatness save in France; such modern neatness, save in Laforgue.

De Gourmont's phrase to the contrary notwithstanding, the supreme test of a book is that we should feel some unusual intelligence working behind the words. By this test various other new books, that I have, or might have, beside me, go to pieces. The barrels of sham poetry that every decade and school and fashion produce, go to pieces. It is sometimes extremely difficult to find any other particular reason for their being so unsatisfactory. I have expressly written here not "intellect" but "intelligence." There is no intelligence without emotion. The emotion may be anterior or concurrent. There may be emotion without much intelligence, but that does not concern us.

Versification:

A conviction as to the rightness or wrongness of *vers libre* is no guarantee of a poet. I doubt if there is much use trying to classify the various kinds of *vers libre,* but there is an anarchy which may be vastly overdone; and there is a monotony of bad usage as tiresome as any typical eighteenth or nineteenth century flatness.

In a recent article Mr. Eliot contended, or seemed to contend, that good *vers libre* was little more than a skilful evasion of the better known English metres. His article was defective in that he omitted all consideration of metres depending on quantity, alliteration, etc.; in fact, he wrote as if metres were measured by accent. This may have been tactful on his part, it may have brought his article nearer to the comprehension of his readers (that is, those of the "New Statesman," people chiefly concerned with sociology of the "button" and "unit" variety). But he came nearer the fact when he wrote elsewhere: "No *vers* is *libre* for the man who wants to do a good job."

Alexandrine and other grammarians have made cubby-holes for va.ious groupings of syllables; they have put names upon them, and have given various labels to "metres" consisting of combinations of these different groups. Thus it would be hard to escape contact with some group or other; only an encyclopedist could ever be half sure he had done so. The known categories would allow a fair liberty to the most conscientious traditional-ist. The most fanatical vers-librist will escape them with difficulty. However, I do not think there is any cry-ing need for verse with absolutely no rhythmical basis.

On the other hand, I do not believe that Chopin wrote to a metronome. There is undoubtedly a sense of music that takes count of the "shape" of the rhythm in a mel-ody rather than of bar divisions, which came rather late in the history of written music and were certainly not the first or most important thing that musicians attempted to record. The creation of such shapes is part of the-matic invention. Some musicians have the faculty of in-vention, rhythmic, melodic. Likewise some poets.

Treatises full of musical notes and of long and short marks have never been convincingly useful. Find a man with thematic invention and all he can say is that he gets what the Celts call a "chune" in his head, and that the words "go into it," or when they don't "go into it" they "stick out and worry him."

You can not force a person to play a musical master-piece correctly, even by having the notes "correctly" printed on the paper before him; neither can you force a person to feel the movement of poetry, be the metre "regular" or "irregular." I have heard Mr. Yeats try-ing to read Burns, struggling in vain to fit the "Birks o'

Aberfeldy" and "Bonnie Alexander" into the mournful
keen of the "Wind among the Reeds." Even in regular
metres there are incompatible systems of music.

I have heard the best orchestral conductor in England
read poems in free verse, poems in which the rhythm was
so faint as to be almost imperceptible. He read them
with the author's cadence, with flawless correctness. A
distinguished statesman read from the same book, with
the intonations of a legal document, paying no attention to
the movement inherent in the words before him. I have
heard a celebrated Dante scholar and mediæval enthusiast read the sonnets of the "Vita Nuova" as if they were
not only prose, but the ignominious prose of a man de-
void of emotions: an utter castration.

The leader of orchestra said to me, "There is more for
a musician in a few lines with something rough or uneven, such as Byron's

> There be none of Beauty's daughters
> With a magic like thee;

than in whole pages of regular poetry."

Unless a man can put some thematic invention into
vers libre, he would perhaps do well to stick to "regular"
metres, which have certain chances of being musical from
their form, and certain other chances of being musical
through his failure in fitting the form. In *vers libre* his
musical chances are but in sensitivity and invention.

Mr. Eliot is one of the very few who have given a
personal rhythm, an identifiable quality of sound as well
as of style. And at any rate, his book is the best thing
in poetry since . . . (for the sake of peace I will leave
that date to the imagination). I have read most of the
poems many times; I last read the whole book at break-
fast time and from flimsy proof-sheets: I believe these
are "test conditions." And, "confound it, the fellow can
write."

JOYCE *

DESPITE the War, despite the paper shortage, and despite those old-established publishers whose god is their belly and whose god-father was the late F. T. Palgrave, there is a new edition of James Joyce's "A Portrait of the Artist as a Young Man." † It is extremely gratifying that this book should have "reached its fourth thousand," and the fact is significant in just so far as it marks the beginning of a new phase of English publishing, a phase comparable to that started in France some years ago by the *Mercure*.

The old houses, even those, or even *more* those, which once had a literary tradition, or at least literary pretensions, having ceased to care a damn about literature, the lovers of good writing have "struck"; have sufficiently banded themselves together to get a few good books into print, and even into circulation. The actual output is small in bulk, a few brochures of translations, Eliot's "Prufrock," Joyce's "A Portrait," and Wyndham Lewis' "Tarr," but I have it on good authority that at least one other periodical will start publishing its authors after the War, so there are new rods in pickle for the old fat-stomached contingent and for the cardboard generation.

Joyce's "A Portrait" is literature; it has become almost the prose bible of a few people, and I think I have encountered at least three hundred admirers of the book, certainly that number of people who, whether they "like" it or not, are wholly convinced of its merits.

Mr. Wells I have encountered in print, where he says that Joyce has a cloacal obsession, *but* he also says that Mr. Joyce writes literature and that his book is to be ranked with the works of Sterne and of Swift.

* *The Future*, May, 1918.
† "A Portrait of the Artist as a Young Man." Egoist, Ltd. London. Huebsch, New York.

Wells is no man to babble of obsessions, but let it stand to his honor that he came out with a fine burst of admiration for a younger and half-known writer.

From England and America there has come a finer volume of praise for this novel than for any that I can remember. There has also come impotent spitting and objurgation from the back-woods and from Mr. Dent's office boy, and, as offset, interesting comment in modern Greek, French and Italian.

Joyce's poems have been reprinted by Elkin Mathews, his short stories re-issued, and a second novel started in "The Little Review."

For all the book's being so familiar, it is pleasant to take up "A Portrait" in its new exiguous form, and one enters many speculations, perhaps more than when one read it initially. It is not that one can open to a forgotten page so much as that wherever one opens there is always a place to start; some sentence like—

"Stephen looked down coldly on the oblong skull beneath him overgrown with tangled twine-colored hair"; *or*

"Frowsy girls sat along the curbstones before their baskets"; *or*

"He drained his third cup of watery tea to the dregs and set to chewing the crusts of fried bread that were scattered near him, staring into the dark pool of the jar. The yellow dripping had been scooped out like a boghole, and the pool under it brought back to his memory the dark turf-colored water of the bath in Clongowes. The box of pawntickets at his elbow had just been rifled, and he took up idly one after another in his greasy fingers the blue and white dockets, scrawled and sanded and creased and bearing the name of the pledger as Daly or MacEvoy.

"1 Pair Buskins, &c."

I do not mean to imply that a novel is necessarily a
bad novel because one can pick it up without being in
this manner caught and dragged into reading; but I do
indicate the curiously seductive interest of the clear-cut
and definite sentences.

Neither, emphatically, is it to be supposed that Joyce's
writing is merely a depiction of the sordid. The sordid
is there in all conscience as you would find it in De Goncourt, but Joyce's power is in his scope. The reach of
his writing is from the fried breadcrusts and from the
fig-seeds in Cranley's teeth to the casual discussion of
Aquinas:

"He wrote a hymn for Maundy Thursday. It begins
with the words *Pange lingua gloriosi*. They say it is the
highest glory of the hymnal. It is an intricate and sooth-
ing hymn. I like it; but there is no hymn that can be put
beside that mournful and majestic processional song, the
Vexilla Regis of Venantius Fortunatus.

"Lynch began to sing softly and solemnly in a deep
bass voice:

'Impleta sunt quae concinit
David fideli carmine . . . .'

"They turned into Lower Mount Street. A few steps
from the corner a fat young man, wearing a silk neck-
cloth, &c."

On almost every page of Joyce you will find just such
swift alternation of subjective beauty and external shab-
biness, squalor, and sordidness. It is the bass and treble
of his method. And he has his scope beyond that of the
novelists his contemporaries, in just so far as whole
stretches of his keyboard are utterly out of their compass.

The conclusion or moral termination from all of which
is that the great writers of any period must be the re-

markable minds of that period; they must know the extremes of their time; they must not represent a *social
status;* they cannot be the "Grocer" or the "Dilettante"
with the egregious and capital letter, nor yet the professor or the professing wearer of Jaeger or professional
eater of herbs.

In the three hundred pages of "A Portrait of the
Artist as a Young Man" there is no omission; there is
nothing in life so beautiful that Joyce cannot touch it
without profanation—without, above all, the profana-
tions of sentiment and sentimentality—and there is
nothing so sordid that he cannot treat it with his metallic exactitude.

I think there are few people who can read Shaw, Wells,
Bennett, or even Conrad (who is in a category apart)
without feeling that there are values and tonalities to
which these authors are wholly insensitive. I do not
imply that there cannot be excellent art within quite distinct limitations, but the artist cannot afford to be or to
appear ignorant of such limitations; he cannot afford a
pretense of such ignorance. He must almost choose his
limitations. If he paints a snuff-box or a stage scene he
must not be ignorant of the fact, he must not think he is
painting a landscape, three feet by two feet, in oils.

I think that what tires me more than anything else in
the writers now past middle age is that they always seem
to imply that they are giving us all modern life, the whole
social panorama, all the instruments of the orchestra.
Joyce is of another donation

His earlier book, "Dubliners," contained several well-
constructed stories, several sketches rather lacking in
form. It was a definite promise of what was to come.
There is very little to be said in praise of it which would
not apply with greater force to "A Portrait." I find that

whoever reads one book inevitably sets out in search of the other.

The quality and distinction of the poems in the first half of Mr. Joyce's "Chamber Music" (new edition, published by Elkin Mathews, 4A, Cork Street, W.I, at 1s. 3d.) is due in part to their author's strict musical training. We have here the lyric in some of its best traditions, and one pardons certain trifling inversions, much against the taste of the moment, for the sake of the clean-cut ivory finish, and for the interest of the rhythms, the cross run of the beat and the word, as of a stiff wind cutting the ripple-tops of bright water.

The wording is Elizabethan, the metres at times suggesting Herrick, but in no case have I been able to find a poem which is not in some way Joyce's own, even though he would seem, and that most markedly, to shun apparent originality, as in:

> Who goes amid the green wood
>   With springtide all adorning her?
> Who goes amid the merry green wood
>   To make it merrier?
>
> Who passes in the sunlight
>   By ways that know the light footfall?
> Who passes in the sweet sunlight
>   With mien so virginal?
>
> The ways of all the woodland
>   Gleam with a soft and golden fire—
> For whom does all the sunny woodland
>   Carry so brave attire?

> O, it is for my true love
>   The woods their rich apparel wear—
> O, it is for my true love,
>   That is so young and fair.

Here, as in nearly every poem, the motif is so slight
that the poem scarcely exists until one thinks of it as set
to music; and the workmanship is so delicate that out of
twenty readers scarce one will notice its fineness. If
Henry Lawes were alive again he might make the suitable music, for the cadence is here worthy of his cunning:

> O, it is for my true love,
>   That is so young and fair.

The musician's work is very nearly done for him, and
yet how few song-setters could be trusted to finish it and
to fill in an accompaniment.

The tone of the book deepens with the poem beginning:

> O sweetheart, hear you
>   Your lover's tale;
> A man shall have sorrow
>   When friends him fail.
>
> For he shall know then
>   Friends be untrue;
> And a little ashes
>   Their words come to.

The collection comes to its end and climax in two pro-
foundly emotional poems; quite different in tonality and

in rhythm-quality from the lyrics in the first part of the book :—

> All day I hear the noise of waters
>   Making moan,
> Sad as the sea-bird is, when going
>   Forth alone,
> He hears the wind cry to the waters'
>   Monotone.
>
> The gray winds, the cold winds are blowing
>   Where I go.
> I hear the noise of many waters
>   Far below.
> All day, all night, I hear them flowing
>   To and fro.

The third and fifth lines should not be read with an end stop. I think the rush of the words will escape the notice of scarcely any one. The phantom hearing in this poem is coupled, in the next poem, to phantom vision, and to a *robustezza* of expression :

> I hear an army charging upon the land,
>   And the thunder of horses plunging, foam about their
>   knees ;
> Arrogant, in black armour, behind them stand,
>   Disdaining the reins, with fluttering whips, the chari-
>   oteers.
>
> They cry unto the night their battle-name ;
>   I moan in sleep when I hear afar their whirling laugh-
>   ter ;
> They cleave the gloom of dreams, a blinding flame,
>   Clanging, clanging upon the heart as upon an anvil.

They come shaking in triumph their long green hair;
   They come out of the sea and run shouting by the
      shore:
My heart, have you no wisdom thus to despair?
   My love, my love, my love, why have you left me
      alone?

In both these poems we have a strength and a fibrous-
ness of sound which almost prohibits the thought of their
being "set to music," or to any music but that which is in
them when spoken; but we notice a similarity of the
technique to that of the earlier poems, in so far as the
beauty of movement is produced by a very skilful, or perhaps we should say a deeply intuitive, interruption of
metric mechanical regularity. It is the irregularity which
has shown always in the best periods.

The book is an excellent antidote for those who find
Mr. Joyce's prose "disagreeable" and who at once fly to
conclusions about Mr. Joyce's "cloacal obsessions." I
have yet to find in Joyce's published works a violent or
malodorous phrase which does not justify itself not only
by its verity, but by its heightening of some opposite effect, by the poignancy which it imparts to some emotion
or to some thwarted desire for beauty. Disgust with the
sordid is but another expression of a sensitiveness to the
finer thing. There is no perception of beauty without a
corresponding disgust. If the price for such artists as
James Joyce is exceeding heavy, it is the artist himself
who pays, and if Armageddon has taught us anything it
should have taught us to abominate the half-truth, and
the tellers of the half-truth in literature.

ULYSSES

Incomplete as I write this. His profoundest work,

most significant—"Exiles" was a side-step, necessary ka-
tharsis, clearance of mind from continental contemporary thought—"Ulysses," obscure, even obscene, as life
itself is obscene in places, but an impassioned meditation
on life.

He has done what Flaubert set out to do in "Bouvard
and Pecuchet," done it better, more succinct. An epitome.

"Bloom" answers the query that people made after
"The Portrait." Joyce has created his second character; he has moved from autobiography to the creation
of the complimentary figure. Bloom on life, death, res-
urrection, immortality. Bloom and the Venus de Milo.

Bloom brings life into the book. All Bloom is vital.
Talk of the other characters, cryptic, perhaps too particular, incomprehensible save to people who know Dublin,
at least by hearsay, and who have university education
plus mediævalism. But unavoidable or almost unavoidable, given the subject and the place of the subject.

NOTE: I am tired of rewriting the arguments for the realist
novel; besides there is nothing to add. The Brothers de Goncourt
said the thing once and for all, but despite the lapse of time
their work is still insufficiently known to the American reader.
The program in the preface to "Germinie Lacerteux" states the
case and the whole case for realism; one can not improve the
statement. I therefore give it entire, ad majoram Dei gloriam.

"PRÉFACE
De la première édition

Il nous faut demander pardon au public de lui donner
ce livre, et l'avertir de ce qu'il y trouvera.

Le public aime les romans faux : ce roman est un roman vrai.

Il aime les livres qui font semblant d'aller dans le
monde : ce livre vient de la rue.

Il aime les petites oeuvres polissonnes, les mémoires de filles, les confessions d'alcôves, les saletés érotiques, le scandale qui se retrousse dans une image aux devantures des libraires, ce qu'il va lire est sévère et pur. Qu'il ne s'attende point à la photographie décolletée du plaisir : l'étude qui suit est la clinique de l'Amour.

Le public aime encore les lectures anodines et consolantes, les aventures qui finissent bien, les imaginations qui ne dérangent ni sa digestion ni sa sérénité : ce livre, avec sa triste et violente distraction, est fait pour contrarier ses habitudes et nuire à son hygiène.

Pourquoi donc l'avons-nous écrit? Est-ce simplement pour choquer le public et scandaliser ses goûts? Non.

Vivant au dix-neuvième siècle, dans un temps de suffrage universel, de démocratie, de libéralisme, nous nous sommes demandé si ce qu'on appelle "les basses classes" n'avait pas droit au roman ; si ce monde sous un monde, le peuple, devait rester sous le coup de l'interdit littéraire et des dédains d'auteurs qui ont fait jusqu'ici le silence sur l'âme et le coeur qu'il peut avoir. Nous nous sommes demandé s'il y avait encore, pour l'écrivain et pour le lecteur, en ces années d'égalité où nous sommes, des classes indignes, des malheurs trop bas, des drames trop mal embouchés, des catastrophes d'une terreur trop peu noble. Il nous est venu la curiosité de savoir si cette forme conventionnelle d'une littérature oubliée et d'une société disparue, la Tragédie, était définitivement morte ; si, dans un pas sans caste et sans aristocratie légale, les misères des petits et des pauvres parleraient à l'intérêt, à l'émotion, à la pitié aussi haut que les misères des grands et des riches ; si, en un mot, les larmes qu'on pleure en bas pourraient faire pleurer comme celles qu'on pleure en haut.

Ces pensées nous avaient fait oser l'humble roman de 'Soeur Philomène,' en 1861 ; elles nous font publier aujourd'hui 'Germinie Lacerteux.' Maintenant, que ce livre soit calomnié : peu lui importe. Aujourd'hui que le Roman s'élargit et grandit, qu'il commence à être la grande forme sérieuse, passionnée, vivante, de l'étude littéraire et de l'enquête sociale, qu'il devient, par l'analyse et par la recherche psychologique, l'Histoire morale contemporaine, aujourd'hui que le Roman s'est imposé les études et les devoirs de la science, il peut en revendiquer les libertés et les franchises. Et qu'il cherche l'Art et la Vérité; qu'il montre des misères bonnes à ne pas laisser oublier aux heureux de Paris ; qu'il fasse voir aux gens du monde ce que les dames de charité ont le courage de voir, ce que les reines d'autre-fois faisaient toucher de l'oeil à leurs enfants dans les hospices : la souffrance humaine, présente et toute vive, qui apprend la charité; que le Roman ait cette religion que le siècle passé appelait de ce large et vaste nom : *Humanité;* il lui suffit de cette conscience : son droit est là.

E. et J. de G."

WYNDHAM LEWIS

The signal omission from my critical papers is an adequate book on Wyndham Lewis; my excuses, apart from the limitations of time, must be that Mr. Lewis is alive and quite able to speak for himself, secondly, that one may print half-tone reproductions of sculpture, for however unsatisfactory they be, they pretend to be only half-tones, and could not show more than they do ; but the reproduction of drawings and painting invites all sorts of expensive process impracticable during the years of war. When the public or the "publishers" are ready for a volume of Lewis, suitably illustrated, I am ready to write in the letterpress, though Mr. Lewis would do it better than I could.

He will rank among the great instigators and great inventors of design; there is mastery in his use of various media (my own interest in his work centres largely in the "drawing" completed with inks, water-color, chalk, etc.). His name is constantly bracketed with that of Gaudier, Piccasso, Joyce, but these are fortuitous couplings. Lewis' painting is further from the public than were the carvings of Gaudier; Lewis is an older artist, maturer, fuller of greater variety and invention. His work is almost unknown to the public. His name is wholly familiar, BLAST is familiar, the "Timon" portfolio has been seen.

I had known him for seven years, known him as an artist, but I had no idea of his scope until he began making his preparations to go into the army; so careless had he been of any public or private approval. The "work" lay in piles on the floor of an attic; and from it we gathered most of the hundred or hundred and twenty drawings which now form the bases of the Quinn collection and of the Baker collection. (now in the South Kensington museum).

As very few people have seen all of these pictures very few people are in any position to contradict me. There are three of his works in this room and I can attest their wearing capacity; as I can attest the duration of my regret for the Red drawing now in the Quinn collection which hung here for some months waiting shipment; as I can attest the energy and vitality that filled this place while forty drawings of the Quinn assortment stood here waiting also; a demonstration of the difference between "cubism," *nature-morte-ism* and the vortex of Lewis: sun, energy, sombre emotion, clean-drawing, disgust, penetrating analysis from the qualities finding literary expression in "Tarr" to the stasis of the Red Duet, from the metallic gleam of the "Timon" portfolio to the velvet-suavity of the later "Timon" of the Baker collection.

The animality and the animal satire, the dynamic and metallic properties, the social satire, on the one hand, the sunlight, the utter cleanness of the Red Duet, are all points in an astounding circumference; which will, until the work is adequately reproduced, have more or less to be taken on trust by the "wider" public.

The novel "Tarr" is in print and no one need bother to read my critiques of it. It contains much that Joyce's work does not contain, but differentiations between the two authors are to the detriment of neither, one tries solely to discriminate qualities: hardness, fullness, abundance, weight, finish, all terms used sometimes with derogatory and sometimes with laudative intonation, or at any rate valued by one auditor and depreciated by another. The English prose fiction of my decade is the work of this pair of authors.

"TARR," BY WYNDHAM LEWIS *

"Tarr" is the most vigorous and volcanic English novel of our time. Lewis is the rarest of phenomena, an Englishman who has achieved the triumph of being also a European. He is the only English writer who can be compared with Dostoievsky, and he is more rapid than Dostoievsky, his mind travels with greater celerity, with more unexpectedness, but he loses none of Dostoievsky's effect of mass and of weight.

* *Little Review.*

Tarr is a man of genius surrounded by the heavy stupidities of the half-cultured latin quarter; the book delineates his explosions in this oleaginous milieu; as well as the débâcle of the unintelligent emotion-dominated Kreisler. They are the two titanic characters in contemporary English fiction. Wells's clerks, Bennett's "cards" and even Conrad's Russian villains do not "bulk up" against them.

Only in James Joyce's "Stephen Dedalus" does one find an equal intensity, and Joyce is, by comparison, cold and meticulous, where Lewis is, if uncouth, at any rate brimming with energy, the man with a leaping mind.

Despite its demonstrable faults I do not propose to attack this novel.* It is a serious work, it is definitely an attempt to express, and very largely a success in expressing, something. The "average novel," the average successful commercial proposition at 6s. per 300 to 600 pages is nothing of the sort; it is merely a third-rate mind's imitation of a perfectly well-known type-novel; of let us say Dickens, or Balzac, or Sir A. Conan-Doyle, or Hardy, or Mr. Wells, or Mrs. Ward, or some other and less laudable proto- or necro-type.

A certain commercial interest attaches to the sale of these mimicries and a certain purely technical or trade or clique interest may attach to the closeness or "skill" of the aping, or to the "application" of a formula. The "work," the opus, has a purely narcotic value, it serves to soothe the tired mind of the reader, to take said "mind" off its "business" (whether that business be lofty, "intellectual," humanitarian, sordid, acquisitive, or other). There is only one contemporary English work

* Egoist, Ltd., 23, Adelphi Terrace House, Robert Street, W. C. 2. 6s. net. Knopf, New York, $1.50. Reviewed in *The Future.*

with which "Tarr" can be compared, namely James
Joyce's utterly different "Portrait of the Artist." The
appearance of either of these novels would be a recognized literary event had it occurred in any other country
in Europe.

Joyce's novel is a triumph of actual writing. The
actual arrangement of the words is worth any author's
study. Lewis on the contrary, is, in the actual writing,
faulty. His expression is as bad as that of Meredith's
floppy sickliness. In place of Meredith's mincing we
have something active and "disagreeable." But we have
at any rate the percussions of a highly energized mind.

In both Joyce and Lewis we have the insistent utterance of men who are once for all through with the particular inanities of Shavian-Bennett, and with the particular oleosities of the Wellsian genre.

The faults of Mr. Lewis' writing can be examined in
the first twenty-five pages. Kreisler is the creation of
the book. He is roundly and objectively set before us.
Tarr is less clearly detached from his creator. The author has evidently suspected this, for he has felt the
need of disclaiming Tarr in a preface.

Tarr, like his author, is a man with an energized
mind. When Tarr talks at length; when Tarr gets
things off his chest, we suspect that the author also is
getting them off his own chest. Herein the technique is
defective. It is also defective in that it proceeds by
general descriptive statements in many cases where the
objective presentment of single and definite acts would
be more effective, more convincing.

It differs from the general descriptiveness of cheap
fiction in that these general statements are often a very
profound reach for the expression of verity. In brief,
the author is trying to get the truth and not merely play-

ing baby-battledore among phrases. When Tarr talks
little essays and makes aphorisms they are often of in-
trinsic interest, are even unforgettable. Likewise, when
the author comments upon Tarr, he has the gift of
phrase, vivid, biting, pregnant, full of suggestion.

The engaging if unpleasant character, Tarr, is placed
in an unpleasant milieu, a milieu very vividly "done."
The reader retains no doubts concerning the verity and
existence of this milieu (Paris or London is no matter,
though the scene is, nominally, in Paris). It is the
existence where:

"Art is the smell of oil paint, Henri Murger's *Vie de
Bohême*, corduroy trousers, the operatic Italian model
. . . quarter given up to Art.—Letters and other things
are round the corner.

". . . permanent tableaux of the place, disheartening
as a Tussaud's of The Flood."

Tarr's first impact is with "Hobson," whose "dastardly
face attempted to portray delicacies of common sense,
and gossamer-like back-slidings into the Inane, that
would have puzzled a bile-specialist. He would occasionally exploit his blackguardly appearance and black-
smith's muscles for a short time . . . his strong piercing laugh threw A.B.C. waitresses into confusion."

This person wonders if Tarr is a "sound bird." Tarr
is not a sound bird. His conversational attack on Hobson proceeds by a brandishing of false dilemma, but
neither Hobson nor his clan, nor indeed any of the critics
of the novel (to date) have observed that this is Tarr's
faulty weapon. Tarr's contempt for Hobson is as adequate as it is justifiable.

"Hobson, he considered, was a crowd.—You could
not say he was an individual.—He was a set. He sat
there a cultivated audience.—He had the aplomb and

absence of self-consciousness of numbers, of the herd—
of those who know they are not alone. . . .

"For distinguishing feature Hobson possessed a distinguished absence of personality. . . . Hobson was an
humble investor."

Tarr addresses him with some frankness on the subject:

"As an off-set for your prying, scurvy way of peeping
into my affairs you must offer your own guts, such as
they are. . . .

"You have joined yourself to those who hush their
voices to hear what other people are saying. . . .

"Your plumes are not meant to fly with, but merely to
slouch and skip along the surface of the earth.—You
wear the livery of a ridiculous set, you are a cunning
and sleek domestic. No thought can come out of your
head before it has slipped on its uniform. All your
instincts are drugged with a malicious languor, an arm,
a respectability, invented by a set of old women and
mean, cadaverous little boys."

Hobson opened his mouth, had a movement of the
body to speak. But he relapsed.

"You reply, 'What is all this fuss about? I have done
the best for myself.'—I am not suited for any heroic
station, like yours. I live sensibly, cultivating my vege-
table ideas, and also my roses and Victorian lilies.—I
do no harm to anybody."

"That is not quite the case. That is a little inexact.
Your proceedings possess a herdesque astuteness; in the
scale against the individual weighing less than the Yellow
Press, yet being a closer and meaner attack. Also you
are essentially *spies*, in a scurvy, safe and well-paid
service, as I told you before. You are disguised to look
like the thing it is your function to betray—What is your

position?—You have bought for eight hundred pounds at an aristocratic educational establishment a complete mental outfit, a program of manners. For four years you trained with other recruits. You are now a perfectly disciplined social unit, with a profound *esprit de corps.* The Cambridge set that you represent is an average specimen, a cross between a Quaker, a Pederast, and a Chelsea artist.—Your Oxford brothers, dating from the Wilde decade, are a stronger body. The Chelsea artists are much less flimsy. The Quakers are powerful rascals. You represent, my Hobson, the *dregs* of Anglo-Saxon civilization! There is nothing softer on earth.—Your flabby potion is a mixture of the lees of Liberalism, the poor froth blown off the decadent nineties, the wardrobe-leavings of a vulgar Bohemianism with its headquarters in Chelsea!

"You are concentrated, systematic slop.—There is nôthing in the universe to be said for you. . . .

"A breed of mild pervasive cabbages, has set up a wide and creeping rot in the West of Europe.—They make it indirectly a peril and a tribulation for live things to remain in the neighborhood. You are a systematizing and vulgarizing of the individual.—You are not an individual. . . ."

and later:

"You are libeling the Artist, by your idleness." Also, "Your pseudo-neediness is a sentimental indulgence."

All this swish and clatter of insult reminds one a little of Papa Karamazoff. Its outrageousness is more Russian than Anglo-Victorian, but Lewis is not a mere echo of Dostoievsky. He hustles his reader, jolts him, snarls at him, in contra-distinction to Dostoievsky, who merely surrounds him with an enveloping dreariness, and imparts his characters by long-drawn osmosis.

Hobson is a minor character in the book, he and Lowndes are little more than a prologue, a dusty avenue of approach to the real business of the book: Bertha, "high standard Aryan female, in good condition, superbly made; of the succulent, obedient, clear peasant type. . . ."

Kreisler, the main character in the book, a "powerful" study in sheer obsessed emotionality, the chief foil to Tarr who has, over and above his sombre emotional spawn-bed, a smouldering sort of intelligence, combustible into brilliant talk, and brilliant invective.

Anastasya, a sort of super-Bertha, designated by the author as "swagger sex."

These four figures move, lit by the flare of restaurants and cafés, against the frowsy background of "Bourgeois Bohemia," more or less Bloomsbury. There are probably such Bloomsburys in Paris and in every large city.

This sort of catalogue is not well designed to interest the general reader. What matters is the handling, the vigor, even the violence, of the handling.

The book's interest is not due to the "style" in so far as "style" is generally taken to mean "smoothness of finish," orderly arrangement of sentences, coherence to the Flaubertian method.

It *is* due to the fact that we have here a highly-energized mind performing a huge act of scavenging; cleaning up a great lot of rubbish, cultural, Bohemian, romantico-Tennysonish, arty, societish, gutterish.

It is not an attack on the *épicier*. It is an attack on a sort of super-*épicier* desiccation. It is by no means a tract. If Hobson is so drawn as to disgust one with the "stuffed-shirt," Kreisler is equally a sign-post pointing to the advisability of some sort of intellectual or at least commonsense management of the emotions.

Tarr, and even Kreisler, is very nearly justified by the depiction of the Bourgeois Bohemian fustiness: Fräulein Lippmann, Fräulein Fogs, etc.

What we are blessedly free from is the red-plush Wellsian illusionism, and the click of Mr. Bennett's cash-register finish. The book does not skim over the surface. If it does not satisfy the mannequin demand for "beauty" it at least refuses to accept margarine substitutes. It will not be praised by Katherine Tynan, nor by Mr. Chesterton and Mrs. Meynell. It will not receive the sanction of Dr. Sir Robertson Nicoll, nor of his despicable paper "The Bookman."

(There will be perhaps some hope for the British reading public, when said paper is no longer to be found in the Public Libraries of the Island, and when Clement Shorter shall cease from animadverting.) "Tarr" does not appeal to these people nor to the audience which they have swaddled. Neither, of course, did Samuel Butler to their equivalents in past decades.

"Bertha and Tarr took a flat in the Boulevard Port Royal, not far from the Jardin des Plantes. They gave a party to which Fräulein Lippmann and a good many other people came. He maintained the rule of four to seven, roughly, for Bertha, with the uttermost punctiliousness. Anastasya and Bertha did not meet.

"Bertha's child came, and absorbed her energies for upwards of a year. It bore some resemblance to Tarr. Tarr's afternoon visits became less frequent. He lived now publicly with his illicit and splendid bride.

"Two years after the birth of the child, Bertha divorced Tarr. She then married an eye-doctor, and lived with a brooding severity in his company, and that of her only child.

"Tarr and Anastasya did not marry. They had no children. Tarr, however, had three children by a Lady of the name of Rose Fawcett, who consoled him eventually for the splendors of his 'perfect woman.' But yet beyond the dim though sordid figure of Rose Fawcett, another rises. This one represents the swing-back of the pendulum once more to the swagger side. The cheerless and stodgy absurdity of Rose Fawcett required the painted, fine and inquiring face of Prism Dirkes."

Neither this well-written conclusion, nor the opening tirade I have quoted, give the full impression of the book's vital quality, but they may perhaps draw the explorative reader.

"Tarr" finds sex a monstrosity, he finds it "a German study": "Sex, Hobson, is a German study. A German study."

At that we may leave it. "Tarr" "had no social machinery, but the cumbrous one of the intellect. . . . When he tried to be amiable he usually only succeeded in being ominous."

"Tarr" really gets at something in his last long discussion with Anastasya, when he says that art "has no inside." This is a condition of art. *"to have no* inside, nothing you cannot see. It is not something impelled like a machine by a little egoistic inside."

"Deadness, in the limited sense in which we use that word, is the first condition of art. The second is absence of *soul*, in the sentimental human sense. The lines and masses of a statue are its soul."

Joyce says something of the sort very differently, he is full of technical scholastic terms: *"stasis, kinesis,"* etc.

Any careful statement of this sort is bound to be *baffoué*,
and fumbled over, but this ability to come to a hard
definition of anything is one of Lewis' qualities lying at
the base of his ability to irritate the mediocre intelligence. The book was written before 1914, but the depiction of the German was not a piece of war propaganda.

AN HISTORICAL ESSAYIST

LYTTON STRACHEY ON LEFT-OVER CELEBRITY

Mr. STRACHEY, acting as funeral director for a group
of bloated reputations, is a welcome addition to the
small group of men who continue what Samuel Butler
began. The howls going up in the Times Lit. Sup. from
the descendants of the ossements are but one curl more
of incense to the new author.

His book is a series of epitomes, even the illustrations,
from the peculiar expression of Mr. Gladstone's rascally
face to the differently, but equally, peculiar expression
of Newman's and the petrified settled fanatic will-to-
power in Cardinal Manning's, are epitomes.

Whatever else we may be sure of, we may be sure that
no age with any intellectual under-pinnings would have
made so much fuss over these "figures." For most of
us, the odor of defunct Victoriania is so unpleasant and
the personal benefits to be derived from a study of the
period so small that we are content to leave the past
where we find it, or to groan at its leavings as they are,
week by week, tossed up in the Conservative papers.
The Victorian era is like a stuffy alley-way which we
can, for the most part, avoid. We do not agitate for its

destruction, because it does not greatly concern us; at least, we have no feeling of responsibility, we are glad to have moved on toward the open, or at least toward the patescent, or to have found solace in the classics or in eighteenth century liberations.

Mr. Strachey, with perhaps the onus of feeling that the "Spectator" was somewhere in his immediate family, has been driven into patient exposition. The heavy gas of the past decades cannot be dispersed by mere "BLASTS" and explosions. Mr. Strachey has undertaken a chemical dispersal of residues.

At the age of nine Manning devoured the Apocalypse. He read Paley at Harrow, and he never got over it. Impeded in a political career, he was told that the Kingdom of Heaven was open to him. "Heavenly ambitions" were suggested. The "Oxford Movement" was, in a minor way, almost as bad as the Italian Counter-Reformation. Zeal was prized more than experience. Manning was the child of his age, the *enfant prodigue* of it, who could take advantage of all its blessings. A fury of "religion" appears to have blazed through the period. This fury must be carefully distinguished from theology, which latter is an elaborate intellectual exercise, and can in its finest developments be used for sharpening the wits, developing the rational faculties (*vide* Aquinas). Theology, straying from the enclosures of religion, enters the purlieus of philosophy, and in some cases exacts stiff definitions.

Froude, Newman and Keble were part of an unfortunate retrogression, or, as Mr. Strachey has written, "Christianity had become entangled in a series of unfortunate circumstances from which it was the plain duty of Newman and his friends to rescue it." Keble desired an England "more superstitious, more bigoted, more gloomy, more fierce in its religion." *Tracts for the Times* were published. Pusey imagined that people practised fasting. It was a curious period. One should take it at length from Mr. Strachey.

The contemporary mind may well fail to note a difference between these retrogradists and the earlier nuisance John Calvin, who conceived the floors of hell paved with unbaptized infants half a span long. Mr. Strachey's patient exposition will put them right in the matter.

We have forgotten how bad it was, the ideas of the Oxford movement have faded out of our class, or at least the free moving men of letters meet no one still embedded in these left-overs. Intent on some system of thought interesting to themselves and their friends, they "lose touch with the public." And the "public," as soon as it is of any size, is full of these left-overs, full of the taste of F. T. Palgrave, of Keble's and Pusey's religion.

To ascertain the under-side of popular opinion, or I had better say popular assumption, one may do worse than read books of a period just old enough to appear intolerable.

(For example, if you wish to understand the taste displayed in the official literature of the last administration you must read anthologies printed between 1785 and 1837.)

Mr. Strachey's study of Manning is particularly valuable in a time when people still persist in not understanding the Papal church as a political organization exploiting a religion; its force, doubtless, has come, through the centuries, from men like Manning, balked in political careers, suffering from a "complex" of power-lust.

Among Strachey's "Eminent" we find one common characteristic, a sort of mulish persistence in any course, however stupid. One might develop the proposition that Nietzsche in his will-to-power "philosophy" was no more than the sentimental, inefficient German of the "old type" expressing an idolization of the British Victorian character.

Still it is hard to see how any people save those

che hanno perduto il ben del intelletto

could have swallowed such shell-game propositions as those of Manning's, quoted on p. 98, concerning response to prayer.

The next essay is a very different matter. Mr. Strachey, without abandoning the acridity of his style, exposes Florence Nightingale as a great constructor of civilization. Her achievement remains, early victim of Christian voodooism, surrounded mainly by cads and imbeciles, it is a wonder her temper was not a great deal worse. She may well be pardoned a few hysterias, a few metaphysical bees in her cap. Even in metaphysics, if she was unable to improve on Confucius and Epicurus, she seems to have been quite as intelligent as many of her celebrated contemporaries who had no more solid basis for reputation than their "philosophic" writing. Our author has so branded Lord Stratford de Redcliffe and the physican Hall that no amount of apologia will reinstate them. Panmure is left as a goose, and Hawes as a goose with a touch of malevolence.

Queen Victoria appears several times in this essay, and effectively:

" 'It will be a very great satisfaction to me,' Her Majesty added, 'to make the acquaintance of one who has set so bright an example to our sex.'

"The brooch, which was designed by the Prince Consort, bore a St. George's cross in red enamel, and the Royal cypher surmounted by diamonds. The whole was encircled by the inscription, 'Blessed are the Merciful.'"

Dr. Arnold of Rugby, to be as brief as possible with a none too pleasant subject, "substituted character for intellect in the training of British youth."

The nineteenth century had a "letch" for unifications, it believed that, in general, "all is one"; when this doctrine failed of a sort of pragmatic sanction *in rem*, it tried to reduce things to the least possible number. True, in the physical world, it did not attempt to use steam and dynamite interchangeably, but, in affairs of the mind, such was the indubitable tendency.

It is, however, a folly to "substitute" character for intelligence and one would rather have been at the Grammar-School of Ashford, in Kent, in 1759, under Stephen Barrett, A.M., than at Rugby, in 1830, under Dr. Arnold, or, later, under any of his successors. And I give thanks to Zeus ὅσις ποτ' ἐσὶν, that being an American, I have escaped the British public school. Mrs. Ward is at liberty to write to the *Times* as much as she likes, I do not envy her Dr. Arnold for grandfather.

Arnold stands pre-eminent as an "educator," and from him the term has gradually taken its present meaning: "a man with no intellectual interests."

Mr. Strachey completes his volume with a study of that extraordinary crank, General Gordon. It takes him two lines to blast the reputation of Lord Elgin. He does it quietly, but Elgin's name will stink in the memory of the reader. It is difficult to attribute this wholly to the author, for the facts are in connivance with him. But if his irony at times descends to sarcasm, one must balance that with the general quietude of his style. One can but hope that this book will not be his last; one would

welcome a treatment, by him, of The Members of the
British Academic Committee, British Publishers, The
Asquith Administration.

The religion of Tien Wang mentioned on p. 221 appears to have been as intelligent as any other form of
Christianity, and to have had much the same active effects. However, Gordon was appointed to oppose it.
Throughout the rest of his life he seems to have been
obsessed by the curious mediæval fallacy that the world
is vanity and the body but ashes and dust. He fell victim to the exaggerated monotheism of his era. But he
had the sense to follow his instinct in a period when
instincts were not thought quite respectable; this made
him an historic figure; it also must have lent him great
charm (with perhaps rather picturesque drawbacks).
This valuable quality, charm, must have been singularly
lacking in Mr. Gladstone.

It is, indeed, difficult to restrain one's growing conviction that Mr. Gladstone was not all his party had
hoped for. Gordon was "difficult," at the time of his
last expedition he was perhaps little better than a lunatic,
but Gladstone was decidedly unpleasant.

In all of the eminent was the quality of a singularly
uncritical era. It was a time when a prominent man
could form himself on a single volume handed to him by
"tradition"; when illiteracy, in the profounder sense of
that term, was no drawback to a vast public career. (An
era, of course, happily closed.)

I do not know that there is much use enquiring into
the causes of the Victorian era, or any good to be got
from speculations. Its disease might seem to have been
an aggravated form of provincialism. Professor Sir
Henry Newbolt has recently pointed out that the English

public is "interested in politics rather than literature";
this may be a lingering symptom.

If one sought, not perhaps to exonerate, but to explain
the Victorian era one might find some contributory cause
in Napoleon. That is to say, the Napoleonic wars had
made Europe unpleasant, England was sensibly glad to
be insular. Geography leaked over into mentality.
Eighteenth century thought had indeed got rid of the
Bourbons, but later events had shown that eighteenth
century thought might be dangerous. England cut off
her intellectual communications with the Continent. An
era of bigotry supervened. We have so thoroughly forgotten, if we ever knew, the mental conditions preceding the Victorian era, save perhaps as they appear in
the scribblings of, let us say, Lady Blessington, that we
cannot tell whether the mentality of the Victorian reign
was an advance or an appalling retrogression. In any
case we are glad to be out of it . . . irregardless of what
we may be into; irregardless of whether the communications among intelligent people are but the mirage of a
minute Thebaid seen from a chaos wholly insuperable.*

A LIST OF BOOKS

WHEN circumstances have permitted me to lift up my
prayer to the gods, of whom there are several, and
whose multiplicity has only been forgotten during the
less felicitous periods, I have requested for contemporary use, some system of delayed book reviewing,
some system whereby the critic of current things is permitted to state that a few books read with pleasure five
or six years ago can still be with pleasure perused, and

* "Eminent Victorians," by Lytton Strachey.

that their claims to status as literature have not been obliterated by half or all of a decade.

GEORGE S. STREET

THERE was in the nineties, the late nineties and during the early years of this century, and still is, a writer named George S. Street. He has written some of the best things that have been thought concerning Lord Byron, he has written them not as a romanticist, not as a Presbyterian, but as a man of good sense. They are worthy of commendation. He has written charmingly in criticism of eighteenth century writers, and of the ghosts of an earlier Piccadilly. He has written tales of contemporary life with a suavity, wherefrom the present writer at least has learned a good deal, even if he has not yet put it into scriptorial practice. (I haste to state this indebtedness.)

The writers of *moeurs contemporaines* are so few, or rather there are so few of them who can be treated under the heading "literature," that the discovery or circulation of any such writer is no mean critical action. Mr. Street is "quite as amusing as Stockton," with the infinite difference that Mr. Street has made literature. Essays upon him are not infrequent in volumes of English essays dealing with contemporary authors. My impression is that he is not widely read in America (his publishers will doubtless put me right if this impression is erroneous) ; I can only conclude that the possession of a style, the use of a suave and pellucid English has erected some sort of barrier.

"The Trials of the Bantocks," "The Wise and the Wayward," "The Ghosts of Piccadilly," "Books of Essays," "The Autobiography of a Boy," "Quales Ego,"

"Miniatures and Moods," are among his works, and in them the rare but intelligent reader may take refuge from the imbecilities of the multitude.

FREDERIC MANNING

In 1910 Mr. Manning published, with the almost defunct and wholly uncommendable firm of John Murray, "Scenes and Portraits," the opening paragraph of which I can still, I believe, quote from memory.

"When Merodach, King of Uruk, sat down to his meals, he made his enemies his footstool, for beneath his table he kept an hundred kings with their thumbs and great toes cut off, as signs of his power and clemency. When Merodach had finished eating he shook the crumbs from his napkin, and the kings fed themselves with two fingers, and when Merodach observed how painful and difficult this operation was, he praised God for having given thumbs to man.

" 'It is by the absence of things,' he said, 'that we learn their use. Thus if we deprive a man of his eyes we deprive him of sight, and in this manner we learn that sight is the function of the eyes.'

"Thus spake Merodach, for he had a scientific mind and was curious of God's handiwork. And when he had finished speaking, his courtiers applauded him."

Adam is afterwards discovered trespassing in Merodach's garden or paradise. The characters of Bagoas, Merodach's high priest, Adam, Eve and the Princess Candace are all admirably presented. The book is divided in six parts: the incident of the Kingdom of

Uruk, a conversation at the house of Euripides, "A Friend of Paul," a conversation between St. Francis and the Pope, another between Thomas Cromwell and Macchiavelli, and a final encounter between Leo XIII and Renan in Paradise.

This book is not to be neglected by the intelligent reader (*avis rarissima*, and in what minute ratio to the population I am still unable to discern).

"Others" Anthology for 1917. This last gives, I think, the first adequate presentation of Mina Loy and Marianne Moore, who have, without exaggerated "nationalism," without waving of banners and general phrases about Columbia gem of the ocean, succeeded in, or fallen into, producing something distinctly American in quality, not merely distinguishable as American by reason of current national faults.

Their work is neither simple, sensuous nor passionate, but as we are no longer governed by the *North American Review* we need not condemn poems merely because they do not fit some stock phrase or rhetorical criticism.

(For example, an infinitely greater artist than Tennyson uses six "s's" and one "z" in a single line. It is one of the most musical lines in Provençal and opens a poem especially commended by Dante. Let us leave the realm of promoted typists who quote the stock phrases of text-books.)

In the verse of Marianne Moore I detect traces of emotion; in that of Mina Loy I detect no emotion whatever. Both of these women are, possibly in unconsciousness, among the followers of Jules Laforgue (whose work shows a great deal of emotion). Or perhaps René Ghil is the "influence" in Miss Moore's case. It is possible, as I have written, or intended to write elsewhere, to divide poetry into three sorts: (1) melopoeia, to wit, poetry which moves by its music, whether it be a music in words or an aptitude for, or suggestion of, accompanying music; (2) imagism, or poetry wherein the feelings of painting and sculpture are predominant (certain men move in phantasmagoria; the images of their gods, whole countrysides, stretches of hill land and forest, travel with them); and there is, thirdly, logopoeia, or poetry that is akin to nothing but language which is a dance of the intelligence among words and ideas and modifications of ideas and characters. Pope and the eighteenth-century writers had in this medium a certain limited range. The intelligence of Laforgue ran through the whole gamut of his time. T. S. Eliot has gone on with it. Browning wrote a condensed form of drama, full of things of the senses, scarcely ever pure logopoeia.

One wonders what the devil any one will make of this sort of thing who has not in their wit all the clues. It has none of the stupidity beloved of the "lyric" enthusiast and the writer and reader who take refuge in scenery, description of nature, because they are unable to cope with the human. These two contributors to the "Others" Anthology write logopoeia. It is, in their case, the utterance of clever people in despair, or hovering upon the brink of that precipice. It is of those who have acceded with Renan "La bêtise humaine est la seule chose qui donne une idée de l'infini." It is a mind cry, more than a heart cry. "Take the world if thou wilt but leave me an asylum for my affection," is not their lamentation, but rather "In the midst of this desolation, give me at least one intelligence to converse with."

The arid clarity, not without its own beauty, of *le tempérament de l'Americaine*, is in the poems of these, I think, graduates or post-graduates. If they have not

IN THE VORTEX 235

received B.A.'s or M.A.'s or B.Sc.'s they do not need
them.

The point of my praise, for I intend this as praise,
even if I do not burst into the phrases of Victor Hugo,
is that without any pretences and without clamors about
nationality, these girls have written a distinctly national
product, they have written something which would not
have come out of any other country, and (while I have
before now seen a deal of rubbish by both of them)
they are, as selected by Mr. Kreymborg, interesting and
readable (by me, that is. I am aware that even the
poems before me would drive numerous not wholly unintelligent readers into a fury of rage-out-of-puzzle-
ment.) Both these poetriæ have said a number of
things not to be found in the current numbers of *Every-
body's*, the *Century* or *McClure's*. "The Effectual Marriage," "French Peacock," "My Apish Cousins," have
each in its way given me pleasure. Miss Moore has
already prewritten her counterblast to my criticism in
her poem "to a Steam Roller."

The anthology displays also Mr. Williams' praise-
worthy opacity.

THE NEW POETRY

ENGLISH and French literature have stood in constant
need of each other, and it is interesting to note, as concurrent but in no way dependent upon the present alliance, a new French vitality among our younger writers
of poetry. As some of these latter are too new to
presuppose the reader's familiarity with them, I quote
a few poems before venturing to open a discussion.
T. S. Eliot is the most finished, the most composed of
these poets; let us observe his poem "The Hippopotamus," as it appears in *The Little Review*.

The Hippopotamus

The broad backed hippopotamus
Rests on his belly in the mud;
Although he seems so firm to us....
Yet he is merely flesh and blood.

Flesh-and-blood is weak and frail,
Susceptible to nervous shock;
While the True Church can never fail
For it is based upon a rock.

The hippo's feeble steps may err
In compassing material ends,
While the True Church need never stir
To gather in its dividends.

The potamus can never reach
The mango on the mango-tree,
But fruits of pomegranate and peach
Refresh the Church from over sea.

At mating time the hippo's voice
Betrays inflexions hoarse and odd,
But every week we hear rejoice
The Church, at being one with God.

The hippopotamus's day
Is past in sleep; at night he hunts;
God works in a mysterious way—
The Church can sleep and feed at once

I saw the potamus take wing
Ascending from the damp savannas,
And quiring angels round him sing
The praise of God, in loud hosannas.

Blood of the Lamb shall wash him clean
And him shall heavenly arms enfold,
Among the saints he shall be seen
Performing on a harp of gold.

He shall be washed as white as snow,
By all the martyr'd virgins kist,
While the True Church remains below
Wrapt in the old miasmal mist.

This cold sardonic statement is definitely of the school of Théophile Gautier; as definitely as Eliot's "Conversation Galante" is in the manner of Jules Laforgue. There is a great deal in the rest of Mr. Eliot's poetry which is personal, and in no wise derivative either from the French or from Webster and Tourneur; just as there is in "The Hippopotamus" a great deal which is not Théophile Gautier. I quote the two present poems simply to emphasize a certain lineage and certain French virtues and qualities, which are, to put it most mildly, a great and blessed relief after the official dullness and Wordsworthian lignification of the "Georgian" Anthologies and their descendants and derivatives as upheld by *The New Statesman*, that nadir of the planet of hebetude, that apogee of the kulturesque.

CONVERSATION GALANTE *

I observe: "Our sentimental friend the moon!
Or possibly (fantastic, I confess)

* From "Prufrock." By T. S. Eliot. Egoist, Ltd.

It may be Prester John's balloon
Or an old battered lantern hung aloft
To light poor travelers to their distress."
    She then: "How you digress!"

And I then: "Some one frames upon the keys
That exquisite nocturne, with which we explain
The night and moonshine, music which we seize
To body forth our own vacuity."
    She then: "Does this refer to me?"
    "Oh no, it is I who am inane."

"You, madam, are the eternal humorist,
The eternal enemy of the absolute,
Giving our vagrant moods the slightest twist!
With your air indifferent and imperious
At a stroke our mad poetics to confute——"
    And——: "Are we then so serious?"

Laforgue's influence or Ghil's or some kindred tendency is present in the whimsicalities of Marianne
Moore, and of Mina Loy. A verbalism less finished
than Eliot's appears in Miss Moore's verses called—

Pedantic Literalist

Prince Rupert's drop, paper muslin ghost,
    White torch "with power to say unkind
    Things with kindness and the most
        Irritating things in the midst of love and
    Tears," you invite destruction.

You are like the meditative man
    With the perfunctory heart; its

Carved cordiality ran
  To and fro at first, like an inlaid and royal
  Immutable production;

Then afterward "neglected to be
  Painful" and "deluded him with
  Loitering formality,
      Doing its duty as if it did not,"
      Presenting an obstruction

To the motive that it served.   What stood
  Erect in you has withered.   A
      Little "palmtree of turned wood"
          Informs your once spontaneous core in its
          Immutable reduction.

The reader accustomed only to glutinous imitations
of Keats, diaphanous dilutations of Shelley, woolly
Wordsworthian paraphrases, or swishful Swinburniania
will doubtless dart back appalled by Miss Moore's departures from custom; custom, that is, as the male or
female devotee of Palgravian insularity understands that
highly elastic term.   The Palgravian will then with disappointment discover that his favorite and conventional
whine is inapplicable.   Miss Moore "rhymes in places."
Her versification does not fit in with preconceived
notions of *vers libre*.   It possesses a strophic structure.
The elderly Newboltian groans.   The all-wool un-
bleached Georgian sighs ominously.   Another author has
been reading French poets, and using words for the
communication of thought.   Alas, times will not stay
anchored.

Mina Loy has been equally subject to something like
international influence; there are lines in her "Ineffectual

Marriage" perhaps better written than anything I have found in Miss Moore, as, for example:—

"So here we might dispense with her
    Gina being a female
But she was more than that
Being an incipience   a correlative
an instigation to the reaction of man
From the palpable to the transcendent
Mollescent irritant of his fantasy

    Gina had her use   Being useful
contentedly conscious
She flowered in Empyrean
From which no well-mated woman ever returns

    Sundays   a warm light in the parlor
From the gritty road   on the white wall
anybody could see it
Shimmered a composite effigy
Madonna   crinolined   a man
    hidden beneath her hoop.

Patience said Gina   is an attribute
And she learned   at any hour to offer
The dish   appropriately delectable

What had Miovanni made of his ego
In his library
What had Gina wondered   among the pots and
    pans
One never asked the other."

These lines are not written as Henry Davray said recently in the "Mercure de France," that the last "Georgian Anthology" poems are written, *i.e.,* in search for "sentiments pour les accommoder à leur vocabulaire." Miss Loy's are distinctly the opposite, they are words set down to convey a definite meaning, and words accommodated to that meaning, even if they do not copy the mannerisms of the five or six by no means impeccable nineteenth century poets whom the British Poetry Society has decided to imitate.

All this is very pleasing, or very displeasing, according to the taste of the reader; according to his freedom from, or his bondage to, custom.

Distinct and as different as possible from the orderly statements of Eliot, and from the slightly acid whimsicalities of these ladies, are the poems of Carlos Williams. If the sinuosities and mental quirks of Misses Moore and Loy are difficult to follow I do not know what is to be said for some of Mr. Williams' ramifications and abruptnesses. I do not pretend to follow all of his volts, jerks, sulks, balks, outblurts and jump-overs; but for all his roughness there remains with me the conviction that there is nothing meaningless in his book, "Al que quiere," not a line. There is whimsicality as we found it in his earlier poems. "The Tempers" (published by Elkin Mathews), in the verse to "The Coroner's Children," for example. There is distinctness and color, as was shown in his "Postlude," in "Des Imagistes"; but there is beyond these qualities the absolute conviction of a man with his feet on the soil, on a soil personally and peculiarly his own. He is rooted. He is at times almost inarticulate, but he is never dry, never without sap in abundance. His course may be well indicated by the change of the last few years; we found

him six years ago in "The Postlude," full of a thick and
opaque color, full of emotional richness, with a maximum of subjective reality:

POSTLUDE

Now that I have cooled to you
Let there be gold of tarnished masonry,
Temples soothed by the sun to ruin
That sleep utterly.
Give me hand for the dances,
Ripples at Philæ, in and out,
And lips, my Lesbian,
Wall flowers that once were flame.

Your hair is my Carthage
And my arms the bow,
And our words the arrows
To shoot the stars,
Who from that misty sea
Swarm to destroy us.

But you there beside me—
Oh! how shall I defy you,
Who wound me in the night
With breasts shining like Venus and like Mars?
The night that is shouting Jason
When the loud eaves rattle
As with waves above me,
Blue at the prow of my desire.

O prayers in the dark!
O incense to Poseidon!
Calm in Atlantis.

From this he has, as some would say, "turned" to a
sort of maximum objective reality in

THE OLD MEN

Old men who have studied
every leg show
in the city
Old men cut from touch
by the perfumed music—
polished or fleeced skulls
that stand before
the whole theatre
in silent attitudes
of attention,—
old men who have taken precedence
over young men
and even over dark-faced
husbands whose minds
are a street with arc-lights.
Solitary old men
for whom we find no excuses . . .

This is less savage than "Les Assis." His "Portrait
of a Woman in Bed" incites me to a comparison with
Rimbaud's picture of an old actress in her "loge." Not
to Rimbaud's disadvantage. I don't know that any,
save the wholly initiated into the cult of anti-exoticism,
would take Williams' poem for an exotic, but there is
no accounting for what may occur in such cases.

PORTRAIT OF A WOMAN IN BED

There's my things
drying in the corner;

that blue skirt
joined to the gray shirt—

I'm sick of trouble!
Lift the covers
if you want me
and you'll see
the rest of my clothes—
though it would be cold
lying with nothing on!

I won't work
and I've got no cash.
What are you going to do
about it?
——and no jewelry
(the crazy fools).

But I've my two eyes
and a smooth face
and here's this! look!
it's high!
There's brains and blood
in there—
my name's Robitza!
Corsets
can go to the devil—
and drawers along with them!
What do I care!

My two boys?
—they're keen!
Let the rich lady
care for them—

they'll beat the school
or
let them go to 'the gutter—
that ends trouble.

This house is empty
isn't it?
Then it's mine
because I need it.
Oh, I won't starve
while there's the Bible
to make them feed me.

Try to help me
if you want trouble
or leave me alone—
that ends trouble.

The county physician
is a damned fool
and you
can go to hell!

You could have closed the door
when you came in;
do it when you go out.
I'm tired.

This is not a little sermon on slums. It conveys
more than two dozen or two hundred magazine stories
about the comedy of slum-work. As the memoir of a
physician, it is keener than Spiess' notes of an advocate
in the Genevan law courts. It is more compact than
Vildrac's "Auberge," and has not Vildrac's tendency to

sentiment. It is a poem that could be translated into French or any other modern language and hold its own with the contemporary product of whatever country one chose.

A DISTINCTION

A journalist has said to me: "We, i.e. we journalists, are like mediums. People go to a spiritist séance and hear what they want to hear. It is the same with a leading article: we write so that the reader will find what he wants to find."

That is the root of the matter; there is good journalism and bad journalism, and journalism that "looks" like "literature" and literature etc. . . .

But the root of the difference is that in journalism the reader finds what he is looking for, whereas in literature he must find at least *a part of* what the author intended.

That is why "the first impression of a work of genius" is "nearly always disagreeable." The public loathe the violence done to their self-conceit whenever any one conveys to them an idea that is his, not their own.

This difference is lasting and profound. Even in the vaguest of poetry, or the vaguest music, where the receiver may, or must make half the beauty he is to receive, there is always something of the author or composer which must be transmitted.

In journalism or the "bad art," there is no such strain on the public.

THE CLASSICS "ESCAPE"

IT is well that the citizen should be acquainted with the laws of his country. In earlier times the laws of a nation were graven upon tablets and set up in the market place. I myself have seen a sign: "Bohemians are not permitted within the precincts of this commune"; but the laws of a great republic are too complex and arcane to permit of this simple treatment. I confess to having been a bad citizen, to just the extent of having been ignorant that at any moment my works might be classed in law's eye with the inventions of the late Dr. Condom.

It is possible that others with only a mild interest in literature may be equally ignorant; I quote therefore the law:

Section 211 of the United States Criminal Code provides:

"Every obscene, lewd, or lascivious, and every filthy book, pamphlet, picture, paper, letter, writing, print, or other publication of an indecent character and every article or thing designed, adapted, or intended for preventing conception or producing abortion, or for any indecent or immoral use; and every article, instrument, substance, drug, medicine, or thing which is advertised or described in a manner calculated to lead another to use or apply it for preventing conception or producing abortion, or for any indecent or immoral purpose; and every written or printed card, letter, circular, book, pamphlet, advertisement, or notice of any kind giving information directly or indirectly, where, or how, or from whom, or by what means any of the hereinbeforementioned matters, articles, or things may be obtained or made, or where or by whom any act or operation of any kind for the procuring or producing of abortion will be done or performed, or how or by what means conception may be prevented or abortion produced, whether sealed or unsealed; and every letter, packet, or package, or other mail matter containing any filthy, vile or indecent thing, device, or substance; any and every paper, writing, advertisement, or representation that any article, instrument, substance, drug, medicine, or thing may, or can, be used or applied for preventing conception or producing abortion or for any indecent or immoral purpose; and every description calculated to induce or incite a person to so use or apply any such article, instrument, substance, drug, medicine, or thing, is hereby declared to be non-mailable matter and shall not be conveyed in the mails or delivered from any post-office or by any letter carrier. Whoever shall knowingly deposit, or cause to be deposited for mailing or delivery, anything declared by this section to be non-mailable, or shall knowingly take, or cause the same to be taken, from the mails for the purpose of circulating or disposing thereof, or of aiding in the circulation or disposition thereof, shall be fined not more than five thousand dollars, or imprisoned not more than five years, or both."

It is well that the citizens of a country should be aware of its laws.

It is not for me to promulgate obiter dicta; to say that whatever the cloudiness of its phrasing, this law was obviously designed to prevent the circulation of immoral advertisements, propaganda for secret cures, and slips of paper that are part of the bawdy house business; that it was not designed to prevent the mailing of Dante, Villon, and Catullus. Whatever the subjective attitude of the framers of this legislation, we have fortunately a decision from a learned judge to guide us in its working.

"I have little doubt that numerous really great writings would come under the ban if tests that are frequently current were applied, and these approved publications doubtless at times escape only because they come within the term "classics," which means, for the purpose of the application of the statute, that they are ordinarily immune from interference, because they have the sanction of age and fame and USUALLY APPEAL TO A COMPARATIVELY LIMITED NUMBER OF READERS."

The capitals are my own.

The gentle reader will picture to himself the state of America IF the classics were widely read; IF these books which in the beginning lifted mankind from savagery, and which from A. D. 1400 onward have gradually redeemed us from the darkness of medievalism, should be read by the millions who now consume Mr. Hearst and the *Ladies' Home Journal! ! ! ! ! !*

Also there are to be no additions. No living man is to contribute or to attempt to contribute to the classics. Obviously even though he acquire fame before publishing, he can not have the sanction of "age."

Our literature does not fall under an inquisition; it does not bow to an index arranged by a council. It is subject to the taste of one individual.

Our hundred and twenty millions of inhabitants desire their literature sifted for them by one individual selected without any examination of his literary qualificatons.

I can not write of this thing in heat. It is a far too serious matter.

The classics "escape." They are "immune" "ordinarily." I can but close with the cadences of that blessed little Brother of Christ, San Francesco d'Assisi:

CANTICO DEL SOLE

The thought of what America would be like
If the classics had a wide circulation
        Troubles my sleep,
The thought of what America,
The thought of what America,
The thought of what America would be like
    If the classics had a wide circulation
        Troubles my sleep,
Nunc dimittis, Now lettest thou thy servant,
Now lettest thou thy servant
        Depart in peace.
The thought of what America,
The thought of what America,
The thought of what America would be like
If the classics had a wide circulation . . .
        Oh well!
        It troubles my sleep.

Oravimus

PART SECOND

V

OUR TETRARCHAL PRÉCIEUSE

(A divagation from Jules Laforgue)

THERE arose, as from a great ossified sponge, the comic-opera, Florence-Nightingale light-house, with junks beneath it clicking in vesperal meretricious monotony; behind them the great cliff obtruded solitary into the oily, poluphloisbious ocean, lifting its confection of pylons; the poplar rows, sunk yards, Luna Parks, etc., of the Tetrarchal Palace polished jasper and basalt, funereal undertakerial, lugubrious, blistering in the highlights under a pale esoteric sun-beat; encrusted, bespattered and damascened with cynocephali, sphinxes, winged bulls, bulbuls, and other sculptural by-laws. The screech-owls from the jungle could only look out upon the shadowed parts of the sea, which they did without optic inconvenience, so deep was the obscured contagion of their afforested blackness.

The two extraneous princes went up toward the stable-yard, gaped at the effulgence of peacocks, glared at the derisive gestures of the horse-cleaners, adumbrated insults, sought vainly for a footman or any one to take up their cards.

The tetrarch appeared on a terrace, removing his ceremonial gloves.

The water, sprinkled in the streets in anticipation of the day's parade, dried in little circles of dust. The tetrarch puffed at his hookah with an exaggeration of dignity; he was disturbed at the presence of princes, he was disturbed by the presence of Jao; he desired to observe his own ruin, the slow deliquescence of his position, with a fitting detachment and lassitude. Jao had distributed pamphlets, the language was incomprehensible; Jao had been stored in the cellarage, his following distributed pamphlets.

In the twentieth century of his era the house of Emeraud Archytypas was about to have its prize bit of fireworks: a war with the other world . . . after so many ages of purely esoteric culture!

Jao had declined both the poisoned coffee and the sacred sword of the Samurai, courtesies offered, in this case, to an incomprehensible foreigner. Even now, with a superlation of form, the sacred kriss had been sent to the court executioner, it was no mere every-day implement. The princes arrived at this juncture. There sounded from the back alleys the preparatory chirping of choral societies, and the wailing of pink-lemonade sellers. To-morrow the galley would be gone.

Leaning over the syrupy clematis, Emeraud crumbled brioches for the fishes, reminding himself that he had not yet collected the remains of his wits. There was no galvanization known to art, science, industry or the ministrations of sister-souls that would rouse his long since respectable carcass.

Yet at his birth a great tempest had burst above the dynastic manor; credible persons had noticed the lightnings scrolling Alpha and Omega above it; and nothing had happened. He had given up flagellation. He walked daily to the family necropolis: a cool place in the summer. He summoned the Arranger of Inanities.

II

Strapped, pomaded, gloved, laced; with patulous beards, with their hair parted at the backs of their heads; with their cork-screw curls pulled back from their foreheads to give themselves tone on their medallions; with helmets against one hip; twirling the musk-balls of their sabres with their disengaged restless fingers, the hyperborean royalties were admitted. And the great people received them, in due order: chief mandarins in clump, the librarian of the palace (Conde de las Navas), the Arbiter Elegantium, the Curator major of Symbols, the Examiner of the High Schools, the Supernumerary priest of the Snow Cult, the Administrator of Death, and the Chief Attendant Collector of Death-duties.

Their Highnesses bowed and addressed the Tetrarch: ". . . felicitous wind . . . day so excessively glorious . . .wafted . . . these isles . . . notwithstanding not also whereof . . . basilica far exceeding . . . Ind, Ormus . . . Miltonesco . . . etc. . . . to say nothing of the seven-stopped barbary organ and the Tedium laudamus . . . etc. . . ."

(Lunch was brought in.)

Kallipagous artichokes, a light collation of tunny-fish, asparagus served on pink reeds, eels pearl-gray and dovegray, gamut and series of compôtes and various wines (without alcohol).

Under impulsion of the Arranger of Inanities the pomaded princes next began their inspection of the buildings. A pneumatic lift hove them upward to the outer rooms of Salome's suite. The lift door clicked on its gilt-brass double expansion-clamps; the procession advanced between rows of wall-facing negresses whose naked shoulder-blades shone like a bronze of oily opacity.

They entered the hall of majolica, very yellow with thick blue incrustations, glazed images, with flushed and protuberant faces; in the third atrium they came upon a basin of joined ivory, a white bath-sponge, rather large, a pair of very pink slippers. The next room was littered with books bound in white vellum and pink satin; the next with mathematical instruments, hydrostats, sextants, astrolabial discs, the model of a gasolene motor, a nickel-plated donkey engine. . . . They proceeded up metal stairs to the balcony, from which a rustling and swaying and melodiously enmousselined figure, jonquil-colored and delicate, preceded or rather predescended them by dumb-waiter, a route which they were not ready to follow. The machine worked for five floors : usage private and not ceremonial.

The pomaded princes stood to attention, bowed with deference and with gallantry. The Arranger ignored the whole incident, ascended the next flight of stairs and began on the telescope:

"Grand equatorial, 22 yards inner tube length, revolvable cupola (frescoes in water-tight paint) weight 200,089 kilos, circulating on fourteen steel castors in a groove of chloride of magnesium, 2 minutes for complete revolution. The princess can turn it herself."

The princes allowed their attention to wander, they noted their ship beneath in the harbor, and calculated the drop, they then compared themselves with the brocaded and depilated denizens of the escort, after which they felt safer. They were led passively into the Small Hall of Perfumes, presented with protochlorine of mercury, bismuth regenerators, cantharides, lustral waters guaranteed free from hydrated lead. Were conducted thence to the hanging garden, where the form hermetically enmousselined, the jonquil-colored gauze with the pea-sized dark spots on it, disappeared from the opposite slope. Molossian hounds yapping and romping about her.

The trees lifted their skinned-salmon trunks, the heavy blackness was broken with a steely, metallic sunshine. A sea wind purred through the elongated forest like an express-train in a tunnel. Polychrome statues obtruded themselves from odd corners. An elephant swayed absentmindedly, the zoo was loose all over the place. The keeper of the aquarium moralized for an hour upon the calm life of his fishes. From beneath the dark tanks the hareem sent up a decomposed odor, and a melancholy slave chantey saturated the corridors, a low droning osmosis. They advanced to the cemetery, wanting all the time to see Jao.

This exhibit came at last in its turn. They were let down in a sling-rope through a musty nitrated grill, observing in this descent the ill-starred European in his bath-robe, his nose in a great fatras of papers overscrawled with illegible pot-hooks.

He rose at their hefty salutation; readjusted his spectacles, blinked; and then it came over him: These damn pustulent princes! Here! and at last! Memory overwhelmed him. How many, on how many rotten December and November evenings had he stopped, had he not stopped in the drizzle, in the front line of workmen, his nose crushed against a policeman, and craning his scraggy neck to see *them* getting out of their state barouche, going up the interminable front stairway to the big-windowed rococo palace; he muttering that the "Times" were at hand.

And now the revolution was accomplished. The proletariat had deputed them. They were here to howk him out of quod; a magnificent action, a grace of royal

humility, performed at the will of the people, the new era
had come into being. He saluted them automatically,
searching for some phrase European, historic, fraternal,
of course, but still noble.

The Royal Nephew, an oldish military man with a
bald-spot, ubiquitarian humorist, joking with every one
in season and out (like Napoleon), hating all doctri-
naires (like Napoleon), was however the first to break
silence: "Huk, heh, old sour bean, bastard of Jean
Jacques Rousseau, is *this* where you've come to be
hanged? Eh? I'm damned if it ain't a good thing."

The unfortunate publicist stiffened.

"Idealogue!" said the Nephew.

The general strike had been unsuccessful. Jao bent
with emotion. Tears showed in his watery eyes, slid
down his worn cheek, trickled into his scraggy beard.
There was then a sudden change in his attitude. He
began to murmur caresses in the gentlest of European
diminutives.

They started. There was a tinkle of keys, and through
a small opposite doorway they discerned the last flash
of the mousseline, the pale, jonquil-colored, blackspotted.

The Nephew readjusted his collar. A subdued cortège
reascended.

III

The ivory orchestra lost itself in gay fatalistic impro-
visation; the opulence of two hundred over-fed tetrarchal
Dining-Companions swished in the Evening salon, and
overflowed coruscated couches. They slithered through
their genuflections to the throne. The princes puffed out
their elbows, simultaneously attempting to disentangle
their Collars-of-the-Fleece in the idea that these would

be a suitable present for their entertainer. Neither succeeded; suddenly in the midst of the so elaborate setting they perceived the æsthetic nullity of the ornament, its connotations were too complex to go into.

The tetrarchal children (superb productions, in the strictly esoteric sense) were led in over the jonquil-colored reed-matting. A water-jet shot up from the centre of the great table, and fell plashing above on the red and white rubber awning. A worn entertainment beset the diminutive music-hall stage: acrobats, flower-dancers, contortionists, comic wrestlers, to save the guests conversation. A trick skater was brought in on real ice, did the split, engraved a gothic cathedral. The Virgin Serpent as she was called, entered singing "Biblis, Biblis"; she was followed by a symbolic Mask of the Graces; which gave place to trapeze virtuosi.

An horizontal geyser of petals was shot over the auditorium. The hookahs were brought in. Jao presumably heard all this over his head. The diners' talk became general, the princes supporting the army, authority, religion a bulwark of the state, international arbitration, the perfectibility of the race; the mandarins of the palace held for the neutralization of contacts, initiated cenacles, frugality and segregation.

The music alone carried on the esoteric undertone, silence spread with great feathers, poised hawk-wise. Salome appeared on the high landing, descended the twisted stair, still stiff in her sheath of mousseline; a small ebony lyre dangled by a gilt cord from her wrist; she nodded to her parent; paused before the Alcazar curtain, balancing, swaying on her anæmic pigeon-toed little feet—until every one had had a good look at her. She looked at no one in particular; her hair dusty with exiguous pollens curled down over her narrow shoulders, ruffled over her forehead, with stems of yellow flowers twisted into it. From the dorsal joist of her bodice, from a sort of pearl matrix socket there rose a peacock tail, moire, azure, glittering with shot emerald: an halo for her marble-white face.

Superior, graciously careless, conscious of her unique-ness, of her autochthonous entity, her head cocked to the left, her eyes fermented with the interplay of contradic-tory expiations, her lips a pale circonflex, her teeth with still paler gums showing their super-crucified half-smile. An exquisite recluse, formed in the island æsthetic, there alone comprehended. Hermetically enmousselined, the black spots in the fabric appeared so many punctures in the soft brightness of her sheath. Her arms of angelic nudity, the two breasts like two minute almonds, the scarf twined just above the adorable umbilical groove (nature desires that nude woman should be adorned with a girdle) composed in a cup-shaped embrace of the hips. Behind her the peacock halo, her pale pigeon-toed feet covered only by the watered-yellow fringe and by the bright-yellow anklet. She balanced, a little budding messiah; her head over-weighted; not knowing what to do with her hands; her petticoat so simple, art long, very long, and life so very inextensive; so obviously ready for the cosy-corner, for little talks in conservatories . . .

And she was going to speak . . .

The Tetrarch bulged in his cushions, as if she had already said something. His attention compelled that of the princes; he brushed aside the purveyor of pine-apples.

She cleared her throat, laughing, as if not to be taken too seriously; the sexless, timbreless voicelet, like that of a sick child asking for medicine, began to the lyre accompaniment:

"Canaan, excellent nothingness; nothingness-latent, circumambient, about to be the day after to-morrow, incipient, estimable, absolving, coexistent . . ."

The princes were puzzled. "Concessions by the five senses to an all-inscribing affective insanity; latitudes, altitudes, nebulæ, Medusæ of gentle water, affinities of the ineradicable, passages over earth so eminently identical with incalculably numerous duplicates, alone in indefinite infinite. Do you take me? I mean that the pragmatic essence attracted self-ward dynamically but more or less in its own volition, whistling in the bagpipes of the soul without termination.—But to be natural passives, to enter into the cosmos of harmonics.— Hydrocephalic theosophies, act it, aromas of populace, phenomena without stable order, contaminated with prudence.—Fatal Jordans, abysmal Ganges—to an end with 'em—insubmersible sidereal currents—nurse-maid cosmogonies."

She pushed back her hair dusty with pollens, the soft handclapping began; her eyelids drooped slightly, her faintly-suggested breasts lifted slightly, showed more rosy through the almond-shaped eyelets of her corsage. She was still fingering the ebony lyre.

"Bis, bis, brava!" cried her audience.

Still she waited.

"Go on! You shall have whatever you like. Go on, my dear," said the Tetrarch; "we are all so damned bored. Go on, Salome, you shall have any blamed thing you like: the Great-Seal, the priesthood of the Snow Cult, a job in the University, even to half of my oil stock. But inoculate us with . . . eh . . . with the gracious salve of this cosmoconception, with this parthenospotlessness."

The company in his wake exhaled an inedited boredom. They were all afraid of each other. Tiaras nodded, but no one confessed to any difficulty in following the thread of her argument. They were, racially, so very correct.

Salome wound on in summary rejection of theogonies, theodicies, comparative wisdoms of nations (short shift, tone of recitative). Nothing for nothing, perhaps one measure of nothing. She continued her mystic loquacity: "O tides, lunar oboes, avenues, lawns of twilight, winds losing caste in November, haymakings, vocations manquées, expressions of animals, chances."

Jonquil colored mousselines with black spots, eyes fermented, smiles crucified, adorable umbilici, peacock aureoles, fallen carnations, inconsequent fugues. One felt reborn, reinitiate and rejuvenate, the soul expiring systematically in spirals across indubitable definitive showers, for the good of earth, understood everywhere, palp of Varuna, air omniversal, assured if one were but ready.

Salome continued insistently: "The pure state, I tell you, sectaries of the consciousness, why this convention of separations, individuals by mere etiquette, indivisible? Breathe upon the thistle-down of these sciences, as you call them, in the orient of my pole-star. Is it life to persist in putting oneself au courant with oneself, constantly to inspect oneself, and then query at each step: am I wrong? Species! Categories! and kingdoms, bah!! Nothing is lost, nothing added, it is all reclaimed in advance. There is no ticket to the confessional for the heir of the prodigies. Not expedients and expiations, but vintages of the infinite, not experimental but in fatality."

The little yellow vocalist with the black funereal spots broke the lyre over her knee, and regained her dignity. The intoxicated crowd mopped their foreheads. An em-

barrassing silence. The hyperboreans looked at each
other: "What time will they put her to bed?" But
neither ventured articulation; they did not even inspect
their watches. It couldn't have been later than six.
The slender voice once more aroused them:

"And now, father, I wish you to send me the head of
Jao Kanan, on any saucer you like. I am going upstairs.
I expect it."

"But . . . but . . . my dear . . . this . . . this . . ."
However—the hall was vigorously of the opinion that
the Tiara should accomplish the will of Salome.

Emeraud glanced at the princes, who gave sign neither
of approbation nor of disapprobation. The cage-birds
again began shrieking. The matter was none of their
business.

Decide!

The Tetrarch threw his seal to the Administrator of
Death. The guests were already up, changing the conversation on their way to the evening tepidarium.

IV

With her elbows on the observatory railing, Salome,
disliking popular fêtes, listened to her familiar poluphloisbious ocean. Calm evening.

Stars out in full company, eternities of zeniths of em-
bers. Why go into exile?

Salome, milk-sister to the Via Lactea, seldom lost herself in constellations. Thanks to photo-spectrum analysis the stars could be classified as to color and magni-
tudes; she had commanded a set of diamonds in the
proportionate sizes to adorn nocturnally her hair and her
person, over mousseline of deep mourning-violet with
gold dots in the surface. Stars below the sixteenth mag-

nitude were not, were not in her world, she envisaged her
twenty-four millions of subjects.

Isolated nebulous matrices, not the formed nebulæ,
were her passion; she ruled out planetiform discs and
sought but the unformed, perforated, tentacular. Orion's
gaseous fog was the Brother Benjamin of her galaxy.
But she was no more the "little" Salome, this night
brought a change of relations, exorcised from her vir-
ginity of tissue she felt peer to these matrices, fecund
as they in gyratory evolutions. Yet this fatal sacrifice
to the cult (still happy in getting out of so discreetly)
had obliged her in order to get rid of her initiator, to
undertake a step (grave perhaps), perhaps homicide;—
finally to assure silence, cool water to contingent people,
—elixir of an hundred nights' distillation. It must serve.

Ah, well, such was her life. She was a specialty, a
minute spécialité.

There on a cushion among the débris of her black
ebony lyre, lay Jao's head, like Orpheus' head in the old
days, gleaming, encrusted with phosphorus, washed,
anointed, barbered, grinning at the 24 million stars.

As soon as she had got it, Salome, inspired by the
true spirit of research, had commenced the renowned experiments after decollation; of which we have heard so
much. She awaited. The electric passes of her hyp-
notic manual brought from it nothing but inconsequential
grimaces.

She had an idea, however.

She perhaps lowered her eyes, out of respect to Orion
stiffening herself to gaze upon the nebulæ of her puber-
ties . . . for ten minutes. What nights, what nights in
the future! Who will have the last word about it?
Choral societies, fire-crackers down there in the city.

Finally Salome shook herself, like a sensible person,

reset, readjusted her fichu, took off the gray gold-spotted
symbol-jewel of Orion, placed it between Jao's lips as
an host, kissed the lips pityingly and hermetically, sealed
them with corrosive wax (a very speedy procedure).

Then with a "Bah!" mutinous, disappointed, she seized
the genial boko of the late Jao Kanan, in delicate feminine hands.

As she wished the head to land plumb in the sea without bounding upon the cliffs, she gave a good swing in
turning. The fragment described a sufficient and phos-
phorescent parabola, a noble parabola. But unfortunately the little astronomer had terribly miscalculated her
impetus, and tripping over the parapet with a cry finally
human she hurtled from crag to crag, to fall, shattered,
into the picturesque anfractuosities of the breakers, far
from the noise of the national festival, lacerated and
naked, her skull shivered, paralyzed with a vertigo, in
short, gone to the bad, to suffer for nearly an hour.

She had not even the viaticum of seeing the phospho-
rescent star, the floating head of Jao on the water. And
the heights of heaven were distant.

.   .   .   .   .   .

Thus died Salome of the Isles (of the White Esoteric
Isles, in especial) less from uncultured misventure than
from trying to fabricate some distinction between herself
and every one else; like the rest of us.

VI

GENESIS, OR, THE FIRST BOOK IN THE BIBLE *

("SUBJECT TO AUTHORITY")

THE sacred author of this work, Genesis, complied with the ideas acceptable to his era; it was almost necessary; for without this condescension he would not have been understood. There remain for us merely a few reflections on the physics of those remote times. As for the theology of the book: we respect it, we believe it most firmly, we would not risk the faintest touch to its surface.

"In the beginning God created heaven and earth." That is the way they translate it, yet there is scarcely any one so ignorant as not to know that the original reads "the gods created heaven and earth"; which reading conforms to the Phœnician idea that God employed lesser divinities to untangle chaos. The Phœnicians had been long established when the Hebrews broke into some few provinces of their land. It was quite natural that these latter should have learned their language and borrowed their ideas of the cosmos.

Did the ancient Phœnician philosophers in "the time of Moses" know enough to regard the earth as a point in relation to the multitude of globes which God has placed in immensity? The very ancient and false idea

* Translated from an eighteenth-century author.

266

that heaven was made for the earth has nearly always prevailed among ignorant peoples. It is scarcely possible that such good navigators as the Phœnicians should not have had a few decent astronomers, but the old prejudices were quite strong, and were gently handled by the author of Genesis, who wrote to teach us God's ways and not to instruct us in physics.

"The earth was all *tohu bohu* and void, darkness was over the face of the deep, the spirit of God was borne on the waters."

"Tohu bohu" means precisely chaos, disorder. The earth was not yet formed as it is at present. Matter existed, the divine power had only to straighten things out. The "spirit of God" is literally the "breath" or "wind" which stirred up the waters. This idea is found in fragments of the Phœnician author, Sanchoniathon. The Phœnicians, like all the other peoples of antiquity, believed matter eternal. There is not one author of all those times who ever said that one could make something of nothing. Even in the Bible there is no passage which claims that matter was made out of nothing, not but what this creation from nothing is true, but its verity was unknown to the carnal Jews.

Men have been always divided on the eternity of the world, but never on the eternity of matter.

"Gigni de nihilo nihilum, et in nihilum nil posse reverti," writes Persius, and all antiquity shared his opinion. God said, "Let there be light," and there was light, and he saw that the light was good, and he divided the light from darkness, and he called the light *day* and the darkness *night*, and this was the evening and the morning of the first day. And God also said that the firmament, etc., the second day . . . saw that it was good.

Let us begin by seeing whether the bishop of Av-

ranches Huet, Leclerc, etc., are right, against those who
claim that this is a sublime piece of eloquence.

.   .   .   .   .   .

The Jewish author lumps in the light with the other
objects of creation; he uses the same turn of phrase,
"saw that it was good." The sublime should lift itself
above the average. Light is no better treated than anything else in this passage. It was another respected
opinion that light did not come from the sun. Men saw
it spread through the air before sunrise and after sunset;
they thought the sun served merely to reinforce it. The
author of Genesis conforms to popular error: he has the
sun and moon made four days after the light. It is un-
likely that there was a morning and evening before the
sun came into being, but the inspired author bows to the
vague and stupid prejudice of his nation. It seems probable that God was not attempting to educate the Jews in
philosophy or cosmogony. He could lift their spirits
straight into truth, *but* he *preferred* to descend to their
level. One can not repeat this answer too often.

The separation of the light from the darkness is not
part of another physical theory; it seems that night and
day were mixed up like two kinds of grain; and that they
were sifted out of each other. It is sufficiently well established that darkness is nothing but the deprivation of
light, and that there is light only in so far as our eyes
receive the sensation, but no one had thought of this at
that time.

The idea of the firmament is also of respectable antiquity. People imagined the skies very solid, because
the same set of things always happened there. The skies
circulated over our heads, they must therefore be very
strong. The means of calculating how many exhalations
of the earth and how many seas would be needed to keep

the clouds full of water? There was then no Halley to write out the equations. There were tanks of water in heaven. These tanks were held up on a good steady dome; but one could see through the dome; it must have been made out of crystal. In order that the water could be poured over the earth there had to be doors, sluices, cataracts which could be opened, turned on. Such was the current astronomy, *and* one was writing for Jews; it was quite necessary to take up their silly ideas, which they had borrowed from other peoples only a little less stupid.

"God made two great lights, one to preside over the day, the other the night, and he made also the stars."

True, this shows the same continuous ignorance of nature. The Jews did not know that the moonlight is merely reflection. The author speaks of the stars as luminous points, which they look like, although they are at times suns with planets swinging about them. But holy spirit harmonized with the mind of the time. If he had said that the sun is a million times as large as the earth, and the moon fifty times smaller, no one would have understood him. They appear to be two stars of sizes not very unequal.

"God said also: let us make man in our image, let him rule over the fishes, etc."

What did the Jews mean by "in our image"? They meant, like all antiquity:

Finxit in effigiem moderantum cuncta deorum.

One can not make "images" save of bodies. No nation then imagined a bodiless god, and it is impossible to picture him as such. One might indeed say "god is nothing of anything we know," but then one would not have any idea what he is. The Jews constantly believed god corporal, as did all the rest of the nations. All the first fathers of the church also believed god corporal, until they had swallowed Plato's ideas, or rather until the lights of Christianity had grown purer.

"He created them male and female."

If God or the secondary gods created man male and female in their resemblance, it would seem that the Jews believed God and the Gods were male and female. One searches to see whether the author meant to say that man was at the start ambisextrous or if he means that God made Adam and Eve the same day. The most natural interpretation would be that god made Adam and Eve at the same time, but this is absolutely contradicted by the formation of woman from the rib, a long time after the first seven days.

"And he rested the seventh day."

The Phœnicians, Chaldeans, and Indians say that God made the world in six periods, which Zoroaster calls the six gahambars, as celebrated among Persians.

It is incontestable that all these people had a theogony long before the Jews got to Horeb and Sinai, and before they could have had writers. Several savants think it likely that the allegory of the six days is imitated from the six periods. God might have permitted great nations to have this idea before he inspired the Jews, just as he had permitted other people to discover the arts before the Jews had attained any.

"The place of delight shall be a river which waters a garden, and from it shall flow four rivers, Phison . . . Gehon . . ., etc., Tigris, Euphrates . . ."

According to this version the terrestrial paradise would have contained about a third of Asia and Africa. The Euphrates and Tigris have their sources sixty miles apart in hideous mountains which do not look the least like a garden. The river which borders Ethiopia can be only the Nile, whose source is a little over a thousand miles from those of the Tigris and the Euphrates; and if Phison is the Phase, it is curious to start a Scythian river from the fount of a river of Africa. One must look further afield for the meaning of all these rivers. Every commentator makes his own Eden.

Some one has said that the Garden was like the gardens of Eden at Saana in Arabia Felix celebrated in antiquity. and that the parvenu Hebrews might have been an Arab tribe taking to themselves credit for the prettiest thing in the best canton of Arabia, as they have always taken to themselves the traditions of all the great peoples who enslaved them. But in any case they were led by the Lord.

"The Lord took man and set him in the midst of the garden, to tend it." It was all very well saying "tend it," "cultivate the garden," but it would have been very difficult for Adam to cultivate a garden 3,000 miles long. Perhaps he had helpers. It is another chance for the commentators to exercise their gifts of divination . . . as they do with the rivers.

"Eat not of the fruit of the knowledge of good and evil." It is difficult to think that there was a tree which taught good and evil; as there are pear trees and peach trees. One asks why God did not wish man to know good from evil. Would not the opposite wish (if one dare say so) appear more worthy of God, and much more needful to man? It seems to our poor reason that God might have ordered him to eat a good deal of this fruit, but one must submit one's reason and conclude that obedience to God is the proper course for us.

"If you eat of the fruit you shall die."
Yet Adam ate, and did not die in the least; they say he lived another nine centuries. Several "Fathers" have

considered all this as an allegory. Indeed, one may say
that other animals do not know that they die, but that
man knows it through his reason. This reason is the
tree of knowledge which makes him foresee his finish.
This explanation may be more reasonable, but we do not
dare to pronounce on it.

"The Lord said also: It is not good that man should
be alone, let us make him an helpmate like to him." One
expects that the Lord is going to give him a woman, but
first he brings up all the beasts. This may be the trans-
position of some copyist.

"And the name which Adam gave to each animal is its
real name." An animal's real name would be one which
designated all the qualifications of its species, or at least
the principal traits, but this does not exist in any language. There are certain imitative words, cock and
cuckoo, and *alali* in Greek, etc. Moreover, if Adam had
known the real names and therefore the properties of
the animals, he must have already eaten of the tree of
knowledge; or else it would seem that God need not
have forbidden him the tree, since he already knew more
than the Royal Society, or the Academy.

Observe that this is the first time Adam is named in
Genesis. The first man according to the Brahmins was
Adimo, son of the earth. Adam and Eve mean the same
thing in Phœnician, another indication that the holy spirit
fell in with the received ideas.

"When Adam was asleep, etc., . . . rib . . . made a
woman." The Lord, in the preceding chapter, had already created them male and female; why should he take
a rib out of the man to make a woman already existing?
We are told that the author announces in one place
what he explains in another. We are told that this allegory shows woman submitted to her husband. Many

people have believed on the strength of these verses that men have one rib less than women, but this is an heresy and anatomy shows us that a woman is no better provided with ribs than her husband.

"Now the serpent was the most subtle of beasts," etc., "he said to the woman," etc.

There is nowhere the least mention of the devil or a devil. All is physical. The serpent was considered not only the subtlest of all beasts by all oriental nations; he was also believed immortal. The Chaldeans had a fable about a fight between God and a serpent; it is preserved by Pherecides. Origen cites it in his sixth book against Celsus. They carried snakes in the feasts of Bacchus. The Egyptians attributed a sort of divinity to the serpent, as Eusebius tells us in his "Evangelical Preparations," book I, chapter X. In India and Arabia, and in China, the serpent was the symbol of life; the Chinese emperors before Moses wore the serpent sign on their breasts.

Eve is not surprised at the serpent's talking to her. Animals are always talking in the old stories; thus when Pilpai and Locman make animals talk no one is ever surprised.

All this tale seems physical and denuded of allegory. It even tells us the reason why the serpent who ramped before this now crawls on its belly, and why we always try to destroy it (at least so they say); precisely as we are told in all ancient metamorphoses why the crow, who was white, is now black, why the owl stays at home in the daytime, etc. But the "Fathers" have believed it an allegory manifest and respectable, and it is safest to believe them.

"I will multiply your griefs and your pregnancies, ye shall bring forth children with grief, ye shall be beneath the power of the man and he shall rule over you." One asks why the multiplication of pregnancies is a punishment. It was on the contrary a very great blessing, and especially for the Jews. The pains of childbirth are alarming only for delicate women; those accustomed to work are brought to bed very easily, especially in hot climates. On the other hand, animals sometimes suffer in littering, and even die of it. As for the superiority of man over woman, this is the quite natural result of his bodily and intellectual forces. The male organs are generally more capable of consecutive effort, more fit for manual and intellectual tasks. But when the woman has fist or wit stronger than those of her husband she rules the roost, and the man is submitted to woman. This is true, *but* before the original sin there may have been neither pain nor submission.

"God made them tunics of skin."
This passage proves very nicely that the Jews believed in a corporal god. A Rabbi named Eliezer has written that God covered Adam and Eve with the skin of the tempter serpent; Origen claims that the "tunic of skin" was a new flesh, a new body which God made for man, but one should have more respect for the text.

"And the Lord said 'Behold Adam, who is become like one of us.'" It seems that the Jews at first admired several gods. It is considerably more difficult to make out what they mean by the word God, *Eloim*. Several commentators state that this phrase, "one of us," means the Trinity, but there is no question of the Trinity in the Bible.*

* The reader will remember in Landor's Chinese dialogues, when the returned mandarin is telling the Emperor's children about England, there is one place where they burst into giggles "because they had been taught some arithmetic."

The Trinity is not a composite of several gods, it is the same god tripled; the Jews never heard tell of a god in three persons. By these words "like unto us" it is probable that the Jews meant angels, Eloïm. For this reason various rash men of learning have thought that the book was not written until a time when the Jews had adopted a belief in inferior gods, but this view is condemned.*

"The Lord set him outside the garden of delights, that he might dig in the earth." Yet some say that God had put him in the garden, in order that he might cultivate *it*. If gardener Adam merely became laborer Adam, he was not so much the worse off. This solution of the difficulty does not seem to us sufficiently serious. It would be better to say that God punished Adam's disobedience by banishing him from his birthplace.

Certain over-temerarious commentators say that the whole of the story refers to an idea once common to all men, i.e., that past times were better than present. People have always bragged of the past in order to run down the present. Men overburdened with work have imagined that pleasure is idleness, not having had wit enough to conceive that man is never worse off than when he has nothing to do. Men seeing themselves not infrequently miserable forged an idea of a time when all men were happy. It is as if they had said, once upon a time no tree withered, no beast fell sick, no animal devoured another, the spiders did not catch flies. Hence the ideal of the Golden Age, of the egg of Arimana, of the serpent who stole the secret of eternal life from the donkey, of the combat of Typhon and Osiris, of Ophionée and the gods, of Pandora's casket, and all these other old stories, sometimes very ingenious and never, in the least way, instruc-

* The reader is referred to our heading: "Subject to authority".

tive. *But* we should believe that the fables of other nations are imitation of Hebrew history, since we still have the Hebrew history and the history of other savage peoples is for the most part destroyed. Moreover, the witnesses in favor of Genesis are quite irrefutable.

"And he set before the garden of delight a cherubin with a turning and flaming sword to keep guard over the gateway to the tree of life." The word "kerub" means bullock. A bullock with a burning sword is an odd sight at a doorway. But the Jews have represented angels as bulls and as sparrow hawks, despite the prohibition to make graven images. Obviously they got these bulls and hawks from Egyptians who imitated all sorts of things, and who worshipped the bull as the symbol of agriculture and the hawk as the symbol of winds. Probably the tale is an allegory, a Jewish allegory, the kerub means "nature." A symbol made of a bull's body, a man's head and a hawk's wings.

"The Lord put his mark upon Cain."
"What a Lord!" say the incredulous. He accepts Abel's offering, rejects that of the elder brother, without giving any trace of a reason. The Lord provided the cause of the first brotherly enmity. This is a moral instruction, most truly, a lesson to be learned from all ancient fables, to wit, that scarcely had the race come into existence before one brother assassinated another, but what appears to the wise of this world, contrary to all justice, contrary to all the common sense principles, is that God has eternally damned the whole human race, and has slaughtered his own son, quite uselessly, for an apple, and that he has pardoned a fratricide. Did I say "pardoned"? He takes the criminal under his own protection. He declares that any one who avenges the murder of Abel shall be punished with seven fold the punishment

inflicted on Cain. He puts on him his sign as a safe-
guard. The impious call the story both execrable and
absurd. It is the delirium of some unfortunate Israelite,
who wrote these inept infamies in imitation of stories so
abundant among the neighboring Syrians. This insen-
sate Hebrew attributed his atrocious invention to Moses,
at a time when nothing was rarer than books. Destiny,
which disposes of all things, has preserved his work till
our day; scoundrels have praised it, and idiots have believed. Thus say the horde of theists, who while ador-
ing God, have been so rash as to condemn the Lord God
of Israel, and who judge the actions of the Eternal Being by the rules of our imperfect ethics, and our erroneous justice. They admit a god but submit god to our
laws. Let us guard against such temerity, and let us
once again learn to respect what lies beyond our comprehension. Let us cry out "O Altitudo!" with all our
strength.

"The Gods, Eloïm, seeing that the daughters of men
were fair, took for spouses those whom they chose."
This flight of imagination is also common to all the nations. There is no race, except perhaps the Chinese,*
which has not recorded gods getting young girls with
child. Corporeal gods come down to look at their domain, they see our young ladies and take the best for
themselves; children produced in this way are better than
other folks' children; thus Genesis does not omit to say

* In Fenollosa's notes on Kutsugen's ode to "Sir in the
Clouds," I am unable to make out whether the girl is more than
a priestess. She bathes in hot water made fragrant by boiling
orchids in it, she washes her hair and binds iris into it, she puts
on the dress of flowery colors, and the god illimitable in his
brilliance descends; she continues her attention to her toilet, in
very reverent manner.

that this commerce bred giants.   Once again the book is
in key with vulgar opinion.

"And I will pour the water floods over the earth."
I would note here that St. Augustin (City of God, No.
8) says, *"Maximum illud diluvium graeca nec latina novit
historia."*   Neither Greek nor Latin history takes note of
this very great flood.   In truth, they knew only Deu-
calion's and Ogyges' in Greece.   These were regarded as
universal in the fables collected by Ovid, but were totally
unknown in Eastern Asia.   St. Augustin is not·in error
when he says history makes no mention thereof.

"God said to Noah: I will make an agreement with
you and with your seed after you, and with all the animals."   God make an agreement with animals!   The unbelievers will exclaim: "What a contract!"   But if he
make an alliance with man, why not with the animals?
What nice feeling, there is something quite as divine in
this sentiment as in the most metaphysical thought.
Moreover, animals feel better than most men think.   It
is apparently in virtue of this agreement that St. Francis
of Assisi, the founder of the seraphic order, said to the
grasshoppers, and hares, "Sing, sister hoppergrass, brouse
brother rabbit."   But what were the terms of the treaty?
That all the animals should devour each other; that they
should live on our flesh; and we on theirs; that after having eaten all we can we should exterminate all the rest,
and that we should only omit the devouring of men stran-
gled with our own·hands.   If there was any such pact it
was presumably made with the devil.

Probably this passage is only intended to show that
God is in equal degree master of all things that breathe.
This pact could only have been a command; it is called
"alliance" merely by an "extension of the word's meaning."   One should not quibble over mere terminology,

but worship the spirit, and go back to the time when they
wrote this work which is scandal to the weak, but quite
edifying to the strong.

"And I will put my bow in the sky, and it shall be a
sign of our pact." Note that the author does not say
"I have put" but "I will put my bow"; this shows that
in common opinion the bow had not always existed. It
is a phenomenon of necessity caused by the rain, and
they give it as a supernatural manifestation that the
world shall never more be covered with water. It is odd
that they should choose a sign of rain as a promise that
one shall not be drowned. But one may reply to this:
when in danger of inundations we may be reassured by
seeing a rainbow.

"Now the Lord went down to see the city which the
children of Adam had builded, and he said, behold a
people with only one speech. They have begun this
and won't quit until it is finished. Let us go down and
confound their language, so that no man may understand
his neighbor." Note merely that the sacred author still
conforms to vulgar opinion. He always speaks of God
as of a man who informs himself of what is going on,
who wants to see with his eyes what is being done on his
estate, and who calls his people together to determine a
course of action.

"And Abraham, having arrayed his people (there
were of them three hundred and eighteen), fell upon the
five kings and slew them and pursued them even to Hoba
on the left side of Damas." From the south side of the
lake of Sodom to Damas is 24 leagues, and they still
had to cross Liban and anti-Liban. Unbelievers exult
over such tremendous exaggeration. But since the Lord
favored Abraham there is *no* exaggeration.

"And that evening two angels came into Sodom, etc."

The history of the two angels whom the Sodomites wanted to ravish is perhaps the most extraordinary which antiquity has produced. But we must remember that all Asia believed in incubi and succubæ demons, and that moreover these angels were creatures more perfect than man, and that they were probably much better looking, and lit more desires in a jaded, corrupt race than common men would have excited. Perhaps this part of the story is only a figure of rhetoric to express the horrible lewdness of Sodom and of Gomorrah. We offer this solution to savants with the most profound self-mistrust.

As for Lot who offered his two daughters to the Sodomites in lieu of the angels, and Lot's wife metamorphosed into the saline image, and all the rest of the story, what can one say of it? The ancient fable of Cinyra and Myrrha has some relation to Lot's incest with his daughters, the adventure of Philemon and Baucis is not without its points of comparison with that of the two angels appearing to Lot and his wife. As for the pillar of salt, I do not know what it compares with, perhaps with the story of Orpheus and Eurydice?

A number of savants think with Newton and the learned Leclerc that the Pentateuch was written by Samuel when the Jews had learned reading and writing, and that all these tales are imitation of Syrian fable.

But it is sufficient for us that it is all Holy Scripture; we therefore revere it without searching in it for anything that is not the work of the Holy Spirit. We should remember, at all times, that these times are not our times, and we should not fail to add our word to that of so many great men who have declared that the Old Testament is true history, and that everything invented by all the rest of the universe is mere fable.

Some savants have pretended that one should remove from the canonical books all incredible matters which might be a stumbling block to the feeble, but it is said that these savants were men of corrupt heart and that they ought to be burned, and that it is impossible to be an honest man unless you believe that the Sodomites desired to ravish the angels. This is the reasoning of a species of monster who wishes to rule over wits.

It is true that several celebrated church fathers have had the prudence to turn all these tales into allegory, like the Jews, and Philo in especial. Popes still more prudent desired to prevent the translation of these books into the everyday tongue, for fear men should be led to pass judgment on what was upheld for their adoration.

One ought surely to conclude that those who perfectly understand this work should tolerate those who do not understand it, for if these latter do not understand it, it is not their fault; also those who do not understand it should tolerate those who understand it most fully.

Savants, too full of their knowledge, have claimed that Moses could not possibly have written the book of Genesis. One of their reasons is that in the story of Abraham, the patriarch pays for his wife's funeral plot in coined money, and that the king of Gerare gives a thousand pieces of silver to Sarah when he returns her, after having stolen her for her beauty in the seventy-fifth year of her age. They say that, having consulted authorities, they find that there was no coined money in those days. But it is quite clear that this is pure chicane on their part, since the Church has always believed most firmly that Moses did write the Pentateuch. They strengthen all the doubts raised by the disciples of Aben-Hesra and Baruch Spinoza. The physician Astruc, father-in-law of the comptroller-general Silhouette, in his book, now very rare, entitled "Conjectures on Genesis," adds new objections, unsolvable to human wisdom; but not to humble submissive piety. The savants dare to contradict every line, the simple revere every line. Guard against falling into the misfortune of trusting our human reason, be contrite in heart and in spirit.

"And Abraham said that Sarah was his sister, and the king of Gerare took her to him." We confess, as we have said in our essay on Abraham, that Sarah was then ninety years old; that she had already been kidnapped by one King of Egypt; and that a king of this same desert Gerare later kidnapped the wife of Abraham's son Isaac. We have also spoken of the servant Agar, by whom Abraham had a son, and of how Abraham treated them both. One knows what delight unbelievers take in these stories; with what supercilious smiles they consider them; how they set the story of Abimelech and this same wife of Abraham's (Sarah) whom he passed off as his sister, above the "1001 nights" and also that of another Abimelech in love with Rebecca, whom Isaac also passed off as his sister. One can not too often reiterate that the fault of all these studious critics lies in their persistent endeavour to bring all these things into accord with our feeble reason and to judge ancient Arabs as they would judge the French court or the English.

"The soul of Sichem, son of King Hemor, cleaved to the soul of Dinah, and he charmed his sadness with her tender caresses, and he went to Hemor his father, and said unto him: Give me this woman for wife." Here the savants are even more refractory. What! a king's son marry a vagabond's daughter, Jacob her father loaded with presents! The king receives into his city these wandering robbers, called patriarchs; he has the incredible and incomprehensible kindness to get himself circum-

cised, he and his son, his court and his people, in order
to condescend to the superstition of this little tribe which
did not own a half league of land! And what reward
do our holy patriarchs make him for such astonishing
kindness? They wait the day when the wound of cir-
cumcision ordinarily produces a fever. Then Simeon
and Levi run throughout the city, daggers in hand; they
massacre the king, the prince, his son, and all the inhabitants. The horror of this St. Bartholemew is only
diminished by its impossibility. It is a shocking romance
but it is obviously a ridiculous romance: It is impossible
that two men could have killed a whole nation. One
might suffer some inconvenience from one's excerpted
foreskin, but one would defend oneself against two
scoundrels, one would assemble, surround them, finish
them off as they deserved.

But there is one more impossible statement: by an
exact supputation of date, we find that Dinah, daughter
of Jacob, was at this time no more than three years of
age; even if one tries to accommodate the chronology,
she could not have been more than five: it is this that
causes complaint. People say: What sort of a book
is this? The book of a reprobate people, a book for so
long unknown to all the earth, a book where right, reason and decent custom are outraged on every page, and
which we have presented us as irrefutable, holy, dictated
by God himself? Is it not an impiety to believe it? Is
it not the dementia of cannibals to persecute sensible,
modest men who do not believe it?

To which we reply: The Church says she believes it.
Copyists may have introduced revolting absurdities into
reverend stories. Only the Holy Church can be judge
of such matters. The profane should be led by her
wisdom. These absurdities, these pretended horrors do

not affect the basis of our religion. Where would men
be if the cult of virtue depended on what happened long
ago to Sichem and little Dinah?

"Behold the Kings who reigned in the land of Edom,
before the children of Israel had a king."

Behold another famous passage, another stone which
doth hinder our feet. It is this passage which determined the great Newton, the pious and sage Samuel
Clarke, the deeply philosophical Bolingbroke, the learned
Leclerc, the savant Frêret, and a great number of other
scholars to argue that Moses could not have been the
author of Genesis.

We do indeed confess that these words could only
have been written at a time when the Jews had kings.

It is chiefly this verse which determined Astruc to
upset the whole book of Genesis, and to hypothecate
memories on which the real author had drawn. His
work is ingenious, exact, but rash. A council would
scarcely have dared to undertake it. And to what end
has it served, this ungrateful. dangerous work of this
Astruc? To redouble the darkness which he set out to
enlighten. This is ever the fruit of that tree of knowledge whereof we all wish to eat. Why should it be
necessary that the fruits of the tree of ignorance should
be more nourishing and more easy to manage?

But what matter to us, after all, whether this verse,
or this chapter, was written by Moses, or by Samuel or
by the priest from Samaria, or by Esdras, or by any one
else? In what way can our government, our laws, our
fortunes, our morals, our well being, be tied up with the
ignorant chiefs of an unfortunate barbarous country,
called Edom or Idumea, always peopled by thieves?
Alas, these poor shirtless Arabs never ask about our
existence, they pillage caravans and eat barley bread,

and we torment ourselves trying to find out whether there were kinglets in one canton of Arabia Petra before they appeared in the neighboring canton to the west of lake Sodom.

O miseras hominium mentes!   O pectora caeca! *

* Our author's treatment of Ezekiel merits equal attention.

VII

ARNAUT DANIEL

RAZO

EN AR. DANIEL was of Ribeyrac in Perigord, under
Lemosi, near to Hautefort, and he was the best fashioner
of songs in the Provençal, as Dante has said of him in
his Purgatorio (XXVI, 140), and Tasso says it was he
wrote "Lancillotto," but this is not known for certain,
but Dante says only "proze di romanzi." Nor is it
known if Benvenuto da Imola speaks for certain when
he says En Arnaut went in his age to a monastery and
sent a poem to the princes, nor if he wrote a satire on
Boniface Castillane; but here are some of his canzos,
the best that are left us; and he was very cunning in his
imitation of birds, as in the poem "Autet," where he
stops in the middle of his singing, crying: "Cadahus, en
son us," as a bird cries, and rhyming on it cleverly, with
no room to turn about on the words, "Mas pel us, estauc
clus," and in the other versets. And in "L'aura amara,"
he cries as the birds in the autumn, and there is some of
this also in his best poem, "Doutz brais e critz."

And in "Breu brisaral," he imitates, maybe, the rough
singing of the *joglar engles*, from whom he learnt "Ac
et no l'ac"; and though some read this "escomes," not
"engles," it is likely enough that in the court of En
Richart there might have been an English joglar, for En

Bertrans calls Richart's brother "joven re Engles," so why should there not be a joglar of the same, knowing alliterations? And he may, in the ending "piula," have had in mind some sort of Arabic singing; for he knew well letters, in Langue d'Oc and in Latin, and he knew Ovid, of whom he takes Atalanta; and may be Virgil; and he talks of the Palux Lerna, though most copyers have writ this "Uzerna," not knowing the place he spoke of. So it is as like as not he knew Arabic music, and perhaps had heard, if he not understood the meaning, some song in rough Saxon letters.

And by making song in *rimas escarsas* he let into Provençal poetry many words that are not found elsewhere and maybe some words half Latin, and he uses many more sounds on the rhyme, for, as Canello or Lavaud has written, he uses ninety-eight rhyme sounds in seventeen canzos, and Peire Vidal makes use of but fifty-eight in fifty-four canzos and Folquet of thirty-three in twenty-two poems, and Raimbaut Orenga uses 129 rhymes in thirty-four poems, a lower proportion than Arnaut's. And the songs of En Arnaut are in some versets wholly free and uneven the whole length of the verset, then the other five versets follow in the track of the first, for the same tune must be sung in them all, or sung with very slight or orderly changes. But after the earlier poems he does not rhyme often inside the stanza. And in all he is very cunning, and has many uneven and beautiful rhythms, so that if a man try to read him like English iambic he will very often go wrong; though En Arnaut made the first piece of "Blank Verse" in the seven opening lines of the "Sols sui"; and he, maybe, in thinning out the rhymes and having but six repetitions to a canzone, made way for Dante who sang his long poem in threes. But this much

is certain, he does not use the rhyme -*atage* and many
other common rhymes of the Provençal, whereby so
many canzos are all made alike and monotonous on one
sound or two sounds to the end from the beginning.

Nor is there much gap from "Lancan vei fueill'" or
"D'autra guiza" to the form of the sonnet, or to the
receipt for the Italian strophes of canzoni, for we have
both the repetition and the unrepeating sound in the
verset. And in two versets the rhymes run *abab cde
abab cde;* in one, and in the other *abba cde abba cde;*
while in sonnets the rhymes run *abab abab cde cde;* or
abba abba cde cde. And this is no very great difference.
A sonetto would be the third of a *son*.

And I do not give "Ac et no l'ac," for it is plainly told
us that he learnt this song from a jongleur, and he says
as much in his coda:

> Miells-de-ben ren
> Sit pren
> Chanssos grazida
> C'Arnautz non oblida.

"Give thanks my song, to Miells-de-ben that Arnaut has
not forgotten thee." And the matter went as a joke,
and the song was given to Arnaut to sing in his reper-
toire "E fo donatz lo cantar an Ar Daniel, qui et aysi
trobaretz en sa obra." And I do not give the tenzon
with Trucs Malecs for reasons clear to all who have
read it; nor do I translate the sestina, for it is a poor
one, but maybe it is interesting to think if the music
will not go through its permutation as the end words
change their places in order, though the first line has only
eight syllables.

And En Arnaut was the best artist among the Provençals, trying the speech in new fashions, and bringing
new words into writing, and making new blendings of
words, so that he taught much to Messire Dante
Alighieri as you will see if you study En Arnaut and the
"De Vulgari Eloquio"; and when Dante was older and
had well thought the thing over he said simply, "il mi-
glior fabbro." And long before Francesco Petrarca,
he, Arnaut, had thought of the catch about *Laura*, laura,
l'aura, and the rest of it, which is no great thing to his
credit. But no man in Provençal has written as he
writes in "Doutz brais": "E quel remir" and the rest
of it, though Ovid, where he recounts Atalanta's flight
from Hippomenes in the tenth book, had written:

> "cum super atria velum
> "Candida purpureum simulatas inficit umbras."

And in Dante we have much in the style of:

> "Que jes Rozers per aiga que l'engrois."

And Dante learned much from his rhyming, and follows
him in *agro* and *Meleagro,* but more in a comprehension,
and Dante has learned also of Ovid: "in Metamor-
phoseos":

> "Velut ales, ab alto
> "Quae teneram prolem produxit in æra nido,"

although he talks so much of Virgil.

I had thought once of the mantle of indigo as of a
thing seen in a vision, but I have now only fancy to

support this. It is like that men slandered Arnaut for
Dante's putting him in his Purgatorio, but the Trucs
Malecs poem is against this.

En Arnaut often ends a canzone with a verset in
different tone from the rest, as markedly in "Si fos
Amors." In "Breu brisaral" the music is very curious,
but is lost for us, for there are only two pieces of his
music, and those in Milan, at the Ambrosiana (in R 71
superiore).

And at the end of "Doutz brais," is a verset like the
verset of a sirvente, and this is what he wrote as a
message, not making a whole sirvente, nor, so far as we
know, dabbling in politics or writing of it, as Bertrans de
Born has; only in this one place is all that is left us.
And he was a joglar, perhaps for his living, and only
composed when he would, and could not to order, as is
shown in the story of his remembering the joglar's canzone when he had laid a wager to make one of his own.

"Can chai la fueilla" is more like a sea song or an
estampida, though the editors call it a canzone, and
"Amors e jois," and some others were so little thought
of, that only two writers have copied them out in the
manuscripts; and the songs are all different one from
another, and their value nothing like even. Dante took
note of the best ones, omitting "Doutz brais," which is
for us perhaps the finest of all, though having some
lines out of strict pertinence. But "Can chai la fueilla"
is very cleverly made with five, six, and four and seven.
And in "Sols sui" and in other canzos verse is syllabic,
and made on the number of syllables, not by stresses, and
the making by syllables cannot be understood by those of
Petramala, who imagine the language they speak was
that spoken by Adam, and that one system of metric was

made in the world's beginning, and has since existed
without change. And some think if the stress fall not
on every second beat, or the third, that they must have
right before Constantine. And the art of En Ar. Daniel
is not literature but the art of fitting words well with
music, well nigh a lost art, and if one will look to the
music of "Chansson doil motz," or to the movement of
"Can chai la fueilla," one will see part of that which I
mean, and if one will look to the falling of the rhymes
in other poems, and the blending and lengthening of the
sounds, and their sequence, one will learn more of this.
And En Arnaut wrote between 1180 and 1200 of the
era, as nearly as we can make out, when the Provençal
was growing weary, and it was to be seen if it could last,
and he tried to make almost a new language, or at least
to enlarge the Langue d'Oc, and make new things possible. And this scarcely happened till Guinicello, and
Guido Cavalcanti and Dante; Peire Cardinal went to
realism and made satirical poems. But the art of singing to music went well nigh out of the words, for
Metastasio has left a few catches, and so has Lorenzo di
Medici, but in Bel Canto in the times of Durante, and
Piccini, Paradeis, Vivaldi, Caldara and Benedetto Mar-
cello, the music turns the words out of doors and strews
them and distorts them to the tune, out of all recognition; and the philosophic canzoni of Dante and his times-
men are not understandable if they are sung, and in
their time music and poetry parted company; the canzone's tune becoming a sonata without singing. And
the ballad is a shorter form, and the Elizabethan lyrics
are but scraps and bits of canzoni much as in the
"nineties" men wrote scraps of Swinburne.

Charles d'Orléans made good roundels and songs, as

in "Dieu qui la fait" and in "Quand j'oie la tambourine,"
as did also Jean Froissart before him in:

> Reviens, ami; trop longue est ta demeure:
> Elle me fait avoir peine et doulour.
> Mon esperit te demande à toute heure.
> Reviens, ami; trop longue est ta demeure.
>
> Car il n'est nul, fors toi, qui me sequerre,
> Ne secourra, jusques à ton retour.
> Reviens, ami; trop longue est ta demeure:
> Elle me fait avoir peine et doulour.

And in:

> Le corps s'en va, mais le cœur vous demeure.

And in:

> On doit le temps ainsi prendre qu'il vient:
> Tout dit que pas ne dure la fortune.
> Un temps se part, et puis l'autre revient:
> On doit le temps ainsi prendre qu'il vient.
>
> Je me comforte en ce qu'il me souvient
> Que tous les mois avons nouvelle lune:
> On doit le temps ainsi prendre qu'il vient:
> Tout dit que pas ne dure la fortune.

Which is much what Bernart de Ventadour has sung:

> "Per dieu, dona, pauc esplecham d'amor
> Va sen lo temps e perdem lo melhor."

And Campion was the last, but in none of the later men
is there the care and thought of En Arnaut Daniel for
the blending of words sung out; and none of them all
succeeded, as indeed he had not succeeded in reviving
and making permanent a poetry that could be sung. But
none of them all had thought so of the sound of the
words with the music, all in sequence and set together
as had En Arnaut of Ribeyrac, nor had, I think, even
Dante Alighieri when he wrote "De Eloquio."

And we find in Provence beautiful poems, as by Vidal
when he sings:

> "Ab l'alen tir vas me l'aire,"

And by the Viscount of St. Antoni:

> "Lo clar temps vei brunezir
>   E'ls auzeletz esperdutz,
>   Que'l fregz ten destregz e mutz
>   E ses conort de jauzir.
>   Donc eu que de cor sospir
>   Per la gensor re qu'anc fos,
>   Tan joios
>   Son, qu'ades m'es vis
>   Que folh' e flor s'espandis.
>   D'amor son tug miei cossir . . ."

and by Bertrans de Born in "Dompna puois di me,"
but these people sang not so many diverse kinds of music
as En Arnaut, nor made so many good poems in different fashions, nor thought them so carefully, though En
Bertrans sings with more vigor, it may be, and in the
others, in Cerclamon, Arnaut of Marvoil, in de Ventadour. there are beautiful passages. And if the art,
now in France, of saying a song—*disia sons,* we find

written of more than one troubadour—is like the art of
En Arnaut, it has no such care for the words, nor such
ear for hearing their consonance.

Nor among the Provençals was there any one, nor had
Dante thought out an æsthetic of sound; of clear sounds
and opaque sounds, such as in "Sols sui," an opaque
sound like Swinburne at his best; and in "Doutz brais"
and in "L'aura amara" a clear sound, with staccato;
and of heavy beats and of running and light beats, as
very heavy in "Can chai la fueilla." Nor do we enough
notice how with his drollery he is in places nearer to
Chaucer than to the Italians, and indeed the Provençal
is usually nearer the English in sound and in feeling,
than it is to the Italian, having a softer humor, not a
bitter tongue, as have the Italians in ridicule.

Nor have any yet among students taken note enough
of the terms, both of love terms, and of terms of the
singing; though theology was precise in its terms, and
we should see clearly enough in Dante's treatise when
he uses such words as *pexa, hirsuta, lubrica,* combed, and
shaggy and oily to put his words into categories, that
he is thinking exactly. Would the Age of Aquinas have
been content with anything less? And so with the love
terms, and so, as I have said in my Guido, with metaphors and the exposition of passion. Cossir, solatz,
plazers, have in them the beginning of the Italian philosophic precisions, and *amors qu'inz el cor mi plou* is not
a vague decoration. By the time of Petrarca the analysis had come to an end, only the vague decorations were
left. And if Arnaut is long before Cavalcanti,

> Pensar de lieis m'es repaus
> E traigom ams los huoills crancs,
> S'a lieis vezer nols estuich.

leads toward "E gli occhi orbati fa vedere scorto,"
though the music in Arnaut is not, in this place, quickly
apprehended. And those who fear to take a bold line
in their interpretation of "Cill de Doma," might do worse
than re-read:

"Una figura de la donna mia"

and what follows it. And for the rest any man who
would read Arnaut and the troubadours owes great
thanks to Emil Levy of Freiburg i/b for his long work
and his little dictionary (Petit Dictionaire Provençal-
Français, Karl Winter's Universitätsbuchhandlung, Hei-
delberg). and to U. A. Canello, the first editor of Arnaut,
who has shown, I think, great profundity in his arrangement of the poems in their order, and has really hit
upon their sequence of composition, and the developments of En Arnaut's trobar; and lastly to René Lavaud
for his new Tolosan edition.

II

THE twenty-three students of Provençal and the seven
people seriously interested in the technic and æsthetic
of verse may communicate with me in person. I give
here only enough to illustrate the points of the *razo*, that
is to say, as much as, and probably more than, the general
reader can be bothered with. The translations are a make-
shift; it is not to be expected that I can do in ten years
what it took two hundred troubadours a century and a
half to accomplish; for the full understanding of Ar-

naut's system of echoes and blending there is no substitute for the original; but in extenuation of the language of
my verses, I would point out that the Provençals were not
constrained by the modern literary sense. Their restraints
were the tune and rhyme-scheme, they were not constrained by a need for certain qualities of writing, without which no modern poem is complete or satisfactory.
They were not competing with De Maupassant's prose.
Their triumph is, as I have said, in an art between literature and music; if I have succeeded in indicating some
of the properties of the latter I have also let the former
go by the board. It is quite possible that if the troubadours had been bothered about "style," they would not
have brought their blend of word and tune to so elaborate
a completion.

"Can chai la fueilla" is interesting for its rhythm, for
the sea-chantey swing produced by simple device of
cæsuræ:

> Can chai la fueilla
> > dels ausors entrecims,
> El freitz s'ergueilla
> > don sechal vais' el vims,
> Dels dous refrims
> > vei sordezir la brueilla;
> Mas ieu soi prims
> > d'amor, qui que s'en tueilla.

The poem does not keep the same rhyme throughout, and
the only reason for giving the whole of it in my English
dither is that one can *not* get the effect of the thumping
and iterate foot-beat from one or two strophes alone.

CAN CHAI LA FUEILLA

When sere leaf falleth
          from the high forkèd tips,
And cold appalleth
          dry osier, haws and hips,
Coppice he strips
          of bird, that now none calleth.
Fordel * my lips
          in love have, though he galleth.

Though all things freeze here,
          I can naught feel the cold,
For new love sees, here
          my heart's new leaf unfold;
So am I rolled
          and lappèd against the breeze here:
Love who doth mould
          my force, force guarantees here.

Aye, life's a high thing,
          where joy's his maintenance,
Who cries 'tis wry thing
          hath danced never my dance,
I can advance
          no blame against fate's tithing
For lot and chance
          have deemed the best thing my thing.

Of love's wayfaring
          I know no part to blame,

* Preëminence.

All other paring,
   compared, is put to shame,
Man can acclaim
   no second for comparing
With her, no dame
   but hath the meaner bearing.

I'ld ne'er entangle
   my heart with other fere,
Although I mangle
   my joy by staying here
I have no fear
   that ever at Pontrangle
You'll find her peer
   or one that's worth a wrangle.

She'd ne'er destroy
   her man with cruelty
'Twixt here 'n' Savoy
   there feeds no fairer she,
Than pleaseth me
   till Paris had ne'er joy
In such degree
   from Helena in Troy.

She's so the rarest
   who holdeth me thus gay,
The thirty fairest
   can not contest her sway;
'Tis right, par fay,
   thou know, O song that wearest
Such bright array,
   whose quality thou sharest.

Chançon, nor stay
       till to her thou declarest :
"Arnaut would say
       me not, wert thou not fairest."

"Lancan son passat" shows the simple and presumably early style of Arnaut, with the kind of reversal from more or less trochaic to more or less iambic movement in fifth and eighth lines, a *kind* of rhythm taken over by Elizabethan lyricists. Terms trochaic and iambic are, however, utterly inaccurate when applied to syllabic metres set to a particular melody :

Lancan son passat li giure
E noi reman puois ni comba,
Et el verdier la flors trembla
Sus el entrecim on poma,
    La flors e li chan eil clar quil
Ab la sazon doussa e coigna
M'enseignon c'ab joi m'apoigna,
    Sai al temps de l'intran d'April.

LANCAN SON PASSAT LI GIURE

When the frosts are gone and over,
And are stripped from hill and hollow,
When in close the blossom blinketh
From the spray where the fruit cometh,
    The flower and song and the clarion
Of the gay season and merry
Bid me with high joy to bear me
    Through days while April's coming on.

Though joy's right hard to discover,
Such sly ways doth false Love follow,
Only sure he never drinketh
At the fount where true faith hometh;
    A thousand girls, but two or one
Of her falsehoods over chary,
Stabbing whom vows make unwary
    Their tenderness is vilely done.

The most wise runs drunkest lover,
Sans pint-pot or wine to swallow,
If a whim her locks unlinketh,
One stray hair his noose becometh.
    When evasion's fairest shown,
Then the sly puss purrs most near ye.
Innocents at heart beware ye,
    When she seems colder than a nun.

See, I thought so highly of her!
Trusted, but the game is hollow,
Not one won piece soundly clinketh;
All the cardinals that Rome hath,
    Yea, they all were put upon.
Her device is "Slyly Wary."
Cunning are the snares they carry,
    Yet while they watched they'd be undone

Whom Love makes so mad a rover,
'Ll take a cuckoo for a swallow,
If she say so, sooth! he thinketh
There's a plain where Puy-de-Dome is.
    Till his eyes and nails are gone,
He'll throw dice and follow fairly

—Sure as old tales never vary—
   For his fond heart he is foredone.

Well I know, sans writing's cover,
What a plain is, what's a hollow.
I know well whose honor sinketh,
And who 'tis that shame consumeth.
   They meet. I lose reception.
'Gainst this cheating I'd not parry
Nor amid such false speech tarry,
   But from her lordship will be gone.

Coda

Sir Bertran,* sure no pleasure's won
Like this freedom naught so merry
'Twixt Nile 'n' where the suns miscarry
   To where the rain falls from the sun.

The fifth poem in Canello's arrangement, "Lanquan vei fueill' e flor e frug." has strophes in the form:

When I see leaf, and flower and fruit
   Come forth upon light lynd and bough,
And hear the frogs in rillet bruit,
   And birds quhitter in forest now,
Love inkirlie doth leaf and flower and bear,
And trick my night from me, and stealing waste it,
Whilst other wight in rest and sleep sojourneth.

The sixth is in the following pattern, and the third strophe translates:

* Presumably De Born.

Hath a man rights at love?   No grain.
Yet gowks think they've some legal lien.
But she'll blame you with heart serene
That, ships for Bari sink, mid-main,
Or 'cause the French don't come from Gascony
And for such crimes I am nigh in my shroud,
Since, by the Christ, I do such crimes or none.

"Autet e bas" is interesting for the way in which
Arnaut breaks the flow of the poem to imitate the bird
call in "Cadahus en son us," and the repetitions of this
sound in the succeeding strophes, highly treble, presumably, Neis Jhezus, Mas pel us, etc.

> Autet e bas entrels prims fuoills
> Son nou de flors li ram eil renc
> E noi ten mut bec ni gola
> Nuills auzels, anz braia e chanta
> Cadahus
> En son us;
> Per joi qu'ai d'els e del temps
> Chant, mas amors mi asauta
> Quils motz ab lo son acorda.

AUTET E BAS ENTRELS PRIMS FUOILLS

"Cadahus En son us."

> Now high and low, where leaves renew,
> Come buds on bough and spalliard pleach
> And no beak nor throat is muted;
> Auzel each in tune contrasted
> Letteth loose
> Wriblis * spruce.

* Wriblis = warblings.

Joy for them and spring would set
Song on me, but Love assaileth
Me and sets my words t' his dancing.

I thank my God and mine eyes too,
Since through them the perceptions reach,
Porters of joys that have refuted
Every ache and shame I've tasted;
They reduce
Pains, and noose
Me in Amor's corded net.
Her beauty in me prevaileth
Till bonds seem but joy's advancing.

My thanks, Amor, that I win through;
Thy long delays I naught impeach;
Though flame's in my marrow rooted
I'd not quench it, well 't hath lasted,
Burns profuse,
Held recluse
Lest knaves know our hearts are met,
Murrain on the mouth that aileth,
So he finds her not entrancing.

He doth in Love's book misconstrue,
And from that book none can him teach,
Who saith ne'er's in speech recruited
Aught, whereby the heart is dasted.
Words' abuse
Doth traduce
Worth, but I run no such debt.
Right 'tis in man over-raileth
He tear tongue on tooth mischancing.*

* This is nearly as bad in the original.

That I love her, is pride, is true,
But my fast secret knows no breach.
Since Paul's writ was executed
Or the forty days first fasted,
Not Cristus
Could produce
Her similar, where one can get
Charms total, for no charm faileth
Her who's memory's enhancing.

Grace and valor, the keep of you
She is, who holds me, each to each,
She sole, I sole, so fast suited,
Other women's lures are wasted,
And no truce
But misuse
Have I for them, they're not let

To my heart, where she regaleth
Me with delights I'm not chancing.

Arnaut loves, and ne'er will fret
Love with o'er-speech, his throat quaileth,
Braggart voust is naught t' his fancy.

In the next poem we have the chatter of birds in autumn, the onomatopoeia obviously depends upon the "-utz, -etz, -ences and -ortz" of the rhyme scheme, 17 of the 68 syllables of each strophe therein included. I was able to keep the English in the same sound as the *Cadahus*, but I have not been able to make more than map of the relative positions in this canzos.

L'aura amara
Fals bruoilss brancutz
Clarzir

Quel doutz espeissa ab fuoills,
Els letz
Becs
Dels auzels ramencs
Ten balps e mutz,
Pars
E non-pars;
Per qu'eu m'esfortz
De far e dir
Plazers
A mains per liei
Que m'a virat bas d'aut,
Don tem morir
Sils afans no m'asoma.

I

The bitter air
Strips panoply
From trees
Where softer winds set leaves,
And glad
Beaks
Now in brakes are coy,
Scarce peep the wee
Mates
And un-mates.
    What gaud's the work?
    What good the glees?
What curse
I strive to shake!
Me hath she cast from high,
In fell disease
I lie, and deathly fearing.

II

So clear the flare
That first lit me
To seize
Her whom my soul believes;
If cad
Sneaks,
Blabs, slanders, my joy
Counts little fee
Baits
And their hates.
   I scorn their perk
    And preen, at ease.
Disburse
Can she, and wake
Such firm delights, that I
Am hers, froth, lees
Bigod! from toe to earring.

III

Amor, look yare!
Know certainly
The keys:
How she thy suit receives;
Nor add
Piques,
'Twere folly to annoy.
I'm true, so dree
Fates;
No debates
   Shake me, nor jerk.
    My verities

Turn terse,
And yet I ache;
Her lips, not snows that fly
Have potencies
To slake, to cool my searing.

IV

Behold my prayer,
(Or company
Of these)
Seeks whom such height achieves;
Well clad
Seeks
Her, and would not cloy.
Heart apertly
States
Thought. Hope waits
  'Gainst death to irk:
  False brevities
And worse!
To her I raik.*
Sole her; all others' dry
Felicities
I count not worth the leering.

V

Ah, visage, where
Each quality
But frees
One pride-shaft more, that cleaves
Me; mad frieks

* Raik = haste precipitate.

(O' thy beck) destroy,
And mockery
Baits
Me, and rates.
  Yet I not shirk
  Thy velleities,
Averse
Me not, nor slake
Desire. God draws not nigh
To Dome,* with pleas
Wherein's so little veering.

VI

Now chant prepare,
And melody
To please
The king, who'll judge thy sheaves.
Worth, sad,
Sneaks
Here; double employ
Hath there. Get thee
Plates
Full, and cates,
  Gifts, go! Nor lurk
  Here till decrees
Reverse,
And ring thou take.
Straight t' Arago I'd ply
Cross the wide seas
But "Rome" disturbs my hearing.

* Our Lady of Poi de Dome? No definite solution of this
reference yet found.

Coda.

At midnight mirk,
In secrecies
I nurse
My served make *
In heart; nor try
My melodies
At other's door nor mearing.†

The eleventh canzo is mainly interesting for the opening bass onomatopoeia of the wind rowting in the autumn branches.   Arnaut may have caught his alliteration
from the joglar engles, a possible hrimm-hramm-hruffer,
though the device dates at least from Naevius.

En breu brisaral temps braus,
Eill bisa busina els brancs
Qui s'entreseignon trastuich
De sobreclaus rams de fuoilla;
    Car noi chanta auzels ni piula
M' enseign' Amors qu'ieu fassa adonc
Chan que non er segons ni tertz
Ans prims d'afrancar cor agre.

The rhythm is too tricky to be caught at the first
reading, or even at the fifth reading; there is only part
of it in my copy.

Briefly bursteth season brisk,
Blasty north breeze racketh branch,
Branches rasp each branch on each

* Make = mate, fere, companion.
† Dante cites this poem in the second book of De Vulgari
Eloquio with poems of his own, De Born's, and Cino Pistoija's.

Tearing twig and tearing leafage,
  Chirms now no bird nor cries querulous;
So Love demands I make outright
A song that no song shall surpass
  For freeing the heart of sorrow.

Love is glory's garden close,
And is a pool of prowess staunch
Whence get ye many a goodly fruit
If true man come but to gather.
  Dies none frost bit nor yet snowily,
.For true sap keepeth off the blight
Unless knave or dolt there pass. . . .

The second point of interest is the lengthening out of
the rhyme in *piula, niula,* etc. In the fourth strophe
we find:

The gracious thinking and the frank
Clear and quick perceiving heart
Have led me to the fort of love.
Finer she is, and I more loyal
Than were Atlanta and Meleager.

Then the quiet conclusion, after the noise of the
opening, Pensar de lieis m'es repaus:

To think of her is my rest
And both of my eyes are strained wry
When she stands not in their sight,
Believe not the heart turns from her,
  For nor prayers nor games nor violing
Can move me from her a reed's-breadth.

The most beautiful passages of Arnaut are in the
canzo beginning:

Doutz brais e critz,
Lais e cantars e voutas
Aug dels auzels qu'en lor latins fant precs
Quecs ab sa par, atressi cum nos fam
A las amigas en cui entendem;
E doncas ieu qu'en la genssor entendi
Dei far chansson sobre totz de bell' obra
Que noi aia mot fals ni rima estrampa.

GLAMOUR AND INDIGO

Sweet cries and cracks
                    and lays and chants inflected
By auzels who, in their Latin belikes,
Chirm each to each, even as you and I
Pipe toward those girls on whom our thoughts attract;
Are but more cause that I, whose overweening
Search is toward the Noblest, set in cluster
Lines where no word pulls wry, no rhyme breaks gauges.

No culs de sacs
                    nor false ways me deflected
When first I pierced her fort within its dykes,
Hers, for whom my hungry insistency
Passes the gnaw whereby was Vivien wracked; *
Day-long I stretch, all times, like a bird preening,
And yawn for her, who hath o'er others thrust her
As high as true joy is o'er ire and rages.

Welcome not lax,
                    and my words were protected
Not blabbed to other, when I set my likes

* Vivien, strophe 2, nebotz Sain Guillem, an allusion to the
romance "Enfances Vivien."

On her. Not brass but gold was 'neath the die.
That day we kissed, and after it she flacked
O'er me her cloak of indigo, for screening
Me from all culvertz' eyes, whose blathered bluster
Can set such spites abroad; win jibes for wages.

God who did tax
          not Longus' sin,* respected
That blind centurion beneath the spikes
And him forgave, grant that we two shall lie
Within one room, and seal therein our pact,
Yes, that she kiss me in the half-light, leaning
To me, and laugh and strip and stand forth in the lustre
Where lamp-light with light limb but half engages.

The flowers wax
          with buds but half perfected;
Tremble on twig that shakes when the bird strikes—
But not more fresh than she! No empery,
Though Rome and Palestine were one compact,
Would lure me from her; and with hands convening
I give me to her. But if kings could muster
In homage similar, you'd count them sages.

Mouth, now what knacks!
          What folly hath infected
Thee? Gifts, that th' Emperor of the Salonikes
Or Lord of Rome were greatly honored by,
Or Syria's lord, thou dost from me distract;
O fool I am! to hope for intervening
From Love that shields not love! Yea, it were juster
To call him mad, who 'gainst his joy engages.

* Longus, centurion in the crucifixion legend.

POLITICAL POSTSCRIPT

The slimy jacks
            with adders' tongues bisected,
I fear no whit, nor have; and if these tykes
Have led Galicia's king to villeiny—— *
His cousin in pilgrimage hath he attacked—
We know—Raimon the Count's son—my meaning
Stands without screen.   The royal filibuster
Redeems not honor till he unbar the cages.

CODA

I should have seen it, but I was on such affair,
Seeing the true king crown'd here in Estampa.†

. Arnaut's tendency to lengthen the latter lines of the
strophe after the diesis shows in: Er vei vermeils, vertz,
blaus, blancs, gruocs, the strophe form being:

Vermeil, green, blue, peirs, white, cobalt,
Close orchards, hewis, holts, hows, vales,
And the bird-song that whirls and turns
Morning and late with sweet accord,
Bestir my heart to put my song in sheen
T'equal that flower which hath such properties,
It seeds in joy, bears love, and pain ameises.

* King of the Galicians, Ferdinand II, King of Galicia, 1157-
88, son of Berangere, sister of Raimon Berenger IV ("quattro
figlie ebbe," etc.) of Aragon, Count of Barcelona. His second
son, Lieutenant of Provence, 1168.
† King crowned at Etampe, Phillipe August, crowned May
29, 1180, at age of 16. This poem might date Arnaut's birth as
early as 1150.

The last cryptic allusion is to the quasi-allegorical descriptions of the tree of love in some long poem like the Romaunt of the Rose.

Dante takes the next poem as a model of canzo construction; and he learned much from its melody:

> Sols sui qui sai lo sobrefan quem sortz
> Al cor d'amor sofren per sobramar,
> Car mos volers es tant ferms et entiers
> C'anc no s'esduis de celliei ni s'estors
> Cui encubric al prim vezer e puois:
> Qu'ades ses lieis dic a lieis cochos motz,
> Pois quan la vei non sai, tant l'ai, que dire.

We note the soft suave sound as against the staccato of "L'aura amara."

Canzon.

> I only, and who elrische pain support
> Know out love's heart o'er borne by overlove,
> For my desire that is so firm and straight
> And unchanged since I found her in my sight
> And unturned since she came within my glance,
> That far from her my speech springs up aflame;
> Near her comes not. So press the words to arrest it.
>
> I am blind to others, and their retort
> I hear not. In her alone, I see, move,
> Wonder. . . . And jest not. And the words dilate
> Not truth; but mouth speaks not the heart outright:
> I could not walk roads, flats, dales, hills, by chance,
> To find charm's sum within one single frame
> As God hath set in her t'assay and test it.

ARNAUT DANIEL

And I have passed in many a goodly court
To find in hers more charm than rumor thereof. . . .
In solely hers. Measure and sense to mate,
Youth and beauty learnèd in all delight,
Gentrice did nurse her up, and so advance
Her fair beyond all reach of evil name,
To clear her worth, no shadow hath oppresst it.

Her contact flats not out, falls not off short . . .
Let her, I pray, guess out the sense hereof
For never will it stand in open prate
Until my inner heart stand in daylight,
So that heart pools him when her eyes entrance,
As never doth the Rhone, fulled and untame,
Pool, where the freshets tumult hurl to crest it.

Flimsy another's joy, false and distort,
No paregale that she springs not above . . .
Her love-touch by none other mensurate.
To have it not? Alas! Though the pains bite
Deep, torture is but galzeardy and dance,
For in my thought my lust hath touched his aim.
God! Shall I get no more! No fact to best it!

No delight I, from now, in dance or sport,
Nor will these toys a tinkle of pleasure prove,
Compared to her, whom no loud profligate
Shall leak abroad how much she makes my right.
Is this too much? If she count not mischance
What I have said, then no. But if she blame,
Then tear ye out the tongue that hath expresst it.

The song begs you: Count not this speech ill chance,
But if you count the song worth your acclaim,
Arnaut cares lyt who praise or who contest it.

The XVIth canto goes on with the much discussed and much too emphasized cryptogram of the ox and the hare. I am content with the reading which gives us a classic allusion in the palux Laerna. The lengthening of the verse in the last three lines of the strophe is, I think, typically Arnaut's. I leave the translation solely for the sake of one strophe.

Ere the winter recommences
And the leaf from bough is wrested,
On Love's mandate will I render
A brief end to long prolusion:
So well have I been taught his steps and paces
That I can stop the tidal-sea's inflowing.
My stot outruns the hare; his speed amazes.

Me he bade without pretences
That I go not, though requested;
That I make no whit surrender
Nor abandon our seclusion:
"Differ from violets, whose fear effaces
Their hue ere winter; behold the glowing
Laurel stays, stay thou. Year long the genet blazes."

"You who commit no offences
'Gainst constancy; have not quested;
Assent not! Though a maid send her
Suit to thee. Think you confusion
Will come to her who shall track out your traces?
And give your enemies a chance for boasts and crowing?
No! After God, see that she have your praises."

Coward, shall I trust not defences!
Faint ere the suit be tested?

Follow! till she extend her
Favour. Keep on, try conclusion
For if I get in this naught but disgraces,
Then must I pilgrimage past Ebro's flowing
And seek for luck amid the Lernian mazes.

If I've passed bridge-rails and fences,
Think you then that I am bested?
No, for with no food or slender
Ration, I'd have joy's profusion
To hold her kissed, and there are never spaces
Wide to keep me from her, but she'd be showing
In my heart, and stand forth before his gazes.

Lovelier maid from Nile to Sences
Is not vested nor divested,
So great is her bodily splendor
That you would think it illusion.
Amor, if she but hold me in her embraces,
I shall not feel cold hail nor winter's blowing
Nor break for all the pair in fever's dazes.

Arnaut hers from foot to face is,
He would not have Lucerne, without her, owing
Him, nor lord the land whereon the Ebro grazes.

The feminine rhyming throughout and the shorter
opening lines keep the strophe much lighter and more
melodic than that of the canzo which Canello prints last
of all.

SIM FOS AMORS DE JOI DONAR TANT LARGA

"Ingenium nobis ipsa puella facit."
                                    Propertius II, I.

Sim fos Amors de joi donar tant larga
Cum ieu vas lieis d'aver fin cor e franc,
Ja per gran ben nom calgra far embarc
Qu'er am tant aut quel pes mi poia em tomba;
Mas quand m' albir cum es de pretz al som
Mout m'en am mais car anc l'ausiei voler,
C'aras sai ieu que mos cors e mos sens
Mi farant far lor grat rica conquesta.

Had Love as little need to be exhorted
To give me joy, as I to keep a frank
And ready heart toward her, never he'd blast
My hope, whose very height hath high exalted,
And cast me down . . . to think on my default,
And her great worth; yet thinking what I dare,
More love myself, and know my heart and sense
Shall lead me to high conquest, unmolested.

I am, spite long delay, pooled and contorted
And whirled with all my streams 'neath such a bank
Of promise, that her fair words hold me fast
In joy, and will, until in tomb I am halted.
As I'm not one to change hard gold for spalt,
And no alloy's in her, that debonaire
Shall hold my faith and mine obedience
Till, by her accolade, I am invested.

Long waiting hath brought in and hath extorted
The fragrance of desire; throat and flank

The longing takes me . . . and with pain surpassed
By her great beauty. Seemeth it hath vaulted
O'er all the rest . . . them doth it set in fault
So that whoever sees her anywhere
Must see how charm and every excellence
Hold sway in her, untaint, and uncontested.

Since she is such; longing no wise detorted
Is in me . . . and plays not the mountebank,
For all my sense is her, and is compassed
Solely in her; and no man is assaulted
(By God his dove!) by such desires as vault
In me, to have great excellence. My care
On her so stark, I can show tolerance
To jacks whose joy 's to see fine loves uncrested.

Miels-de-Ben, have not your heart distorted
Against me now; your love has left me blank,
Void, empty of power or will to turn or cast
Desire from me . . . not brittle,* nor defaulted.
Asleep, awake, to thee do I exalt
And offer me. No less, when I lie bare
Or wake, my will to thee, think not turns thence,
For breast and throat and head hath it attested.

Pouch-mouthed blubberers, culrouns and aborted,
May flame bite in your gullets, sore eyes and rank
T' the lot of you, you've got my horse, my last
Shilling, too; and you'd see love dried and salted.
God blast you all that you can't call a halt!
God's itch to you, chit-cracks that overbear

* "Brighter than glass, and yet as glass is, brittle." The comparisons to glass went out of poetry when glass ceased to be a rare, precious substance. (*Cf.* Passionate Pilgrim, III.)

And spoil good men, ill luck your impotence!!
More told, the more you've wits smeared and congested.

CODA

Arnaut has borne delay and long defence
And will wait long to see his hopes well nested.

[In De Vulgari Eloquio II, 13, Dante calls for freedom
in the rhyme order within the strophe, and cites this
canzo of Arnaut's as an example of poem where there
is no rhyme within the single strophe. Dante's "Rithimorum quoque relationi vacemus" implies no careless-
ness concerning the blending of rhyme sounds, for we
find him at the end of the chapter "et tertio rithimorum
asperitas, nisi forte sit lenitati permista: nam lenium
asperorumque rithimorum mixtura ipsa tragoedia nite-
scit," as he had before demanded a mixture of shaggy
and harsh words with the softer words of a poem.
"Nimo scilicet eiusdem rithimi repercussio, nisi forte
novum aliquid atque intentatum artis hoc sibi praeroget."
The De Eloquio is ever excellent testimony of the way
in which a great artist approaches the detail of métier.]

VIII

TRANSLATORS OF GREEK

EARLY TRANSLATORS OF HOMER

I. HUGHES SALEL

THE dilection of Greek poets has waned during the last pestilent century, and this decline has, I think, kept pace with a decline in the use of Latin cribs to Greek authors. The classics have more and more become a baton exclusively for the cudgelling of schoolboys, and less and less a diversion for the mature.

I do not imagine I am the sole creature who has been well taught his Latin and very ill-taught his Greek (beginning at the age, say, of twelve, when one is unready to discriminate matters of style, and when the economy of the adjective cannot be wholly absorbing). A child may be bulldozed into learning almost anything, but man accustomed to some degree of freedom is loath to approach a masterpiece through five hundred pages of grammar. Even a scholar like Porson may confer with former translators.

We have drifted out of touch with the Latin authors as well, and we have mislaid the fine English versions: Golding's *Metamorphoses*; Gavin Douglas' *Æneids*; Marlowe's *Eclogues* from Ovid, in each of which books a great poet has compensated, by his own skill, any loss in transition; a new beauty has in each case been created. Greek in English remains almost wholly unsuccessful, or rather, there are glorious passages but no long or whole satisfaction. Chapman remains the best English "Homer," marred though he may be by excess of added ornament, and rather more marred by parentheses and inversions, to the point of being hard to read in many places.

And if one turn to Chapman for almost any favorite passage one is almost sure to be disappointed; on the other hand I think no one will excel him in the plainer passages of narrative, as of Priam's going to Achilles in the XXIVth Iliad. Yet he breaks down in Priam's prayer at just the point where the language should be the simplest and austerest.

Pope is easier reading, and, out of fashion though he is, he has at least the merit of translating Homer into *something*. The nadir of Homeric translation is reached by the Leaf-Lang prose; Victorian faddism having persuaded these gentlemen to a belief in King James fustian; their alleged prose has neither the concision of verse nor the virtues of direct motion. In their preface they grumble about Chapman's "mannerisms," yet their version is full of "Now behold I" and "yea even as" and "even as when," tushery possible only to an affected age bent on propaganda. For, having, despite the exclusion of the *Dictionnaire Philosophique* from the island, finally found that the Bible couldn't be retained either as history or as private Reuter from J'hvh's Hebrew Press bureau, the Victorians tried to boom it, and even its wilfully bowdlerized translations, as literature.

"So spake he, and roused Athene that already was set

thereon. . . . Even as the son of . . . even in such guise. . . ."

perhaps no worse than

"With hollow shriek the steep of Delphos leaving"* but bad enough anyway.

Of Homer two qualities remain untranslated: the magnificent onomatopœia, as of the rush of the waves on the sea-beach and their recession in:

$$\pi\alpha\rho\grave{\alpha}\ \theta\hat{\imath}\nu\alpha\ \pi o\lambda\upsilon\phi\lambda o\acute{\imath}\sigma\beta o\iota o\ \theta\alpha\lambda\acute{\alpha}\sigma\sigma\eta s$$

untranslated and untranslatable; and, secondly, the authentic cadence of speech; the absolute conviction that the words used, let us say by Achilles to the "dog-faced" chicken-hearted Agamemnon, are in the actual swing of words spoken. This quality of actual speaking is *not* untranslatable. Note how Pope fails to translate it:

There sat the seniors of the Trojan race
(Old Priam's chiefs, and most in Priam's grace):
The king, the first; Thymœtes at his side;
Lampus and Clytius, long in counsel try'd;
Panthus and Hicetaon, once the strong;
And next, the wisest of the reverend throng,
Antenor grave, and sage Ucalegon,
Lean'd on the walls, and bask'd before the sun.
Chiefs, who no more in bloody fights engage,
But wise through time, and narrative with age,
In summer days like grasshoppers rejoice,
A bloodless race, that send a feeble voice.
These, when the Spartan queen approach'd the tower,
In secret own'd resistless beauty's power:

* Milton, of course, whom my detractors say I condemn without due circumspection.

They cried, No wonder, such celestial charms
For nine long years have set the world in arms!
What winning graces! What majestic mien!
She moves a goddess, and she looks a queen!
Yet hence, oh Heaven, convey that fatal face,
And from destruction save the Trojan race.

This is anything but the "surge and thunder," but it is,
on the other hand, a definite idiom, within the limits of
the rhymed pentameter couplet it is even musical in
parts; there is imbecility in the antithesis, and bathos in
"she looks a queen," but there is fine accomplishment in:

"Wise through time, and narrative with age,"

Mr. Pope's own invention, and excellent. What we
definitely can *not* hear is the voice of the old men speaking. The simile of the grasshoppers is well rendered, but
the old voices do not ring in the ear.

Homer (iii. 156-160) reports their conversation:

> Οὐ νέμεσις, Τρῶας καὶ ἐϋκνήμιδας Ἀχαιοὺς
> Τοιῇδ ἀμφὶ γυναικὶ πολὺν χρόνον ἄλγεα πάσχειν·
> Αἰῶς ἀθανάτῃσι θεῇς εἰς ὦπα ἔοικεν.
> Ἀλλὰ καὶ ὧς, τοίη περ εοῦσ', ἐν νηυσὶ νεέσθω·
> Μηδ' ἡμῖν τεκέεσσι τ' 'οπίσσω πῆμα λίποιτο.

Which is given in Sam. Clark's *ad verbum* translation:
"Non *est* indigne ferendum, Trojanos et bene-ocreatos
    Archivos
Tali de muliere longum tempus dolores pati:
Omnino immortalibus deabus ad vultum similis est.
Sed et sic, talis quamvis sit, in navibus redeat,
Neque nobis liberisque in posterum detrimentum
    relinquatur."

Mr. Pope has given six short lines for five long ones, but he has added "fatal" to face (or perhaps only lifted it from νέμεσις), he has added "winning graces," "majestic," "looks a queen." As for owning beauty's resistless power secretly or in the open, the Greek is:

Τοῖοι ἄρα Τρώων ἡγήτορες ἧντ' ἐπὶ πύργῳ.
Οἱ δ' ὡς οὖν εἶδον Ἑλένην ἐπὶ πύργον ἰοῦσαν,
Ἦκα πρὸς ἀλλήλους ἔπεα πτερόεντ' ἀγόρευον·

and Sam. Clark as follows:

"Tales utique Trojanorum proceres sedebant in turri.
Hi autem ut viderunt Helenam ad turrim venientem,
Submisse inter se verbis alatis dixerunt;"

Ἦκα is an adjective of sound, it is purely objective, even *submisse** is an addition; though Ἦκα might, by a slight strain, be taken to mean that the speech of the old men cāme little by little, a phrase from each of the elders. Still it would be purely objective. It does not even say they spoke humbly or with resignation.

Chapman is no closer than his successor. He is so *galant* in fact, that I thought I had found his description in Rochefort. The passage is splendid, but splendidly unhomeric:

"All grave old men, and soldiers they had been, but for
    age
Now left the wars; yet counsellors they were exceed-
    ingly sage.
And as in well-grown woods, on trees, cold spiny grass-
    hoppers

* *I. e.* Clark is "correct," but the words shade differently. Ἦκα means low, quiet, with a secondary meaning of "little by little." *Submisse* means low, quiet, with a secondary meaning of modesty, humbly.

Sit chirping, and send voices out, that scarce can pierce
        our ears
For softness, and their weak faint sounds; so, talking
        on the tow'r,
These seniors of the people sat; who when they saw
        the pow'r
Of beauty, in the queen, ascend, ev'n those cold-spirited
        peers,
Those wise and almost wither'd men, found this heat
        in their years,
That they were forc'd (though whispering) to say:
        'What man can blame
The Greeks and Trojans to endure, for so admir'd a
        dame,
So many mis'ries, and so long? In her sweet
        count'nance shine
Looks like the Goddesses. And yet (though never so
        divine)
Before we boast, unjustly still, of her enforced prise,
And justly suffer for her sake, with all our progenies,
Labor and ruin, let her go; the profit of our land
Must pass the beauty.' Thus, though these could bear
        so fit a hand
On their affections, yet, when all their gravest powers
        were us'd,
They could not choose but welcome her, and rather they
        accus'd
The Gods than beauty; for thus spake the most-fam'd
        king of Troy:"

The last sentence representing mostly Ὣς ἄρ ἔφα in the
line:

Ὣς ἄρ ἔφαν· Πρίαμος δ' Ἑλένην ἐκαλέσσατο φωνῇ·

"Sic dixerunt: Priamus autem Helenam vocavit voce,"

Chapman is nearer Swinburne's ballad with:

"But those three following men," etc.

than to his alleged original.

Rochefort is as follows (*Iliade,* Livre iii, M. de Rochefort, 1772):

"Hélène a ce discours sentit naître en son âme
Un doux ressouvenir de sa première flamme;
Le désir de revoir les lieux qu'elle a quittés
Jette un trouble inconnu dans ses sens agités.
Tremblante elle se lève et les yeux pleins de larmes,
D'un voile éblouissant elle couvre ses charmes;
De deux femmes suivie elle vole aux remparts.
La s'étaient assemblés ces illustres vieillards
Qui courbés sous le faix des travaux et de l'age
N'alloient plus au combat signaler leur courage,
Mais qui, près de leur Roi, par de sages avis,
Mieux qu'en leurs jeunes ans défendoient leur païs.
  Dans leurs doux entretiens, leur voix toujours égale
Ressembloit aux accents que forme la cigale,
Lorsqu'aux longs jours d'été cachée en un buisson,
Elle vient dans les champs annoncer la moisson.
Une tendre surprise enflamma leurs visages;
Frappés de ses appas, ils se disoient entre eux:
'Qui pourroit s'étonner que tant de Rois fameux,
Depuis neuf ans entiers aient combattu pour elle?
Sur le trône des cieux Vénus n'est pas plus belle.
Mais quelque soit l'amour qu'inspirent ses attraits,
Puisse Illion enfin la perdre pour jamais,
Puisse-t-elle bientôt à son époux rendue,
Conjurer l'infortune en ces lieux attendue.'"

Hugues Salel (1545), praised by Ronsard, is more pleasing:

"Le Roi Priam, et auec luy bon nombre
De grandz Seigneurs estoient à l'ombre
Sur les Crenaulx, Tymoetes et Panthus,
Lampus, Clytus, excellentz en vertus,
Hictaon renomme en bataille,
Ucalegon iadis de fort taille,
Et Antenor aux armes nompareil
Mais pour alors ne seruantz qu'en conseil.

La, ces Vieillards assis de peur du Hasle
Causoyent ensemble ainsi que la Cignalle
Ou deux ou trois, entre les vertes fueilles,
En temps d'Esté gazouillant a merveilles;
Lesquelz voyans la diuine Gregeoise,
Disoient entre eux que si la grande noise
De ces deux camps duroit longe saision,
Certainement ce n'estoit sans raision:
Veu la Beaulté, et plus que humain outrage,
Qui reluysoit en son diuin visaige.
Ce neantmoins il vauldrait mieulx la rendre,
(Ce disoyent ilz) sans guères plus attendre.
Pour éviter le mal qui peult venir,
Qui la voudra encores retenir."

Salel is a most delightful approach to the Iliads; he is still absorbed in the subject-matter, as Douglas and Golding were absorbed in their subject-matter. Note how exact he is in the rendering of the old men's mental attitude. Note also that he is right in his era. I mean simply that Homer *is* a little *rustre*, a little, or perhaps a good deal, mediæval, he has not the dovetailing of Ovid. He has onomatopœia, as of poetry sung out; he

has authenticity of conversation as would be demanded
by an intelligent audience not yet laminated with
æsthetics; capable of recognizing reality. He has the
repetitions of the *chanson de geste*. Of all the French
and English versions I think Salel alone gives any hint
of some of these characteristics. Too obviously he is not
onomatopœic, no. But he is charming, and readable,
and "Briseis Fleur des Demoiselles" has her reality.

Nicolo Valla is, for him who runs, closer:

"Consili virtus, summis de rebus habebant
  Sermones, et multa inter se et magna loquentes,
  Arboribus quales ǫracili stridere cicadæ
  Sæᵣe solent cantu, postquam sub moenibus altis
  Tyndarida aspiciunt, procerum tum quisque fremebat,
  Mutuasque exorsi, Decuit tot funera Teucros
  Argolicasque pati, longique in tempore bellum
  Tantuɜ in ore decor cui non mortalis in artus
  Est honor et vultu divina efflagrat imago.
  Diva licet facies, Danauum cum classe recedat
  Longius excido ne nos aut nostra fatiget
  Pignora sic illi tantis de rebus agebant."

This hexameter is rather heavily accented. It shows,
perhaps, the source of various "ornaments" in later English and French translations. It has indubitable sonority
even though monotonous.

It is the earliest Latin verse rendering I have yet come
upon, and is bound in with Raphael of Volterra's first
two Iliads, and some further renderings by Obsopeo.

Odyssea (Liber primus) (1573).

"Dic mihi musa uirum captae post tempora Troiae
  Qui mores hominum multorum uidit et urbes

Multa quoque et ponto passus dum naufragus errat
Ut sibi tum sociis uitam seruaret in alto
Non tamen hos cupens fato deprompsit acerbo
Ob scelus admissum extinctos ausumque malignum
Qui fame compulsu solis rapuere iuvencos
Stulti ex quo reditum ad patrias deus abstulit oras.
Horum itaque exitium memora mihi musa canenti."

Odyssea (Lib. sec.) (1573).

"Cumprimum effulsit roseis aurora quadrigis
Continuo e stratis proles consurgit Ulyxis
Induit et uestes humerosque adcomodat ensem
Molia denin pedibus formosis uincula nectit
Parque deo egrediens thalamo praeconibus omnis
Concilio cognant extemplo mandat Achaeos
Ipse quoque ingentem properabat ad aedibus hastam
Corripiens: gemenique canes comitantor euntem
Quumque illi mirum Pallas veneranda decorem
Preberer populus venientem suspicit omnis
Inque throno patrio ueteres cessere sedenti."

The charm of Salel is continued in the following excerpts. They do not cry out for comment. I leave
Ogilby's English and the lines of Latin to serve as contrast or cross-light.

Iliade (Livre I). Hugues Salel (1545).*

THE IRE

"Je te supply Déesse gracieuse,
Vouloir chanter l'Ire pernicieuse,

* Later continued by l'Abbé de St. Chérroc.

Dont Achille fut tellement espris,
Que par icelle, ung grand nombre d'espritz
Des Princes Grecs, par dangereux encombres,
Feit lors descente aux infernales Umbres.
Et leurs beaulx Corps privéz de Sépulture
Furent aux chiens et aux oiseaulx pasture."

Iliade (Lib. III).   John Ogilby (1660).

HELEN

"Who in this chamber, sumpteously adornd
Sits on your ivory bed, nor could you say,
By his rich habit, he had fought to-day:
A reveller or masker so comes drest,
From splendid sports returning to his rest.
Thus did love's Queen warmer desires prepare.
But when she saw her neck so heavenly faire,
Her lovely bosome and celestial eyes,
Amazed, to the Goddess, she replies:
Why wilt thou happless me once more betray,
And to another wealthy town convey,
Where some new favourite must, as now at Troy
With utter loss of honour me enjoy."

Iliade (Livre VI).   Salel.

GLAUCUS RESPOND À DIOMÈDE

"Adonc Glaucus, auec grace et audace,
Luy respondit: 'T'enquiers tu de ma race?
Le genre humain est fragile et muable
Comme la fueille et aussi peu durable.

Car tout ainsi qu'on uoit les branches uertes
Sur le printemps de fueilles bien couuertes
Qui par les uents d'automne et la froidure
Tombent de l'arbre et perdent leur uerdure
Puis de rechef la gelée passée,
Il en reuient à la place laissée :
Ne plus ne moins est du lignage humain :
Tel est huy uif qui sera mort demain.
S'il en meurt ung, ung autre reuint naistre.
Voylà comment se conserue leur estre.' "

Iliade (Lib. VI). As in Virgil, Dante, and others.

"Quasim gente rogas?   Quibus et natalibus ortus?
Persimile est foliis hominum genus omne caduciis
Quae nunc nata uides, pulchrisque, uirescere sylvis
Automno ueniente cadunt, simul illa perurens
Incubuit Bóreas : quaedam sub uerna renasci
Tempora, sic uice perpetua succrescere lapsis,
Semper item nova, sic alliis obeuntibus, ultro
Succedunt alii luuenes aetate grauatis.
Quod si forte iuvat te qua sit quisque suorum
Stirpe satus, si natales cognoscere quaeris
Forte meos, referam, quae sunt notissima multis."

Iliade (Livre IX). Salel.

CALYDON

"En Calydon règnoit
Oenéus, ung bon Roy qui donnoit
De ses beaulx Fruictz chascun an les Primices
Aux Immortelz, leur faisant Sacrifices.

Or il aduint (ou bien par son uouloir,
Ou par oubly) qu'il meit à nonchalloir
Diane chaste, et ne luy feit offrande,
Dont elle print Indignation grande
Encontre luy, et pour bien le punir
Feit ung Sanglier dedans ses Champs uenir
Horrible et fier qui luy feit grand dommage
Tuant les Gens et gastant le Fruictage.
Maintz beaulx Pomiers, maintz Arbres reuestuz
De Fleur et Fruict, en furent abattuz,
Et de la Dent aguisée et poinctue,
Le Bléd gasté et la Vigne tortue.
Méléager, le Filz de ce bon Roy,
Voyant ainsi le piteux Désarroy
De son Pays et de sa Gent troublée
Proposa lors de faire une Assemblée
De bons Veneurs et Leutiers pour chasser
L'horrible Beste et sa Mort pourchasser.
Ce qui fut faict. Maintes Gens l'y trouvèrent
Qui contre luy ses Forces éprouvèrent;
Mais à la fin le Sanglier inhumain
Receut la Mort de sa Royale Main.
Estant occis, deux grandes Nations
Pour la Dépouille eurent Contentions
Les Curetois disoient la mériter,
Ceulx d'Etolie en uouloient hériter."

Iliade (Livre X). Salel.

THE BATHERS

"Quand Ulysses fut en la riche tente
Du compaignon, alors il diligente

De bien lier ses cheuaulx et les loge
Soigneusement dedans la même loge
Et au rang même ou la belle monture
Du fort Gregeois mangeoit pain et pasture
Quand aux habitz de Dolon, il les pose
Dedans la nef, sur la poupe et propose
En faire ung jour à Pallas sacrifice,
Et luy offrir à jamais son seruice
Bien tost après, ces deux Grecs de ualeur
Se cognoissant oppresséz de chaleur,
Et de sueur, dedans la mer entrèrent
Pour se lauer, et très bien so frotèrent
Le col, le dos, les jambes et les cuisses,
Ostant du corps toutes les immondices,
Estans ainsi refreichiz et bien netz,
Dedans des baingz souefs bien ordonnéz,
S'en sont entréz, et quand leurs corps
Ont esté oinctz d'huyle par le dehors.
Puis sont allez manger prians Minerue
Qu'en tous leurs faictz les dirige et conserue
En respandant du uin à pleine tasse,
(pour sacrifice) au milieu de la place."

II. ANDREAS DIVUS

In the year of grace 1906, '08, or '10 I picked from
the Paris quais a Latin version of the *Odyssey* by Andreas Divus Justinopolitanus (Parisiis, In officina Chris-
tiani Wecheli, M, D, XXXVIII), the volume containing
also the Batrachomyomachia, by Aldus Manutius, and
the "Hymni Deorum" rendered by Georgius Dartona
Cretensis. I lost a Latin *Iliads* for the economy of four
francs, these coins being at that time scarcer with me

than they ever should be with any man of my tastes
and abilities.

In 1911 the Italian savant, Signore E. Teza, published
his note, "Quale fosse la Casata di Andreas Divus Justinopolitanus?" This question I am unable to answer,
nor do I greatly care by what name Andreas was known
in the privacy of his life: Signore Dio, Signore Divino,
or even Mijnheer van Gott may have served him as
patronymic. Sannazaro, author of *De Partu Virginis*,
and also of the epigram ending *hanc et sugere,* translated himself as Sanctus Nazarenus; I am myself known
as Signore Sterlina to James Joyce's children, while the
phonetic translation of my name into the Japanese tongue
is so indecorous that I am seriously advised not to use
it, lest it do me harm in Nippon. (Rendered back *ad
verbum* into our maternal speech it gives for its meaning, "This picture of a phallus costs ten yen." There is
no surety in shifting personal names from one idiom
to another.)

Justinopolis is identified as Capodistria; what matters
is Divus' text. We find for the "Nekuia" (*Odys.* xi):
"At postquam ad navem descendimus, et mare,

Nauem quidem primum deduximus in mare diuum,

Et malum posuimus et vela in navi nigra:

Intro autem oues accipientes ire fecimus, intro et ipsi

Iuimus dolentes, huberes lachrymas fundentes:

Nobis autem a tergo navis nigræ proræ

Prosperum ventum imisit pandentem velum bonum
        amicum

Circe benecomata gravis Dea altiloqua.

Nos autem arma singula expedientes in navi

Sedebamus: hanc autem ventusque gubernatorque
        dirigebat:

Huius at per totum diem extensa sunt vela pontum
    transientis:
Occidit tunc Sol, ombratæ sunt omnes viæ:
Hæc autem in fines pervenit profundi Oceani:
Illic autem Cimmeriorum virorum populusque civi-
    tasque,
Caligine et nebula cooperti, neque unquam ipsos
Sol lucidus aspicit radiis,
Neque quando tendit ad cœlum stellatum,
Neque quando retro in terram a cœlo vertitur:
Sed nox pernitiosa extenditur miseris hominibus:
Navem quidem illuc venientes traximus, extra autem
    oves
Accepimus: ipsi autem rursus apud fluxum Oceani
Iuimus, ut in locum perveniremus quem dixit Circe:
Hic sacra quidem Perimedes Eurylochusque
Faciebant: ego autem ensem acutum trahens a fœmore,
Foveam fodi quantum cubiti mensura hinc et inde:
Circum ipsam autem libamina fundimus omnibus mor-
    tuis;
Primum mulso, postea autem dulci vino:
Tertio rursus aqua, et farinas albas miscui:
Multum autem oravi mortuorum infirma capita:
Profectus in Ithicam, sterilem bovem, quæ optima
    esset,
Sacrificare in domibus, pyramque implere bonis:
Tiresiæ autem seorsum ovem sacrificare vovi
Totam nigram, quæ ovibus antecellat nostris:
Has autem postquam votis precationibusque gentes
    mortuorum
Precatus sum, oves autem accipiens obtruncavi:
In fossam fluebat autem sanguis niger, congregatæque
    sunt
Animæ ex Erebo cadaverum mortuorum,

Nymphæque iuvenesque et multa passi senes,
Virginesque teneræ, nuper flebilem animum habentes,
Multi autem vulnerati æreis lanceis
Viri in bello necati, cruenta arma habentes,
Qui multi circum foveam veniebant aliunde alius
Magno clamore, me autem pallidus timor cepit.
Iam postea socios hortans iussi
Pecora, quæ iam iacebant iugulata sævo ære,
Excoriantes combuere: supplicare autem Diis,
Fortique Plutoni, et laudatæ Proserpinæ.
At ego ensem acutum trahens a foemore,
Sedi, neque permisi mortuorum impotentia capita
Sanguinem prope ire, antequam Tiresiam audirem:
Prima autem anima Elpenoris venit socii:
Nondum enim sepultus erat sub terra lata,
Corpus enim in domo Circes reliquimus nos
Infletum et insepultum, quoniam labor alius urgebat:
Hunc quidem ego lachrymatus sum videns, misertusque
    sum aio,
Et ipsum clamando verba velocia allocutus sum:
  Elpenor, quomodo venisti sub caliginem obscuram:
Prævenisti pedes existens quam ego in navi nigra?
  Sic dixi: hic autem mini lugens respondit verbo:
Nobilis Laertiade, prudens Ulysse,
Nocuit mihi dei fatum malum, et multum vinum:
Circes autem in domo dormiens, non animadverti
Me retrogradum descendere eundo per scalam longam,
Sed contra murum cecidi ast autem mihi cervix
Nervorum fracta est, anima autem in infernum
    descendit:
Nunc autem his qui venturi sunt postea precor non
    præsentibus
Per uxorem et patrem, qui educavit parvum existentem,
Telemachumque quem solum in domibus reliquisti.

Scio enim quod hinc iens domo ex inferni
Insulam in Æaeam impellens benefabricatam navim:
Tunc te postea Rex iubeo recordari mei
Ne me infletum, insepultum, abiens retro, relinquas
Separatus, ne deorum ira fiam
Sed me combure con armis quæcunque mihi sunt,
Sepulchramque mihi accumula cani in litore maris,
Viri infelicis, et cuius apud posteros fama sit:
Hæcque mihi perfice, figeque in sepulchro remum,
Quo et vivus remigabam existens cum meis sociis.
    Sic dixit: at ego ipsum, respondens, allocutus sum:
Hæc tibi infelix perficiamque et faciam:
Nos quidem sic verbis respondentes molestis
Sedebamus: ego quidem seperatim supra sanguinem
        ensem tenebam:
Idolum autem ex altera parte socii multa loquebatur:
Venit autem insuper anima matris mortuæ
Autolyci filia magnanimi Anticlea,
Quam vivam dereliqui iens ad Ilium sacrum,
Hac quidem ego lachrymatus sum videns miseratusque
        sum aio:
Sed neque sic sivi priorem licet valde dolens
Sanguinem prope ire, antequam Tiresiam audirem:
Venit autem insuper anima Thebani Tiresiæ,
Aureum sceptrum tenens, me autem novit et allocuta
        est:
Cur iterum o infelix linquens lumen Solis
Venisti, ut videas mortuos, et iniucundam regionem?
Sed recede a fossa, remove autem ensem acutum,
Sanguinem ut bibam, et tibi vera dicam.
    Sic dixi: ego autem retrocedens, ensem argenteum
Vagina inclusi: hic autem postquam bibit sanguinem
        nigrum,
Et tunc iam me verbis allocutus est vates verus:

Reditum quæris dulcem illustris Ulysse:
Hanc autem tibi difficilem faciet Deus, non enim
    puto
Latere Neptunum, quam iram imposuit animo
Iratus, quem ei filium dilectum excæcasti:
    Sed tamen et sic mala licet passi pervenientis,
    Si volveris tuum animum continere et sociorum."

The meaning of the passage is, with a few abbrevia-
tions, as I have interpolated it in my Third Canto.

"And then went down to the ship, set keel to breakers,
  Forth on the godly sea,
We set up mast and sail on the swart ship,
Sheep bore we aboard her, and our bodies also,
Heavy with weeping; and winds from sternward
Bore us out onward with bellying canvas,
Circe's this craft, the trim-coifed goddess.
Then sat we amidships—wind jamming the tiller—
Thus with stretched sail we went over sea till day's end.
Sun to his slumber, shadows o'er all the ocean,
Came we then to the bounds of deepest water,
To the Kimmerian lands and peopled cities
Covered with close-webbed mist, unpierced ever
With glitter of sun-rays,
Nor with stars stretched, nor looking back from heaven,
Swartest night stretched over wretched men there,
The ocean flowing backward, came we then to the place
Aforesaid by Circe.
Here did they rites, Perimedes and Eurylochus,
And drawing sword from my hip
I dug the ell-square pitkin,
Poured we libations unto each the dead,

First mead and then sweet wine, water mixed with
    white flour,
Then prayed I many a prayer to the sickly death's-
    heads,
As set in Ithaca, sterile bulls of the best
For sacrifice, heaping the pyre with goods.
Sheep, to Tiresias only; black and a bell sheep.
Dark blood flowed in the fosse,
Souls out of Erebus, cadaverous dead,
Of brides, of youths, and of much-bearing old;
Virgins tender, souls stained with recent tears,
Many men mauled with bronze lance-heads,
Battle spoil, bearing yet dreary arms,
These many crowded about me,
With shouting, pallor upon me, cried to my men for
    more beasts.
Slaughtered the herds, sheep slain of bronze,
Poured ointment, cried to the gods,
To Pluto the strong, and praised Proserpine,
Unsheathed the narrow sword,
I sat to keep off the impetuous, impotent dead
Till I should hear Tiresias.
But first Elpenor came, our friend Elpenor,
Unburied, cast on the wide earth,
Limbs that we left in the house of Circe,
Unwept, unwrapped in sepulchre, since toils urged
    other.
Pitiful spirit, and I cried in hurried speech:
'Elpenor, how art thou come to this dark coast?
Cam'st thou a-foot, outstripping seamen?'
                    And he in heavy speech:
'Ill fate and abundant wine! I slept in Circe's ingle,
Going down the long ladder unguarded, I fell against
    the buttress,

Shattered the nape-nerve, the soul sought Avernus.
But thou, O King, I bid remember me, unwept, unburied,
Heap up mine arms, be tomb by sea-board, and inscribed:
"A man of no fortune and with a name to come."
And set my oar up, that I swung mid fellows.'
Came then another ghost, whom I beat off, Anticlea,
And then Tiresias, Theban,
Holding his golden wand, knew me and spoke first:
'Man of ill hour, why come a second time,
Leaving the sunlight, facing the sunless dead, and this joyless region?
Stand from the fosse, move back, leave me my bloody bever,
And I will speak you true speeches.'
                                   And I stepped back,
Sheathing the yellow sword. Dark blood he drank then,
And spoke: 'Lustrous Odysseus
Shalt return through spiteful Neptune, over dark seas,
Lose all companions.' Foretold me the ways and the signs.
Came then Anticlea, to whom I answered:
'Fate drives me on through these deeps. I sought Tiresias,'
Told her the news of Troy. And thrice her shadow
Faded in my embrace."

It takes no more Latin than I have to know that Divus'
Latin is not the Latin of Catulius and Ovid; that it is
illepidus to chuck Latin nominative participles about in
such profusion; that Romans did not use *habentes* as the
Greeks used ἔχοντες, etc. And *nos* in line 53 is un-

necessary. Divus' Latin has, despite these wems, its
quality; it is even singable, there are constant suggestions
of the poetic motion; it is very simple Latin, after all,
and a crib of this sort may make just the difference of
permitting a man to read fast enough to get the swing
and mood of the subject, instead of losing both in a
dictionary.

Even *habentes* when one has made up one's mind to
it, together with less obvious exoticisms, does not upset
one as

"the steep of Delphos leaving."

One is, of necessity, more sensitive to botches in one's
own tongue than to botches in another, however carefully learned.

For all the fuss about Divus' errors of elegance
Samuelis Clarkius and Jo. Augustus Ernestus do not
seem to have gone him much better—with two hundred
years extra Hellenic scholarship at their disposal.

The first Aldine Greek Iliads appeared I think in
1504, Odyssey possibly later.* My edition of Divus is
of 1538, and as it contains Aldus' own translation of the
Frog-fight, it may indicate that Divus was in touch with
Aldus in Italy, or quite possibly the French edition is
pirated from an earlier Italian printing. A Latin
Odyssey in some sort of verse was at that time infinitely worth doing.

Raphael of Volterra had done a prose Odyssey with
the opening lines of several books and a few other brief

---

* My impression is that I saw an Iliad by Andreas Divus on
the Quais in Paris, at the time I found his version of the Odyssey, but an impression of this sort is, after eight years, un-
trustworthy, it may have been only a Latin Iliad in similar
binding.

passages in verse. This was printed with Laurenzo
Valla's prose Iliads as early as 1502. He begins:

"Dic mihi musa virum captæ post tempora Troiae
Qui mores hominum multorum vidit et urbes
Multa quoque et ponto passus dum naufragus errat
Ut sibi tum sotiis (sociis) vitam servaret in alto
Non tamen hos cupiens fato deprompsit acerbo."

Probably the source of "Master Watson's" English
quantitative couplet, but obviously not copied by Divus:

"Virum mihi dic musa multiscium qui valde multum
Erravit ex quo Troiae sacram urbem depopulatus est:
Multorum autem virorum vidit urbes et mentem
    cognovit:
Multos autem hic in mare passus est dolores, suo in
    animo,
Liberans suamque animam et reditum sociorum."

On the other hand, it is nearly impossible to believe
that Clark and Ernestus were unfamiliar with Divus.
Clark calls his Latin crib a composite "non elegantem
utique et venustam, sed ita Romanam, ut verbis verba."
A good deal of Divus' *venustas* has departed. Clark's
hyphenated compounds are, I think, no more Roman
than are some of Divus' coinage; they may be a trifle
more explanatory, but if we read a shade more of color
into ἀθέσφατος οἶνος than we can into *multum vinum*,
it is not restored to us in Clark's *copiosum vinum*, nor
does *terra spatiosa* improve upon *terra lata*, εὐρυδείης
being (if anything more than *lata*): "with wide ways or
streets," the wide ways of the world, traversable, open
to wanderers. The participles remain in Clark-Ernestus,

many of the coined words remain unchanged. Georgius
Dartona gives, in the opening of the second hymn to
Aphrodite:

"Venerandam auream coronam habentem pulchram
        Venerem
  Canam, quae totius Cypri munimenta sortita est
  Maritimae ubi illam zephyri vis molliter spirantis
  Suscitavit per undam multisoni maris,
  Spuma in molli: hanc autem auricurae Horae
  Susceperunt hilariter, immortales autem vestes in-
        duere:
  Capite vero super immortali coronam bene construc-
        tam posuere
  Pulchram, auream: tribus autem ansis
  Donum orichalchi aurique honorabilis:
  Collum autem molle, ac pectora argentea
  Monilibus aureis ornabant . . ." etc.

Ernestus, adding by himself the appendices to the Epics,
gives us:

"Venerandam auream coronam habentem pulchram
        Venerem
  Canam, quae totius Cypri munimenta sortita est
  Maritimae, ubi illam zephyri vis molliter spirantis
  Tulit per undam multisoni maris
  Spuma in molli: hanc autem auro comam religatae
        Horae
  Susceperunt hilariter, immortales autem vestes in-
        duere:
  Caput autem super immortale coronam bene construc-
        tam posuere

Pulchram, auream, perforatis autem auriculis
Donum orichalci preciosi:
Collum autem molle ac pectora candida *
Monilibus aureis ornabant . . ." etc.

"Which things since they are so" lead us to feel that
we would have had no less respect for Messrs. Clarkius
and Ernestus if they had deigned to mention the names
of their predecessors. They have not done this in their
prefaces, and if any mention is made of the sixteenth-
century scholars, it is very effectually buried somewhere
in the voluminous Latin notes, which I have not gone
through *in toto*. Their edition (Glasgow, 1814) is, however, most serviceable.

TRANSLATION OF AESCHYLUS

A SEARCH for Aeschylus in English is deadly, ac-
cursed, mind-rending. Browning has "done" the Agamemnon, or "done the Agamemnon in the eye" as the
critic may choose to consider. He has written a modest
and an apparently intelligent preface:
"I should hardly look for an impossible transmission
of the reputed magniloquence and sonority of the Greek;
and this with the less regret, inasmuch as there is abundant musicality elsewhere, but nowhere else than in his
poem the ideas of the poet."
He quotes Matthew Arnold on the Greeks: "their expression is so excellent, because it is so simple and so
well subordinated, because it draws its force directly
from the pregnancy of the matter which it conveys . . .
not a word wasted, not a sentiment capriciously thrown
in, stroke on stroke."

* Reading ἀργυφέοισιν, variant ἀργυρέοισιν, offered in footnote.
In any case *argentea* is closer than *candida*.

He is reasonable about the Greek spelling. He points
out that γόνον ἰδὼν κάλλιστον ἀνδρῶν sounds very poorly
as "Seeing her son the fairest of men" but is out-
shouted in "Remirando il figliuolo bellissimo degli
uomini," and protests his fidelity to the meaning of
Aeschylus.

His weakness in this work is where it essentially lay
in all of his expression, it rests in the term "ideas"—
"Thought" as Browning understood it—"ideas" as the
term is current, are poor two dimensional stuff, a scant,
scratch covering. "Damn ideas, anyhow." An idea is
only an imperfect induction from fact.

The solid, the "last atom of force verging off into the
first atom of matter" is the force, the emotion, the objective sight of the poet. In the Agamemnon it is the
whole rush of the action, the whole wildness of Kassandra's continual shrieking, the flash of the beacon fires
burning unstinted wood, the outburst of

Τροίαν Αχαιῶν οὖσαν,

or the later

Τροίαν 'Αχαιοὶ τῆδ' ἔχουσ' ἐν ἡτέρα.

"Troy is the greeks'." Even Rossetti has it better than
Browning: "Troy's down, tall Troy's on fire," anything,
literally anything that can be shouted, that can be
shouted uncontrolledly and hysterically. "Troy is the
Greeks'" is an ambiguity for the ear. "Know that our
men are in Ilion."

Anything but a stilted unsayable jargon. Yet with
Browning we have

"Troia the Achaioi hold," and later,

"Troia do the Achaioi hold," followed by:

> "this same day
> I think a noise—no mixture—reigns i' the city
> Sour wine and unguent pour thou in one vessel——"

And it does not end here. In fact it reaches the nadir of its bathos in a later speech of Klutaimnestra in the line

"The perfect man his home perambulating!"

We may add several exclamation points to the one which Mr. Browning has provided. But then all translation is a thankless, or is at least most apt to be a thankless and desolate undertaking.

What Browning had not got into his sometimes excellent top-knot was the patent, or what should be the patent fact that inversions of sentence order in an uninflected language like English are not, simply and utterly *are not* any sort of equivalent for inversions and perturbations of order in a language inflected as Greek and Latin are inflected. That is the chief source of his error. In these inflected languages order has other currents than simple sequence of subject, predicate, object; and all sorts of departures from this Franco-English natural position are in Greek and Latin neither confusing nor delaying; they may be both simple and emphatic, they do not obstruct one's apperception of the verbal relations.

Obscurities *not inherent in* the matter, obscurities due not to the thing but to the wording, are a botch, and are *not* worth preserving in a translation. The work lives not by them but despite them.

Rossetti is in this matter sounder than Browning, when he says that the only thing worth bringing over is the beauty of the original; and despite Rossetti's purple plush and molasses trimmings he meant by "beauty" something fairly near what we mean by the "emotional intensity" of his original.

Obscurities inherent in the thing occur when the author is piercing, or trying to pierce into, uncharted regions; when he is trying to express things not yet current, not yet worn into phrase; when he is ahead of the emotional, or philosophic sense (as a painter might be ahead of the color-sense) of his contemporaries.

As for the word-sense and phrase-sense, we still hear workmen and peasants and metropolitan bus-riders repeating the simplest sentences three and four times, back and forth between interlocutors: trying to get the sense "I sez to Bill, I'm goin' to 'Arrow" or some other such subtlety from one occiput into another.

"You sez to Bill, etc."

"Yus, I sez . . . etc."

"O!"

The first day's search at the Museum reveals "Aeschylus" printed by Aldus in 1518; by Stephanus in 1557, no English translation before 1777, a couple in the 1820's, more in the middle of the century, since 1880 past counting, and no promising names in the list. Sophocles falls to Jebb and does not appear satisfactory.

From which welter one returns thankfully to the Thomas Stanley Greek and Latin edition, with Saml. Butler's notes, Cambridge, "typis ac sumptibus academicis," 1811—once a guinea or half a guinea per volume, half leather, but now mercifully, since people no

longer read Latin, picked up at 2s. for the set (eight
volumes in all), rather less than the price of their
postage. Quartos in excellent type.

Browning shows himself poet in such phrases as "dust,
mud's thirsty brother," which is easy, perhaps, but is
English, even Browning's own particular English, as
"dust, of mud brother thirsty," would not be English
at all; and if I have been extremely harsh in dealing
with the first passage quoted it is still undisputable that
I have read Browning off and on for seventeen years
with no small pleasure and admiration, and am one of
the few people who know anything about his Sordello,
and have never read his Agamemnon, have not even
now when it falls into a special study been able to get
through his Agamemnon.

Take another test passage:

Οὗτός ἐσιν Ἀγαμέμνων, ἐμὸs
Πόσιs, νεκρὸs δέ τῆσδε δεξιᾶs χερόs
Ἔργον δικαίναs τέκτονοs. Τάδ' ὧδ ἔχει. 1415

"Hicce est Agamemnon, maritus
Meus, hac dextra mortuus,
Facinus justae artificis. Haec ita se habent."

We turn to Browning and find:

"—this man is Agamemnon,
My husband, dead, the work of this right hand here,
Aye, of a just artificer: so things are."

To the infinite advantage of the Latin, and the complete explanation of why Browning's Aeschylus, to say
nothing of forty other translations of Aeschylus, is un-
readable.

Any bungling translation:

> "This is Agamemnon,
> My husband,
> Dead by this hand,
> And a good job.   These, gentlemen, are the facts."

No, that is extreme, but the point is that any natural wording, anything which keeps the mind off theatricals and on Klutaimnestra actual, dealing with an actual situation, and not pestering the reader with frills and festoons of language, is worth all the convoluted tushery that the Victorians can heap together.

I can conceive no improvement on the Latin, it saves by *dextra* for δεξιᾶς χερός, it loses a few letters in "se habent," but it has the same drive as the Greek.

The Latin can be a whole commentary on the Greek, or at least it can give one the whole parsing and order, and let one proceed at a comfortable rate with but the most rudimentary knowledge of the original language. And I do not think this a trifle; it would be an ill day if men again let the classics go by the board; we should fall into something worse than, or as bad as, the counter-reformation: a welter of gum-shoes, and cocoa, and Y. M. C. A. and Webbs, and social theorizing committees, and the general hell of a groggy doctrinaire obfuscation; and the very disagreeablizing of the classics, every pedagogy which puts the masterwork further from us, either by obstructing the schoolboy, or breeding affectation in dilettante readers, works toward such a detestable end.   I do not know that strict logic will cover all of the matter, or that I can formulate anything beyond a belief that we test a translation by the feel, and particularly by the feel of being in contact with the force of a great original, and it does not seem to me that one can open this Latin text of the Agamemnon without getting such sense of contact:

"Mox sciemus lampadum luciferarum 498
 Signorumque per faces et ignis vices,
 An vere sint, an somniorum instar,
 Gratum veniens illud lumen eluserit animum nostrum.
 Praeconem hunc a littore video obumbratum
 Ramis olivae: testatur autem haec mihi frater
 Luti socius aridus pulvis,
 Quod neque mutus, neque accendens facem
 Materiae montanae signa dabit per fumum ignis."

or

"Apollo, Apollo! 1095
 Agyieu Apollo mi!
 Ah! quo me tandem duxisti? ad qualem domum?

 . . . . . .

"Heu, heu, ecce, ecce, cohibe a vacca 1134
 Taurum: vestibus involens
 Nigricornem machina
 Percutit; cadit vero in aquali vase.
 Insidiosi lebetis casum ut intelligas velim.

 . . . . . .

Heu, heu, argutae lusciniae fatum *mihi tribuis:*

 . . . . . .

"Heu nuptiae, nuptiae Paridis exitiales 1165
 Amicis! eheu Scamandri patria unda!"

All this howling of Kassandra comes at one from the page, and the grimness also of the Iambics:

 "Ohime! lethali intus percussus sum vulnere." 1352
 "Tace: quis clamat vulnus lethaliter vulneratus?"

"Ohime! iterum secundo ictu sauciatus."
"Patrari facinus mihi videtur regis ex ejulatu.   1355
"At tuta communicemus consilia."
"Ego quidem vobis meam dico sententiam," etc.

Here or in the opening of the play, or where you
like in this Latin, we are at once in contact with the
action, something real is going on, we are keen and
curious on the instant, but I cannot get any such impact
from any part of the Browning.

"In bellum nuptam,
    Auctricem que contentionum, Helenam: 695
    Quippe quae congruenter
    Perditrix navium, perditrix virorum, perditrix urbium.
    E delicatis
    Thalami ornamentis navigavit
    Zephyri terrigenae aura.
    Et numerosi scutiferi,
    Venatores secundum vestigia,
    Remorum inapparentia
    Appulerunt ad Simoentis ripas
    Foliis abundantes
    Ob jurgium cruentum."

"War-wed, author of strife,
    Fitly Helen, destroyer of ships, of men,
    Destroyer of cities,
    From delicate-curtained room
    Sped by land breezes.

"Swift the shields on your track,
    Oars on the unseen traces,
    And leafy Simois

Gone red with blood." *

Contested Helen, 'Αμφινεικῆ.

"War-wed, contested,
  (Fitly) Helen, destroyer of ships; of men;
Destroyer of cities,

"From the delicate-curtained room
  Sped by land breezes.

"Swift on the shields on your track,
  Oars on the unseen traces.

"Red leaves in Simois!"

"Rank flower of love, for Troy."

"Quippe leonem educavit . . .   726
  Mansuetum, pueris amabilem . . .
  . . . divinitus sacerdos Ates (i.e. Paris)
  In aedibus enutritus est.

"Statim igitur venit   746
  Ad urbem Ilii,
  Ut ita dicam, animus
  Tranquillae serenitatis, placidum
  Divitiarum ornamentum
  Blandum oculourum telum,

* "H. D.'s" translations from Euripides should be mentioned
either here or in connection with "The New Poetry"; she has
obtained beautiful strophes for First Chorus of Iphigenia in
Aulis, 1-4 and 9, and for the first of the second chorus. Elsewhere she retains certain needless locutions, and her versification permits too many dead stops in its current.

Animum pungens flos amoris
(*Helena*) accubitura. Perfecit autem
Nuptiarum acerbos exitus,
Mala vicina, malaque socia,
Irruens in Priamidas,
Ductu Jovis Hospitalis,
Erinnys luctuosa sponsis."

It seems to me that English translators have gone wide
in two ways, first in trying to keep every adjective, when
obviously many adjectives in the original have only
melodic value, secondly they have been deaved with syntax; have wasted time, involved their English, trying
first to evolve a definite logical structure for the Greek
and secondly to preserve it, *and all its grammatical relations,* in English.

One might almost say that Aeschylus' Greek is agglu-
tinative, that his general drive, especially in choruses, is
merely to remind the audience of the events of the Trojan war; that syntax is subordinate, and duly subordinated, left out, that he is not austere, but often even verbose after a fashion (not Euripides' fashion).

A reading version might omit various things which
would be of true service only if the English were actually
to be sung on a stage, or chanted to the movements of
the choric dance or procession.

Above suggestions should *not* be followed with intem-
perance. But certainly more sense and less syntax (good
or bad) in translations of Aeschylus might be a relief.

Chor. Anapest:
"O iniquam Helenam. una quae multas,   1464
Multas admodum animas
Perdidisti ad Trojam!
Nunc vero nobilem memorabilem *(Agam. animam),*

Deflorasti per caedem inexpiabilem.
Talis erat tunc in aedibus
Eris viri domitrix aerumna."

Clytemnestra:
"Nequaquam mortis sortem exopta   1470
Hisce gravatus;
Neque in Helenam iram convertas,
Tanquam viriperdam, ac si una multorum
Virorum animas Graecorum perdens,
Intolerabilem dolorem effecerit."

.   .   .   .   .   .

Clytemnestra:
"Mortem haud indignam arbitrar   1530
Huic contigisse:
Neque enim ille insidiosam cladem
Aedibus intulit; sed meum ex ipso
Germen sublatum, multum defletam
Iphigeniam cum indigne affecerit,
Digna passus est, nihil in inferno
Glorietur, gladio inflicta
Morte luens quae prior perpetravit."

"Death not unearned, nor yet a novelty in this house;
Let him make talk in hell concerning Iphigenia."

(If we allow the last as ironic equivalent of the literal
"let him not boast in hell.")
   "He gets but a thrust once given (by him)
     Back-pay, for Iphigenia."

One can further condense the English but at the cost of
  obscurity.

Morshead is bearable in Clytemnestra's description of the beacons.

"From Ida's top Hephaestos, Lord of fire,
Sent forth his sign, and on, and ever on,
Beacon to beacon sped the courier-flame
From Ida to the crag, that Hermes loves
On Lemnos; thence into the steep sublime
Of Athos, throne of Zeus, the broad blaze flared.
Thence, raised aloft to shoot across the sea
The moving light, rejoicing in its strength
Sped from the pyre of pine, and urged its way,
In golden glory, like some strange new sun,
Onward and reached Macistus' watching heights."

IX

THE CHINESE WRITTEN CHARACTER AS A MEDIUM FOR POETRY

BY ERNEST FENOLLOSA

[*This essay was practically finished by the late Ernest Fenollosa; I have done little more than remove a few repetitions and shape a few sentences.*

We have here not a bare philological discussion, but a study of the fundamentals of all æsthetics. In his search through unknown art Fenollosa, coming upon unknown motives and principles unrecognized in the West, was already led into many modes of thought since fruitful in "new" western painting and poetry. He was a forerunner without knowing it and without being known as such.

*He discerned principles of writing which he had scarcely time to put into practice. In Japan he restored, or greatly helped to restore, a respect for the native art. In America and Europe he cannot be looked upon as a mere searcher after exotics. His mind was constantly filled with parallels and comparisons between eastern and western art. To him the exotic was always a means of fructification. He looked to an American renaissance. The vitality of his outlook can be judged from the fact that although this essay was written some time before his death in 1908 I have not had to change the allusions to western conditions. The later movements in art have corroborated his theories.—*EZRA POUND.]

THIS twentieth century not only turns a new page in the book of the world, but opens another and a startling chapter. Vistas of strange futures unfold for man, of world-embracing cultures half weaned from Europe, of hitherto undreamed responsibilities for nations and races.

The Chinese problem alone is so vast that no nation can afford to ignore it. We in America, especially, must face it across the Pacific, and master it or it will master us. And the only way to master it is to strive with patient sympathy to understand the best, the most hopeful and the most human elements in it.

It is unfortunate that England and America have so long ignored or mistaken the deeper problems of Oriental culture. We have misconceived the Chinese for a materialistic people, for a debased and worn-out race. We have belittled the Japanese as a nation of copyists. We have stupidly assumed that Chinese history affords no glimpse of change in social evolution, no salient epoch of moral and spiritual crisis. We have denied the essential humanity of these peoples; and we have toyed with their ideals as if they were no better than comic songs in an "opera bouffe."

The duty that faces us is not to batter down their forts or to exploit their markets, but to study and to come to sympathize with their humanity and their generous aspirations. Their type of cultivation has been high. Their harvest of recorded experience doubles our own. The Chinese have been idealists, and experimenters in the making of great principles; their history opens a world of lofty aim and achievement, parallel to that of the ancient Mediterranean peoples. We need their best ideals to supplement our own—ideals enshrined in their art, in their literature and in the tragedies of their lives.

We have already seen proof of the vitality and practical value of oriental painting for ourselves and as a key to the eastern soul. It may be worth while to approach their literature, the intensest part of it, their poetry, even in an imperfect manner.

I feel that I should perhaps apologize * for presuming to follow that series of brilliant scholars, Davis, Legge, St. Denys and Giles, who have treated the subject of Chinese poetry with a wealth of erudition to which I can proffer no claim. It is not as a professional linguist nor as a sinologue that I humbly put forward what I have to say. As an enthusiastic student of beauty in Oriental culture, having spent a large portion of my years in close relation with Orientals, I could not but breathe in something of the poetry incarnated in their lives.

I have been for the most part moved to my temerity by personal considerations. An unfortunate belief has spread both in England and in America that Chinese and Japanese poetry are hardly more than an amusement, trivial, childish, and not to be reckoned in the world's serious literary performance. I have heard well-known sinologues state that, save for the purposes of professional linguistic scholarship, these branches of poetry are fields too barren to repay the toil necessary for their cultivation.

Now my own impression has been so radically and diametrically opposed to such a conclusion, that a sheer enthusiasm of generosity has driven me to wish to share with other Occidentals my newly discovered joy. Either I am pleasingly self-deceived in my positive delight, or else there must be some lack of æsthetic sympathy and of poetic feeling in the accepted methods of presenting the poetry of China. I submit my causes of joy.

Failure or success in presenting any alien poetry in English must depend largely upon poetic workmanship in the chosen medium. It was perhaps too much to

* [*The apology was unnecessary, but Professor Fenollosa saw fit to make it, and I therefore transcribe his words.—E. P.*]

expect that aged scholars who had spent their youth in gladiatorial combats with the refractory Chinese characters should succeed also as poets. Even Greek verse might have fared equally ill had its purveyors been perforce content with provincial standards of English rhyming. Sinologues should remember that the purpose of poetical translation is the poetry, not the verbal definitions in dictionaries.

One modest merit I may, perhaps, claim for my work: it represents for the first time a Japanese school of study in Chinese culture. Hitherto Europeans have been somewhat at the mercy of contemporary Chinese scholarship. Several centuries ago China lost much of her creative self, and of her insight into the causes of her own life, but her original spirit still lives, grows, interprets, transferred to Japan in all its original freshness. The Japanese to-day represent a stage of culture roughly corresponding to that of China under the Sung dynasty. I have been fortunate in studying for many years as a private pupil under Professor Kainan Mori, who is probably the greatest living authority on Chinese poetry. He has recently been called to a chair in the Imperial University of Tokio.

My subject is poetry, not language, yet the roots of poetry are in language. In the study of a language so alien in form to ours as is Chinese in its written character, it is necessary to inquire how those universal elements of form which constitute poetics can derive appropriate nutriment.

In what sense can verse, written in terms of visible hieroglyphics, be reckoned true poetry? It might seem that poetry, which like music is a *time art*, weaving its unities out of successive impressions of sound, could with difficulty assimilate a verbal medium consisting largely of semi-pictorial appeals to the eye.

Contrast, for example, Gray's line:

The curfew tolls the knell of parting day

with the Chinese line:

Moon   Rays   Like   Pure   Snow

Moon rays like pure snow.

Unless the sound of the latter be given, what have they in common? It is not enough to adduce that each contains a certain body of prosaic meaning; for the question is, how can the Chinese line imply, *as form,* the very element that distinguishes poetry from prose?

On second glance, it is seen that the Chinese words, though visible, occur in just as necessary an order as the phonetic symbols of Gray. All that poetic form requires is a regular and flexible sequence, as plastic as thought itself. The characters may be seen and read, silently by the eye, one after the other:

Moon rays like pure snow.

Perhaps we do not always sufficiently consider that thought is successive, not through some accident or weakness of our subjective operations but because the operations of nature are successive. The transferences of force from agent to object which constitute natural phenomena, occupy time. Therefore, a reproduction of them in imagination requires the same temporal order.*

* [Style, that is to say, limpidity, as opposed to rhetoric.— E. P.]

Suppose that we look out of a window and watch a man. Suddenly he turns his head and actively fixes his attention upon something. We look ourselves and see that his vision has been focussed upon a horse. We saw, first, the man before he acted; second, while he acted; third, the object toward which his action was directed. In speech we split up the rapid continuity of this action and of its picture into its three essential parts or joints in the right order, and say:

Man sees horse.

It is clear that these three joints, or words, are only three phonetic symbols, which stand for the three terms of a natural process. But we could quite as easily denote these three stages of our thought by symbols equally arbitrary, *which had no basis in sound;* for example, by three Chinese characters:

Man   Sees   Horse

If we all knew *what division* of this mental horse-picture each of these signs stood for, we could communicate continuous thought to one another as easily by drawing them as by speaking words. We habitually employ the visible language of gesture in much this same manner.

But Chinese notation is something much more than arbitrary symbols. It is based upon a vivid shorthand picture of the operations of nature. In the algebraic figure and in the spoken word there is no natural connection between thing and sign: all depends upon sheer convention. But the Chinese method follows natural suggestion. First stands the man on his two legs. Second, his eye moves through space: a bold figure represented by running legs under an eye, a modified picture of an eye, a modified picture of running legs but unforgettable once you have seen it. Third stands the horse on his four legs.

The thought picture is not only called up by these signs as well as by words but far more vividly and concretely. Legs belong to all three characters: they are *alive*. The group holds something of the quality of a continuous moving picture.

The untruth of a painting or a photograph is that, in spite of its concreteness, it drops the element of natural succession.

Contrast the Laocoon statue with Browning's lines:

"I sprang to the saddle, and Jorris, and he

.   .   .   .   .   .

And into the midnight we galloped abreast."

One superiority of verbal poetry as an art rests in its getting back to the fundamental reality of *time*. Chinese poetry has the unique advantage of combining both elements. It speaks at once with the vividness of painting, and with the mobility of sounds. It is, in some sense, more objective than either, more dramatic. In reading Chinese we do not seem to be juggling mental counters, but to be watching *things* work out their own fate.

Leaving for a moment the form of the sentence, let us look more closely at this quality of vividness in the structure of detached Chinese words. The earlier forms of these characters were pictorial, and their hold upon the imagination is little shaken, even in later conventional modifications. It is not so well known, perhaps, that the great number of these ideographic roots carry in them a *verbal idea of action.* It might be thought that a picture is naturally the picture of a *thing,* and that therefore the root ideas of Chinese are what grammar calls nouns.

But examination shows that a large number of the primitive Chinese characters, even the so-called radicals, are shorthand pictures of actions or processes.

For example, the ideograph meaning "to speak" is a mouth with two words and a flame coming out of it. The sign meaning "to grow up with difficulty" is grass with a twisted root. But this concrete *verb* quality, both in nature and in the Chinese signs, becomes far more striking and poetic when we pass from such simple, original pictures to compounds. In this process of compounding, two things added together do not produce a third thing but suggest some fundamental relation between them. For example, the ideograph for a "messmate" is a man and a fire.

A true noun, an isolated thing, does not exist in nature. Things are only the terminal points, or rather the meeting points of actions, cross-sections cut through actions, snap-shots. Neither can a pure verb, an abstract motion, be possible in nature. The eye sees noun and verb as one: things in motion, motion in things, and so the Chinese conception tends to represent them.

The sun underlying the bursting forth of plants = spring.

The sun sign tangled in the branches of the tree sign = east.

"Rice-field" plus "struggle" = male.

"Boat" plus "water," boat-water, a ripple.

Let us return to the form of the sentence and see what

power it adds to the verbal units from which it builds. I wonder how many people have asked themselves why the sentence form exists at all, why it seems so universally necessary *in all languages?* Why *must* all possess it, and what is the normal type of it? If it be so universal it ought to correspond to some primary law of nature.

I fancy the professional grammarians have given but a lame response to this inquiry. Their definitions fall into two types: one, that a sentence expresses a "complete thought"; the other, that in it we bring about a union of subject and predicate.

The former has the advantage of trying for some natural objective standard, since it is evident that a thought can not be the test of its own completeness. But in nature there is *no* completeness. On the one hand, practical completeness may be expressed by a mere interjection, as "Hi! there!", or "Scat!", or even by shaking one's fist. No sentence is needed to make one's meaning more clear. On the other hand, no full sentence really completes a thought. The man who sees and the horse which is seen will not stand still. The man was planning a ride before he looked. The horse kicked when the man tried to catch him. The truth is that acts are successive, even continuous; one causes or passes into another. And though we may string never so many clauses into a single compound sentence, motion leaks everywhere, like electricity from an exposed wire. All processes in nature are inter-related; and thus there could be no complete sentence (according to this definition) save one which it would take all time to pronounce.

In the second definition of the sentence, as "uniting a subject and a predicate," the grammarian falls back on pure subjectivity. *We* do it all; it is a little private juggling between our right and left hands. The subject is that about which *I* am going to talk; the predicate is that which *I* am going to say about it. The sentence according to this definition is not an attribute of nature but an accident of man as a conversational animal.

If it were really so, then there could be no possible test of the truth of a sentence. Falsehood would be as specious as verity. Speech would carry no conviction.

Of course this view of the grammarians springs from the discredited, or rather the useless, logic of the middle ages. According to this logic, thought deals with abstractions, concepts drawn out of things by a sifting process. These logicians never inquired how the "qualities" which they pulled out of things came to be there. The truth of all their little checker-board juggling depended upon the natural order by which these powers or properties or qualities were folded in concrete things, yet they despised the "thing" as a mere "particular," or pawn. It was as if Botany should reason from the leaf-patterns woven into our table-cloths. Valid scientific thought consists in following as closely as may be the actual and entangled lines of forces as they pulse through things. Thought deals with no bloodless concepts but watches *things move* under its microscope.

The sentence form was forced upon primitive men by nature itself. It was not we who made it; it was a reflection of the temporal order in causation. All truth has to be expressed in sentences because all truth is the *transference of power*. The type of sentence in nature is a flash of lightning. It passes between two terms, a cloud and the earth. No unit of natural process can be less than this. All natural processes are, in their units, as much as this. Light, heat, gravity, chemical affinity, human will have this in common, that they redistribute force. Their unit of process can be represented as:

term	transference	term
from	of	to
which	force	which

If we regard this transference as the conscious or unconscious act of an agent we can translate the diagram into:

agent	act	object

In this the act is the very substance of the fact denoted. The agent and the object are only limiting terms.

It seems to me that the normal and typical sentence in English as well as in Chinese expresses just this unit of natural process. It consists of three necessary words; the first denoting the agent or subject from which the act starts; the second embodying the very stroke of the act; the third pointing to the object, the receiver of the impact. Thus:

Farmer	pounds	rice.

The form of the Chinese transitive sentence, and of the English (omitting particles) exactly corresponds to this universal form of action in nature. This brings language close to *things*, and in its strong reliance upon verbs it erects all speech into a kind of dramatic poetry.

A different sentence order is frequent in inflected languages like Latin, German or Japanese. This is because they are inflected, i.e., they have little tags and word-endings, or labels to show which is the agent, the object, etc. In uninflected languages, like English and Chinese, there is nothing but the order of the words to distinguish their functions. And this order would be no sufficient indi-

cation, were it not the *natural order*—that is, the order
of cause and effect.

It is true that there are, in language, intransitive and
passive forms, sentences built out of the verb "to be,"
and, finally, negative forms. To grammarians and logicians these have seemed more primitive than the transitive, or at least exceptions to the transitive. I had long
suspected that these apparently exceptional forms had
grown from the transitive or worn away from it by
alteration or modification. This view is confirmed by
Chinese examples, wherein it is still possible to watch the
transformation going on.

The intransitive form derives from the transitive by
dropping a generalized, customary, reflexive or cognate
object. "He runs (a race)." "The sky reddens (itself)." "We breathe (air)." Thus we get weak and
incomplete sentences which suspend the picture and lead
us to think of some verbs as denoting states rather than
acts. Outside grammar the word "state" would hardly
be recognized as scientific. Who can doubt that when
we say, "The wall shines," we mean that it actively re-
flects light to our eye?

The beauty of Chinese verbs is that they are all transitive or intransitive at pleasure. There is no such
thing as a naturally intransitive verb. The passive form
is evidently a correlative sentence, which turns about and
makes the object into a subject. That the object is not
in itself passive, but contributes some positive force of
its own to the action, is in harmony both with scientific
law and with ordinary experience. The English passive
voice with "is" seemed at first an obstacle to this hypothesis, but one suspected that the true form was a generalized transitive verb meaning something like "re-

ceive," which had degenerated into an auxiliary. It was a delight to find this the case in Chinese.

In nature there are no negations, no possible transfers of negative force. The presence of negative sentences in language would seem to corroborate the logicians' view that assertion is an arbitrary subjective act. *We* can assert a negation, though nature can not. But here again science comes to our aid against the logician: all apparently negative or disruptive movements bring into play other positive forces. It requires great effort to annihilate. Therefore we should suspect that, if we could follow back the history of all negative particles, we should find that they also are sprung from transitive verbs. It is too late to demonstrate such derivations in the Aryan languages, the clue has been lost, but in Chinese we can still watch positive verbal conceptions passing over into so-called negatives. Thus in Chinese the sign meaning "to be lost in the forest" relates to a state of non-existence. English "not" = the Sanskrit *na*, which may come from the root *na*, to be lost, to perish.

Lastly comes the infinitive which substitutes for a specific colored verb the universal copula "is," followed by a noun or an adjective. We do not say a tree "greens itself," but "the tree is green;" not that "monkeys bring forth live young," but that "the monkey is a mammal." This is an ultimate weakness of language. It has come from generalizing all intransitive words into one. As "live," "see," "walk," "breathe," are generalized into states by dropping their objects, so these weak verbs are in turn reduced to the abstractest state of all, namely, bare existence.

There is in reality no such verb as a pure copula, no such original conception, our very word *exist* means "to stand forth," to show oneself by a definite act. "Is" comes from the Aryan root *as,* to breathe. "Be" is from *bhu,* to grow.

In Chinese the chief verb for "is" not only means actively "to have," but shows by its derivation that it expresses something even more concrete, namely, "to snatch from the moon with the hand." Here the baldest symbol of prosaic analysis is transformed by magic into a splendid flash of concrete poetry.

I shall not have entered vainly into this long analysis of the sentence if I have succeeded in showing how poetical is the Chinese form and how close to nature. In translating Chinese, verse especially, we must hold as closely as possible to the concrete force of the original, eschewing adjectives, nouns and intransitive forms wherever we can, and seeking instead strong and individual verbs.

Lastly we notice that the likeness of form between Chinese and English sentences renders translation from one to the other exceptionally easy. The genius of the two is much the same. Frequently it is possible by omitting English particles to make a literal word-for-word translation which will be not only intelligible in English, but even the strongest and most poetical English. Here, however, one must follow closely what is said, not merely what is abstractly meant.

Let us go back from the Chinese sentence to the individual written word. How are such words to be classified? Are some of them nouns by nature, some verbs and some adjectives? Are there pronouns and prepositions and conjunctions in Chinese as in good Christian languages?

One is led to suspect from an analysis of the Aryan languages that such differences are not natural, and that they have been unfortunately invented by grammarians to confuse the simple poetic outlook on life. All nations have written their strongest and most vivid literature before they invented a grammar. Moreover, all Aryan etymology points back to roots which are the equivalents of simple Sanskrit verbs, such as we find tabulated at the back of our Skeat. Nature herself has no grammar.* Fancy picking up a man and telling him that he is a noun, a dead thing rather than a bundle of functions! A "part of speech" is only *what it does*. Frequently our lines of cleavage fail, one part of speech acts for another. They *act for* one another because they were originally one and the same.

Few of us realize that in our own language these very differences once grew up in living articulation; that they still retain life. It is only when the difficulty of placing some odd term arises or when we are forced to translate into some very different language, that we attain for a moment the inner heat of thought, a heat which melts down the parts of speech to recast them at will.

One of the most interesting facts about the Chinese language is that in it we can see, not only the forms of sentences, but literally the parts of speech growing up, budding forth one from another. Like nature, the Chinese words are alive and plastic, because *thing* and *action* are not formally separated. The Chinese language naturally knows no grammar. It is only lately that foreigners, European and Japanese, have begun to torture this vital speech by forcing it to fit the bed of their definitions.

* Even Latin, living Latin had not the network of rules they foist upon unfortunate school-children. These are borrowed sometimes from Greek grammarians, even as I have seen English grammars borrowing oblique cases from Latin grammars. Sometimes they sprang from the grammatizing or categorizing passion of pedants. Living Latin had only the feel of the cases: the ablative and dative emotion.—E. P.

We import into our reading of Chinese all the weakness of our own formalisms. This is especially sad in poetry, because the one necessity, even in our own poetry, is to keep words as flexible as possible, as full of the sap of nature.

Let us go further with our example. In English we call "to shine" a *verb in the infinitive,* because it gives the abstract meaning of the verb without conditions. If we want a corresponding adjective we take a different word, "bright." If we need a noun we say "luminosity," which is abstract, being derived from an adjective.* To get a tolerably concrete noun, we have to leave behind the verb and adjective roots, and light upon a thing arbitrarily cut off from its power of action, say "the sun" or "the moon." Of course there is nothing in nature so cut off, and therefore this nounizing is itself an abstraction. Even if we did have a common word underlying at once the verb "shine," the adjective "bright" and the noun "sun," we should probably call it an "infinitive of the infinitive." According to our ideas, it should be something extremely abstract, too intangible for use.

The Chinese have one word, *ming* or *mei.* Its ideograph is the sign of the sun together with the sign of the moon. It serves as verb, noun, adjective. Thus you write literally, "the sun and moon of the cup" for "the cup's brightness." Placed as a verb, you write "the cup sun-and-moons," actually "cup sun-and-moon," or in a weakened thought, "is like sun," i.e., shines. "Sun-and-moon cup" is naturally a bright cup. There is no possible confusion of the real meaning, though a stupid

* [A good writer would use "shine" (i. e., to shine), shining, and "the shine" or "sheen", possibly thinking of the German "*schöne*' and *Schönheit*"; but this does not invalidate Prof. Fenollosa's next contention.—E. P.]

scholar may spend a week trying to decide what "part of speech" he should use in translating a very simple and direct thought from Chinese to English.

The fact is that almost every written Chinese word is properly just such an underlying word, and yet it is *not* abstract. It is not exclusive of parts of speech, but comprehensive; not something which is neither a noun, verb, or adjective, but something which is all of them at once and at all times. Usage may incline the full meaning now a little more to one side, now to another, according to the point of view, but through all cases the poet is free to deal with it richly and concretely, as does nature.

In the derivation of nouns from verbs, the Chinese language is forestalled by the Aryan. Almost all the Sanskrit roots, which seem to underlie European languages, are primitive verbs, which express characteristic actions of visible nature. The verb must be the primary fact of nature, since motion and change are all that we can recognize in her. In the primitive transitive sentence, such as "Farmer pounds rice," the agent and the object are nouns only in so far as they limit a unit of action. "Farmer" and "rice" are mere hard terms which define the extremes of the pounding. But in themselves, apart from this sentence-function, they are naturally verbs. The farmer is one who tills the ground, and the rice is a plant which grows in a special way. This is indicated in the Chinese characters. And this probably exemplifies the ordinary derivation of nouns from verbs. In all languages, Chinese included, a noun is originally "that which does something," that which performs the verbal action. Thus the moon comes from the root *ma*, and means "the measurer." The sun means that which begets.

The derivation of adjectives from the verb need hardly

be exemplified. Even with us, to-day, we can still watch
participles passing over into adjectives. In Japanese the
adjective is frankly part of the inflection of the verb, a
special mood, so that every verb is also an adjective.
This brings us close to nature, because everywhere the
quality is only a power of action regarded as having an
abstract inherence. Green is only a certain rapidity of
vibration, hardness a degree of tenseness in cohering.
In Chinese the adjective always retains a substratum of
verbal meaning. We should try to render this in translation, not be content with some bloodless adjectival abstraction plus "is."

Still more interesting are the Chinese "prepositions,"
they are often post-positions. Prepositions are so important, so pivotal in European speech only because we
have weakly yielded up the force of our intransitive
verbs. We have to add small supernumerary words to
bring back the original power. We still say "I see a
horse," but with the weak verb "look," we have to add
the directive particle "at" before we can restore the
natural transitiveness.*

Prepositions represent a few simple ways in which incomplete verbs complete themselves. Pointing toward
nouns as a limit they bring force to bear upon them.
That is to say, they are naturally verbs, of generalized
or condensed use. In Aryan languages it is often difficult to trace the verbal origins of simple prepositions.
Only in *"off"* do we see a fragment of the thought "to
throw off." In Chinese the preposition is frankly a
verb, specially used in a generalized sense. These verbs

* [This is a bad example. We can say "I look a fool",
"look", transitive, now means resemble. The main contention
is however correct. We tend to abandon specific words like
resemble and substitute, for them, vague verbs with prepo-
sitional directors, or riders.—E. P.]

are often used in their specially verbal sense, and it greatly weakens an English translation if they are systematically rendered by colorless prepositions.

Thus in Chinese: By = to cause; to = to fall toward; in = to remain, to dwell; from = to follow; and so on.

Conjunctions are similarly derivative, they usually serve to mediate actions between verbs, and therefore they are necessarily themselves actions. Thus in Chinese: Because = to use; and = to be included under one; another form of "and" = to be parallel; or = to partake; if = to let one do, to permit. The same is true of a host of other particles, no longer traceable in the Aryan tongues.

Pronouns appear a thorn in our evolution theory, since they have been taken as unanalyzable expressions of personality. In Chinese even they yield up their striking secrets of verbal metaphor. They are a constant source of weakness if colorlessly translated. Take, for example, the five forms of "I." There is the sign of a "spear in the hand" = a very emphatic I; five and a mouth = a weak and defensive I, holding off a crowd by speaking; to conceal = a selfish and private I; self (the cocoon sign) and a mouth = an egoistic I, one who takes pleasure in his own speaking; the self presented is used only when one is speaking to one's self.

I trust that this digression concerning parts of speech may have justified itself. It proves, first, the enormous interest of the Chinese language in throwing light upon our forgotten mental processes, and thus furnishes a new chapter in the philosophy of language. Secondly, it is indispensable for understanding the poetical raw material which the Chinese language affords. Poetry differs from prose in the concrete colors of its diction. It is not enough for it to furnish a meaning to philosophers.

It must appeal to emotions with the charm of direct impression, flashing through regions where the intellect can only grope.* Poetry must render what is said, not what is merely meant. Abstract meaning gives little vividness, and fullness of imagination gives all. Chinese poetry demands that we abandon our narrow grammatical categories, that we follow the original text with a wealth of concrete verbs.

But this is only the beginning of the matter. So far we have exhibited the Chinese characters and the Chinese sentence chiefly as vivid shorthand pictures of actions and processes in nature. These embody true poetry as far as they go. Such actions are *seen,* but Chinese would be a poor language and Chinese poetry but a narrow art, could they not go on to represent also what is unseen. The best poetry deals not only with natural images but with lofty thoughts, spiritual suggestions and obscure relations. The greater part of natural truth is hidden in processes too minute for vision and in harmonies too large, in vibrations, cohesions and in affinities. The Chinese compass these also, and with great power and beauty.

You will ask, how could the Chinese have built up a great intellectual fabric from mere picture writing? To the ordinary western mind, which believes that thought is concerned with logical categories and which rather condemns the faculty of direct imagination, this feat seems quite impossible. Yet the Chinese language with its peculiar materials has passed over from the seen to the unseen by exactly the same process which all ancient races employed. This process is metaphor, the use of material images to suggest immaterial relations.†

* [*Cf.* principle of Primary apparition, "Spirit of Romance".— E. P.]

† [Compare Aristotle's *Poetics.*—E. P.]

The whole delicate substance of speech is built upon substrata of metaphor. Abstract terms, pressed by etymology, reveal their ancient roots still embedded in direct action. But the primitive metaphors do not spring from arbitrary subjective processes. They are possible only because they follow objective lines of relations in nature herself. Relations are more real and more important than the things which they relate. The forces which produce the branch-angles of an oak lay potent in the acorn. Similar lines of resistance, half curbing the out-pressing vitalities, govern the branching of rivers and of nations. Thus a nerve, a wire, a roadway, and a clearing-house are only varying channels which communication forces for itself. This is more than analogy, it is identity of structure. Nature furnishes her own clues. Had the world not been full of homologies, sympathies, and identities, thought would have been starved and language chained to the obvious. There would have been no bridge whereby to cross from the minor truth of the seen to the major truth of the unseen. Not more than a few hundred roots out of our large vocabularies could have dealt directly with physical processes. These we can fairly well identify in primitive Sanskrit. They are, almost without exception, vivid verbs. The wealth of European speech grew, following slowly the intricate maze of nature's suggestions and affinities. Metaphor was piled upon metaphor in quasi-geological strata.

Metaphor, the revealer of nature, is the very substance of poetry. The known interprets the obscure, the universe is alive with myth. The beauty and freedom of the observed world furnish a model, and life is pregnant with art. It is a mistake to suppose, with some philosophers of æsthetics, that art and poetry aim to deal with the general and the abstract. This misconception has

been foisted upon us by mediæval logic. Art and poetry
deal with the concrete of nature, not with rows of sep-
arate "particulars," for such rows do not exist. Poetry
is finer than prose because it gives us more concrete
truth in the same compass of words. Metaphor, its chief
device, is at once the substance of nature and of language. Poetry only does consciously * what the primitive races did unconsciously. The chief work of literary men in dealing with language, and of poets especially,
lies in feeling back along the ancient lines of advance.†
He must do this so that he may keep his words enriched
by all their subtle undertones of meaning. The original
metaphors stand as a kind of luminous background, giving color and vitality, forcing them closer to the concreteness of natural processes. Shakespeare everywhere
teems with examples. For these reasons poetry was the
earliest of the world arts; poetry, language and the care
of myth grew up together.

I have alleged all this because it enables me to show
clearly why I believe that the Chinese written language
has not only absorbed the poetic substance of nature and
built with it a second world of metaphor, but has, through
its very pictorial visibility, been able to retain its original
creative poetry with far more vigor and vividness than
any phonetic tongue. Let us first see how near it is to
the heart of nature in its metaphors. We can watch it
passing from the seen to the unseen, as we saw it pass-

* [Vide also an article on "Vorticism" in the *Fortnightly Review* for September, 1914. "The language of exploration" now
in my "Gaudier-Brzeska."—E. P.]

† [I would submit in all humility that this applies in the
rendering of ancient texts. The poet in dealing with his own
time, must also see to it that language does not petrify on his
hands. He must prepare for new advances along the lines of
true metaphor that is interpretative metaphor, or image, as diametrically opposed to untrue, or ornamental metaphor.—E. P.]

ing from verb to pronoun. It retains the primitive sap, it is not cut and dried like a walking-stick. We have been told that these people are cold, practical, mechanical, literal, and without a trace of imaginative genius. That is nonsense.

Our ancestors built the accumulations of metaphor into structures of language and into systems of thought. Languages to-day are thin and cold because we think less and less into them. We are forced, for the sake of quickness and sharpness, to file down each word to its narrowest edge of meaning. Nature would seem to have become less like a paradise and more and more like a factory. We are content to accept the vulgar misuse of the moment. A late stage of decay is arrested and embalmed in the dictionary. Only scholars and poets feel painfully back along the thread of our etymologies and piece together our diction, as best they may, from forgotten fragments. This anemia of modern speech is only too well encouraged by the feeble cohesive force of our phonetic symbols. There is little or nothing in a phonetic word to exhibit the embryonic stages of its growth. It does not bear its metaphor on its face. We forget that personality once meant, not the soul, but the soul's mask. This is the sort of thing one can not possibly forget in using the Chinese symbols.

In this Chinese shows its advantage. Its etymology is constantly visible. It retains the creative impulse and process, visible and at work. After thousands of years the lines of metaphoric advance are still shown, and in many cases actually retained in the meaning. Thus a word, instead of growing gradually poorer and poorer as with us, becomes richer and still more rich from age to age, almost consciously luminous. Its uses in national philosophy and history, in biography and in poetry, throw about it a nimbus of meanings. These centre about the graphic symbol. The memory can hold them and use them. The very soil of Chinese life seems entangled in the roots of its speech. The manifold illustrations which crowd its annals of personal experience, the lines of tendency which converge upon a tragic climax, moral character as the very core of the principle —all these are flashed at once on the mind as reinforcing values with an accumulation of meaning which a phonetic language can hardly hope to attain. Their ideographs are like blood-stained battle flags to an old campaigner. With us, the poet is the only one for whom the accumulated treasures of the race-words are real and active. Poetic language is always vibrant with fold on fold of overtones, and with natural affinities, but in Chinese the visibility of the metaphor tends to raise this quality to its intensest power.

I have mentioned the tyranny of mediæval logic. According to this European logic thought is a kind of brickyard. It is baked into little hard units or concepts. These are piled in rows according to size and then labeled with words for future use. This use consists in picking out a few bricks, each by its convenient label, and sticking them together into a sort of wall called a sentence by the use either of white mortar for the positive copula "is," or of black mortar for the negative copula "is not." In this way we produce such admirable propositions as "A ring-tailed baboon is not a constitutional assembly."

Let us consider a row of cherry trees. From each of these in turn we proceed to take an "abstract," as the phrase is, a certain common lump of qualities which we may express together by the name cherry or cherry-ness. Next we place in a second table several such characteristic concepts: cherry, rose, sunset, iron-rust, flamingo.

From these we abstract some further common quality, dilutation or mediocrity, and label it "red" or "redness." It is evident that this process of abstraction may be carried on indefinitely and with all sorts of material. We may go on forever building pyramids of attenuated concept until we reach the apex "being."

But we have done enough to illustrate the characteristic process. At the base of the pyramid lie *things,* but stunned, as it were. They can never know themselves for things until they pass up and down among the layers of the pyramids. The way of passing up and down the pyramid may be exemplified as follows: We take a concept of lower attenuation, such as "cherry"; we see that it is contained under one higher, such as "redness." Then we are permitted to say in sentence form, "Cherryness is contained under redness," or for short, "(the) cherry is red." If, on the other hand, we do not find our chosen subject under a given predicate we use the black copula and say, for example, "(The) cherry is not liquid."

From this point we might go on to the theory of the syllogism, but we refrain. It is enough to note that the practised logician finds it convenient to store his mind with long lists of nouns and adjectives, for these are naturally the names of classes. Most text-books on language begin with such lists. The study of verbs is meagre, for in such a system there is only one real working verb, to-wit, the quasi-verb "is." All other verbs can be transformed into participles and gerunds. For example, "to run" practically becomes a case of "running." Instead of thinking directly, "The man runs," our logician makes two subjective equations, namely: The individual in question is contained under the class "man"; and the class "man" is contained under the class of "running things."

The sheer loss and weakness of this method is apparent and flagrant. Even in its own sphere it can not think half of what it wants to think. It has no way of bringing together any two concepts which do not happen to stand one under the other and in the same pyramid. It is impossible to represent change in this system or any kind of growth. This is probably why the conception of evolution came so late in Europe. *It could not make way until it was prepared to destroy the inveterate logic of classification.*

Far worse than this, suoh logic can not deal with any kind of interaction or with any multiplicity of function. According to it, the function of my muscles is as isolated from the function of my nerves, as from an earthquake in the moon. For it the poor neglected things at the bases of the pyramids are only so many particulars or pawns.

Science fought till she got at the things. All her work has been done from the base of the pyramids, not from the apex. She has discovered how functions cohere in things. She expresses her results in grouped sentences which embody no nouns or adjectives but verbs of special character. The true formula for thought is: The cherry tree is all that it does. Its correlated verbs compose it. At bottom these verbs are transitive. Such verbs may be almost infinite in number.

In diction and in grammatical form science is utterly opposed to logic. Primitive men who created language agreed with science and not with logic. Logic has abused the language which they left to her mercy. Poetry agrees with science and not with logic.

The moment we use the copula, the moment we express subjective inclusions, poetry evaporates. The more concretely and vividly we express the interactions of things the better the poetry. We need in poetry thousands of active words, each doing its utmost to show forth the motive and vital forces. We can not exhibit the wealth of nature by mere summation, by the piling of sentences. Poetic thought works by suggestion, crowding maximum meaning into the single phrase pregnant, charged, and luminous from within.

In Chinese character each work accumulated this sort of energy in itself.

Should we pass formally to the study of Chinese poetry, we should warn ourselves against logicianized pitfalls. We should beware of modern narrow utilitarian meanings ascribed to the words in commercial dictionaries. We should try to preserve the metaphoric overtones. We should beware of English grammar, its hard parts of speech, and its lazy satisfaction with nouns and adjectives. We should seek and at least bear in mind the verbal undertone of each noun. We should avoid "is" and bring in a wealth of neglected English verbs. Most of the existing translations violate all of these rules.*

The development of the normal transitive sentence rests upon the fact that one action in nature promotes another; thus the agent and the object are secretly verbs. For example, our sentence, "Reading promotes writing," would be expressed in Chinese by three full verbs. Such a form is the equivalent of three expanded clauses and can be drawn out into adjectival, participial, infinitive, relative or conditional members. One of many possible examples is, "If one reads it teaches him how to write." Another is, "One who reads becomes one who writes."

* [These precautions should be broadly conceived. It is not so much their letter, as the underlying feeling of objectification and activity, that matters.—E. P.]

But in the first condensed form a Chinese would write, "Read promote write." The dominance of the verb and its power to obliterate all other parts of speech give us the model of terse fine style.

I have seldom seen our rhetoricians dwell on the fact that the great strength of our language lies in its splendid array of transitive verbs, drawn both from Anglo-Saxon and from Latin sources. These give us the most individual characterizations of force. Their power lies in their recognition of nature as a vast storehouse of forces. We do not say in English that things seem, or appear, or eventuate, or even that they are; but that they *do*. Will is the foundation of our speech.* We catch the Demiurge in the act. I had to discover for myself why Shakespeare's English was so immeasurably superior to all others. I found that it was his persistent, natural, and magnificent use of hundreds of transitive verbs. Rarely will you find an "is" in his sentences. "Is" weakly lends itself to the uses of our rhythm, in the unaccented syllables; yet he sternly discards it. A study of Shakespeare's verbs should underlie all exercises in style.

We find in poetical Chinese a wealth of transitive verbs, in some way greater even than in the English of Shakespeare. This springs from their power of combining several pictorial elements in a single character. We have in English no verb for what two things, say the sun and moon, both do together. Prefixes and affixes merely direct and qualify. In Chinese the verb can be more minutely qualified. We find a hundred variants clustering about a single idea. Thus "to sail a boat for purposes of pleasure" would be an entirely different verb

* [Compare Dante's definition of "rectitudo" as the direction of the will, probably taken from Aquinas.—E. P.]

from "to sail for purposes of commerce." Dozens of Chinese verbs express various shades of grieving, yet in English translations they are usually reduced to one mediocrity. Many of them can be expressed only by periphrasis, but what right has the translator to neglect the overtones? There are subtle shadings. We should strain our resources in English.

It is true that the pictorial clue of many Chinese ideographs can not now be traced, and even Chinese lexicographers admit that combinations frequently contribute only a phonetic value. But I find it incredible that any such minute subdivision of the idea could have ever existed alone as abstract sound without the concrete character. It contradicts the law of evolution. Complex ideas arise only gradually. as the power of holding them together arises. The paucity of Chinese sound could not so hold them. Neither is it conceivable that the whole list was made at once, as commercial codes of cipher are compiled. Therefore we must believe that the phonetic theory is in large part unsound. The metaphor once existed in many cases where we can not now trace it. Many of our own etymologies have been lost. It is futile to take the ignorance of the Han dynasty for omniscience.* It is not true, as Legge said, that the

* [Professor Fenollosa is well borne out by chance evidence. The vorticist sculptor Gaudier-Brzeska sat in my room before he went off to the war. He was able to read the Chinese radicals and many compound signs almost at pleasure. He was of course, used to consider all life and nature in the terms of planes and of bounding lines. Nevertheless he had spent only a fortnight in the museum studying the Chinese characters. He was amazed at the stupidity of lexicographers who could not discern for all their learning the pictorial values which were to him perfectly obvious and apparent. Curiously enough, a few weeks later Edmond Dulac, who is of a totally different tradition, sat here, giving an im-

386 INSTIGATIONS

original picture characters could never have gone far in building up abstract thought. This is a vital mistake. We have seen that our own languages have all sprung from a few hundred vivid phonetic verbs by figurative derivation. A fabric more vast could have been built up in Chinese by metaphorical composition. No attenuated idea exists which it might not have reached more vividly and more permanently than we could have been expected to reach with phonetic roots. Such a pictorial method, whether the Chinese exemplified it or not, would be the ideal language of the world.

Still, is it not enough to show that Chinese poetry gets back near to the processes of nature by means of its vivid figure, its wealth of such figure? If we attempt to follow it in English we must use words highly charged, words whose vital suggestion shall interplay as nature interplays. Sentences must be like the mingling of the fringes of feathered banners, or as the colors of many flowers blended into the single sheen of a meadow.

The poet can never see too much or feel too much. His metaphors are only ways of getting rid of the dead white plaster of the copula. He resolves its indifference into a thousand tints of verb. His figures flood things with jets of various light, like the sudden up-blaze of fountains. The prehistoric poets who created language discovered the whole harmonious framework of nature, they sang out her processes in their hymns. And

promptu panegyric on the elements of Chinese art, on the units of composition, drawn from the written characters. He did not use Professor Fenollosa's own words, he said "bamboo" instead of 'rice'. He said the essence of the bamboo is in a certain way it grows, they have this in their sign for bamboo, all designs of bamboo proceed from it. Then he went on rather to disparage vorticism, on the grounds that it could not hope to do for the Occident, in one life-time, what had required centuries of development in China.—E. P.]

this diffused poetry which they created, Shakespeare has condensed into a more tangible substance. Thus in all poetry a word is like a sun, with its corona and chromosphere; words crowd upon words, and enwrap each other in their luminous envelopes until sentences become clear, continuous light-bands.

Now we are in condition to appreciate the full splendor of certain lines of Chinese verse. Poetry surpasses prose especially in that the poet selects for juxtaposition those words whose overtones blend into a delicate and lucid harmony. All arts follow the same law; refined harmony lies in the delicate balance of overtones. In music the whole possibility and theory of harmony is based on the overtones. In this sense poetry seems a more difficult art.

How shall we determine the metaphorical overtones of neighboring words? We can avoid flagrant breaches like mixed metaphor. We can find the concord or harmonizing at its intensest, as in Romeo's speech over the dead Juliet.

Here also the Chinese ideography has its advantage, in even a simple line, for example, "The sun rises in the east."

The overtones vibrate against the eye. The wealth of composition in characters makes possible a· choice of words in which a single dominant overtone colors every plane of meaning. That is perhaps the most conspicuous quality of Chinese poetry. Let us examine our line.

Sun   Rises   (in the)   East

The sun, the shining, on one side, on the other the sign of the east, which is the sun entangled in the branches of a tree. And in the middle sign, the verb "rise," we have further homology; the sun is above the horizon, but beyond that the single upright line is like the growing trunk-line of the tree sign. This is but a beginning, but it points a way to the method, and to the method of intelligent reading.